Black American Writing from the Nadir

DICKSON D. BRUCE, JR.

Black American Writing from the Nadir

The Evolution
of a Literary
Tradition
1877–1915

LOUISIANA STATE UNIVERSITY PRESS
Baton Rouge and London

98 97 96 95 94 93 92 91 90 89 88   5 4 3 2 1

Designer: Laura Roubique Gleason
Typeface: ITC Garamond
Typesetter: The Composing Room of Michigan, Inc.
Printer: Thomson-Shore, Inc.
Binder: John H. Dekker & Sons, Inc.

Library of Congress Cataloging-in-Publication Data

Bruce, Dickson D., 1946–
    Black American writing from the nadir : the evolution of a
literary tradition, 1877–1915 / Dickson D. Bruce, Jr.
        p. cm.
    Includes index.
    ISBN 0-8071-1450-2 (alk. paper)
    1. American literature—Afro-American authors—History and
criticism.   2. American literature—19th century—History and
criticism.   3. American literature—20th century—History and
criticism.   4. Afro-Americans—Intellectual life.   I. Title.
PS153.N5B77 1989
810'.9'896073—dc19   88-22039
                                                           CIP

The author gratefully acknowledges permission to reprint the following excerpts: Lines from poems in *St. Peter Relates an Incident* by James Weldon Johnson, copyright 1935 by James Weldon Johnson, copyright renewed © 1963 by Grace Nail Johnson, all rights reserved, reprinted by permission of Viking Penguin, Inc. Excerpts from Charles W. Chesnutt's Journal and Notebook, from his "The Future American," and from his letter to William Brown, Nov. 7, 1909, in the Charles W. Chesnutt Collection, Fisk University Library Special Collections, reprinted by permission of Fisk University Library Special Collections. An excerpt from "Paying the Fiddler," in the Daniel Webster Davis Papers, Virginia Historical Society, reprinted by permission of the Virginia Historical Society. Lines from Paul Laurence Dunbar's poems, reprinted by permission of Dodd, Mead & Company, Inc. from *The Complete Poems of Paul Laurence Dunbar.* Excerpt from Andrew F. Hilyer, "Analysis of American Color Prejudice and How to Suppress," in Andrew F. Hilyer Papers; excerpt from Archibald H. Grimké, "Paul Laurence Dunbar: The Poet," and "El Beso" by Angelina Grimké, in Archibald H. Grimké Papers; stanza from Anna Julia Cooper, "Aunt Charlotte," in Anna Julia Cooper Papers; excerpt from letter from Arthur Schomburg to John W. Cromwell, Dec. 23, 1915, in the Cromwell Family Papers—all reprinted by permission of the Moorland-Spingarn Research Center, Howard University. Excerpts from letters from Booker T. Washington, Charles Chesnutt, and W. S. Braithwaite to James Weldon Johnson, and from Johnson to Joel Spingarn, Grace Nail Johnson, and Sherman, and from marginal notes to poetry in Johnson's Notebook No. 5, in the James Weldon Johnson Collection, the Beinecke Rare Book and Manuscript Library—all reprinted by permission of the Collection of American Literature, the Beinecke Rare Book and Manuscript Library, Yale University.

The paper in this book meets the guidelines for permanence and durability of the Committee on Production Guidelines for Book Longevity of the Council on Library Resources.

To Harold and Aline Watson

Contents

Illustrations

Preface

This book examines ways in which black Americans responded to the growing virulence of white racism in late nineteenth and early twentieth century America. The subject is hardly esoteric; nor is it of only academic interest. Many historians have acknowledged that this period was especially crucial for the course of American race relations. Much of white American racial ideology and many of the practices that have made America, for so long, a biracial society took shape during this period. Its legacy continues to mark the nation's life.

Our understanding of the dynamics of post-Reconstruction white racism is increasingly near completion. Its intellectual roots, its social and cultural character, even its psychological sources have been explored thoroughly by historians and other students of society. However, our knowledge of black responses to the racism of the period is less complete, even though much essential and fascinating work has been done. Historians have, for example, fully investigated the main contours of Afro-American ideology from the period after Reconstruction, as well as some of the more prominent social and political movements. But there remains a need to go below the surface of black thought and action in the post-Reconstruction period and to explore the underlying structures of ideas and feelings behind the more visible responses to white racial oppression. I have tried to do this, through a survey and interpretation of the large amount of literary work—especially poetry and fiction—produced by black Americans between the close of Reconstruction and the early days of World War I.

This literature has not been easy to read. For one thing, it is marked by tensions and ambiguities that defy systematization. These tensions and ambiguities provided the key structural framework for black literary composition during this period and created, as well, the major impetus for continuity and change. The ambivalences of early black writing show how profoundly black men and women were affected by the character of race relations that developed in America before World War I, as, confronting the racism of American society, they found it difficult to resolve powerful contradictions in their lives, their thoughts, and their feelings. Much of what post-Reconstruction literature reveals about black American thought and action lies in its unresolved contradictions, not in the answers it gave to the pressing problems of racial injustice. An account of those contradictions runs through the chapters, providing the book's central interpretive focus.

At the same time, one of the exciting aspects of studying this literature has been the realization that a great deal of creative work was done by black Americans in the post-Reconstruction era. Much of this writing is of intrinsic interest. The men and women who produced it were educated, often sophisticated, and always motivated to make a literary mark for themselves while artfully expressing their deepest ideals and passions. These simple facts have much to do with the organization and content of this book. The literature that is its subject is, for the most part, unknown. To be sure, such prominent figures from this era as Paul Laurence Dunbar, Charles Chesnutt, W. E. B. Du Bois, James Weldon Johnson, and, perhaps, Frances Ellen Watkins Harper are fairly familiar to many students of American history and literature. But most of their contemporaries labored in obscurity and have remained obscure to all but a few scholars. As a result, our picture of black life in the late nineteenth and early twentieth centuries remains partial and uninformed by a sense of the volume of creative and intellectual activity going on behind the veil that white America threw over black communities and their histories.

An examination of the literature from this period helps pull aside that veil in order to show the great breadth and diversity of black writing between 1877 and 1915. Many people wrote many things during that era and, indeed, succeeded in creating a rich literary tradition. One purpose here is to make that tradition better known.

Research for this book was generously supported by funds from several sources. Funding for a lengthy trip to important manuscript collections was provided by the National Endowment for the Humanities, the Penrose Fund of the American Philosophical Society, and the Academic Senate Committee on Research at the University of California, Irvine (UCI). Additional, indispensable support was provided by the School of

Social Sciences and the Program in Comparative Culture at UCI. Research was done at The Moorland-Spingarn Research Center at Howard University, the Library of Congress, the Schomburg Center for Research in Black Culture of the New York Public Library, the Beinecke Rare Book and Manuscript Library at Yale University, the Library Company of Philadelphia, and the Special Collections department of the Fisk University Library. I am grateful to the staffs at each of those institutions for courtesy and assistance. I am also grateful to the staff members of the UCI Library—especially those in interlibrary loan and in acquisitions—for making a great deal of material available to me.

In addition, my efforts have been significantly aided by the comments and encouragement of friends and colleagues, among them Roger Abrahams, Margaret Creel, James Flink, David Rankin, Dickran Tashjian, Bertram Wyatt-Brown, and Richard Yarborough. I should also note that a portion of the editing of the manuscript occurred while I was a visiting lecturer in the English Department at Attila József University in Szeged, Hungary, and I thank my colleagues there for being both helpful and patient. I hope no one will be offended if I say, however, that my deepest gratitude is to my wife, Mary, and my daughter, Emily, whose support and aid have been far beyond what I've had any right to expect.

Black American Writing from the Nadir

Prologue

Black fiction and poetry written between 1877 and 1915 occupies an important place in the history of the black literary tradition. To be sure, it was not the earliest creative work by black writers to be published in the United States. The first black poets began to publish during the colonial period and the first black novelists during the 1850s. Black writers made important literary contributions to the antislavery movement almost as soon as it began to gather strength, in the 1830s. But historical conditions converged, beginning in about 1877, to produce an unprecedented burst of literary activity among black Americans, leading to the formation of a literary tradition whose main lines of development would not be significantly modified until about 1915, when urbanization and the Great War began to effect those changes in black life and thought that later flowered into the Harlem Renaissance of the 1920s. And even then, the tradition post-Reconstruction writers had created was not wholly shelved.

Black literature in the late nineteenth and early twentieth centuries was a product of complex and difficult times. Above all, black writers, like all black Americans, faced a severe test from a white racism so virulent that the historian Rayford W. Logan has labeled this period the "nadir" of black American history.[1] Excluded, with increasing vehemence, from social and economic institutions, black Americans also had to live within a society in which the majority was convinced that black people were inferior to whites and should therefore be consigned to a place of permanent social, economic, and political subordination.

The virulence of white racism was a powerful spur to literary activity, as black writers sought to use their pens to fight against racist practices

1. Rayford W. Logan, *The Betrayal of the Negro from Rutherford B. Hayes to Woodrow Wilson* (New York, 1965).

1

and ideas. Literature, black writers believed, could strike a blow against what one poet termed "the hydra-headed monster, prejudice."[2] Writers could help reveal how wrong white racial ideas were by attacking those ideas and the assumptions that lay behind them. Writers also could see the very existence of a vital black literature as being strong evidence against the ideology of black inferiority. A group of prominent black men, evaluating the course of black literature through the 1890s, declared, "It is manifest that although our literature is in its infancy, and has thus far occupied but limited space in the region of art, science, philosophy and poetry, it has yet demonstrated the existence amongst us of a capacity for a larger scope and higher aims and greater perfections than it has yet attained."[3] They believed that literary achievement, demonstrating that blacks could handle the highest level of thought and culture, would go a long way toward helping to dispel notions that blacks were an inferior and dependent people.

But challenging white beliefs in black inferiority was only one aspect of the relationship between black literature and racism during the years after 1877. What made those years so crucial—what makes labeling them as the nadir so apt—was that they were the setting for a visible deterioration in the position of black people in American society. The Reconstruction period itself had been a hopeful time for blacks. Although white racism had been a constant, there were reasons during Reconstruction to believe that it was in retreat. Many public facilities were, for example, equally accessible to blacks and whites during Reconstruction. In politics, especially, black men reached high levels of influence and were elected to major offices. But these attainments only made post-Reconstruction events more devastating, as the years after 1877 witnessed a snowballing of racist ideas and practices, both of which reached unprecedented vehemence in the 1890s.

Post-Reconstruction-era attacks on black aspirations came from several fronts. In politics, black voters were disfranchised throughout the South, a process that began in the 1890s and was complete by 1910. During the same period, segregation was fixed by custom or by law in most areas of American life. Especially during the 1890s, the South saw the rise of "Jim Crow" legislation, which required segregation in every-

2. Lizelia Augusta Jenkins Moorer, *Prejudice Unveiled and Other Poems* (Boston, 1907), [unpaginated].

3. "A Call for Afro-American Authors of America: To Meet with the American Association of Educators of Colored Youth, in Wilmington, N.C., December 27–30, 1892," pamphlet, in Frederick Douglass Papers, Manuscript Division, Library of Congress.

thing from residential areas to places of amusement, hospitals, schools, and public transportation. United States Supreme Court decisions in 1883 and 1896—the latter the *Plessy* vs. *Ferguson* decision, in which the principle of "separate but equal" was acknowledged as an appropriate measure of civil rights for blacks—meant that such southern legislation was secure from constitutional challenge.[4] In the North, black Americans did not suffer from such restrictive legislation; but even there, segregation took a decided upturn during the 1890s and, particularly, after about 1900.

Added to this growing pattern of segregation was an increasing level of racial violence directed against black people. Although racial violence had marked even the era of Reconstruction (not to mention that of slavery), such violence seemed to reach new heights after Reconstruction ended and, especially, as the century drew to a close. A real upsurge in lynching, for example, occurred during the post-Reconstruction period. The worst decade was, again, the 1890s, during which there were almost two hundred lynchings a year, the bulk of them in the South. At another level, racial violence flared up into a series of race riots in various parts of the United States. In a 1900 race riot, mobs of white men roamed New Orleans for black victims; a similar riot broke out that same year in New York City. The most spectacular riot of this period occurred in Atlanta in 1906. More than ten thousand whites took to the streets in September of that year, mobbing black passersby, pulling people off streetcars and beating them, even attacking people in their homes.[5]

Supporting these racist practices was the racist ideology of black inferiority, an ideology that itself increased in strength during the late nineteenth century, playing a role in political oratory, popular culture, and even American intellectual life. At its most benign, this ideology evoked images of the old-time "plantation Negro," stressing his supposed loyalty to and dependence on the white master class of the old South or portraying such quaintly humorous "characteristics" as inveterate laziness and a propensity for chicken stealing. Little of this ideology was overtly hostile; much—particularly in the works of such planta-

4. C. Vann Woodward, *Origins of the New South, 1877–1915* (Baton Rouge, 1951), 321–22; Woodward, *The Strange Career of Jim Crow* (3rd rev. ed; New York, 1974), 97–102.

5. Woodward, *Origins of the New South*, 351; Gilbert Osofsky, *Harlem: The Making of a Ghetto, Negro New York, 1890–1930* (New York, 1968), 47–49; John Dittmer, *Black Georgia in the Progressive Era, 1900–1920* (Urbana, 1977), 123–29.

tion-tradition writers as Irwin Russell, Thomas Nelson Page, and Joel Chandler Harris—was even intended to pay affectionate tribute to the humble black people who, these writers claimed, had served their masters well during slavery and who continued to give their former masters respect and devotion after emancipation. The affection, of course, made such portrayals no less insidious, for, in their affection and sympathy for the blacks of the old regime, the self-proclaimed white admirers of the plantation Negro presented blacks as a dependent people who found fulfillment only by identifying with white people and whose well-being depended wholly upon white largesse.[6]

But as the nineteenth century drew to a close, the notion of black inferiority came to focus steadily on the belief that, with freedom, black people were showing signs of an ugly degeneracy, signs most visible in an alleged propensity for criminality, sexual brutality, and violence. This message was not entirely new. It had even played a role in the defense of slavery, before the Civil War. But it undoubtedly came into its own during the 1890s, when it was used to great effect in support of disfranchisement and Jim Crow. It also justified the orgies of racial violence that marked turn-of-the-century American life. They were required, racists declared, to keep the Negro in a subordinate place in American society. This ideological development was certainly an important part of the more general deterioration of racial conditions in the closing years of the nineteenth century and the early years of the twentieth.[7]

The story of worsening conditions is important to tell, because it provides an inescapable background for black literature in the late nineteenth century and early twentieth. In their works, black writers directly confronted the conditions of an increasingly racist society in everything from their choice of subjects to the way they drew their characters and the kinds of moods they tried to portray. Black writing during the nadir not only protested against racism but created a protest that took account of changing conditions. It would be difficult to understand the main lines of development in pre–World War I black writing without an awareness of the deteriorating racial situation in which its creation took place.

It would also be difficult to understand much about black writing from 1877 to 1915 without some sense of the characteristics of its creators. Black writers were hardly representative of the black popula-

6. See Logan, *Betrayal of the Negro*, 242–44.
7. *Ibid.*; Joel Williamson, *The Crucible of Race: Black-White Relations in the American South Since Emancipation* (New York, 1984), 111ff.

tion as a whole during this period. They may be described without oversimplification as members of the black middle class that was taking shape and growing in size in the post-Reconstruction era. This class was composed of black ministers, teachers, and other professionals, as well as black businessmen, who increasingly supplied many of the essential services for the segregated black community. Encouraged in its growth by the needs of that community and by the opportunities resulting from the development of black institutions—including churches and colleges—this group, although small in size prior to World War I, was nevertheless visible and influential, a significant part of prewar black life.

A survey of black writers of this period, based on biographical and autobiographical remarks in their books, along with sketches in magazines and in such standard biographical sources as William J. Simmons' 1887 *Men of Mark* and Frank L. Mather's 1915 *Who's Who of the Colored Race*, provides a fairly clear picture of them. Most—about 80 percent—held professional positions, chiefly as ministers and educators, but with some physicians and attorneys among them. Over three-quarters were college educated—most at black colleges but about one-third at predominantly white institutions—a striking figure when one considers W. E. B. Du Bois' 1900 estimate that there was "about one college trained person in every 3600 Negroes." Even in regard to religion, these writers showed a middle-class character. Although, not surprisingly, about half belonged to Baptist churches or to the African Methodist Episcopal Church—the major religious organizations of black Americans at the time—a surprising number belonged to such middle-class, white-dominated organizations as the Episcopal, Congregational, and Presbyterian churches (denominations singled out for their middle-class character in the mid-twentieth century by sociologist E. Franklin Frazier in his study of the "black bourgeoisie"). These religious bodies served less than 1 percent of the black churchgoing population, according to a census published in 1903. But almost one-quarter of the writers surveyed here belonged to one or another of them.[8]

8. William Johnson Simmons, *Men of Mark: Eminent, Progressive, and Rising* (1887; rpr. Chicago, 1970); Frank Lincoln Mather (ed.), *Who's Who of the Colored Race* (Chicago, 1915); W. E. B. Du Bois (ed.), *The College-Bred Negro*, Atlanta University Publication No. 5 (1900; rpr. New York, 1968), 42; E. Franklin Frazier, *Black Bourgeoisie: The Rise of a New Middle Class in the United States* (1957; rpr. New York, 1962), 79–80; W. E .B. Du Bois (ed.), *The Negro Church*, Atlanta University Publication No. 8 (1903; rpr. New York, 1968), 38.

I do not want to conclude too much from such figures. Black writers were, after all, individuals. As creative men and women, they brought their own individuality to their efforts to capture and communicate their ideas and feelings. Nevertheless, such a collective portrait helps indicate a common body of experience upon which they drew and helps illuminate their work.

There is much to indicate that the black middle class shared in and lived life according to the dominant values of the larger society. Scattered comments indicate, for example, that members of this group took great pride in achieving a middle-class decorum in religious life; and similar evidence exists in regard to other areas of life as well. The Howard University scholar Andrew F. Hilyer described a fairly general middle-class orientation for himself and his contemporaries when he remarked in an essay that middle-class black and white Americans "speak the same language, read and enjoy the same literature, venerate and supplicate the same Deity, have the same religion, the same ideals, the same standards of taste, the same manners and customs, love the same country and worship the same flag." Highly conscious about status, moreover, members of this black middle class often expressed a troubled alienation from, as one put it, "the rank and file whom we commonly denominate as *our people*." People who spoke in such terms saw themselves as Victorian Americans and resented suggestions that, because of color, they differed in any significant way from middle-class Americans who happened to be white. And even in terms of color, they were not all that distinct from white Americans. A substantial part of the black middle class of this period had noticeable white ancestry, and its members often drew a "color line" between themselves and darker individuals.[9]

This middle-class orientation was formed and reinforced in a number of ways. If one looks, for example, at letters and diaries from the

9. Comments on religion appeared, for example, in Charlotte Forten Grimké, Diary Number 5, November, 1885, to July, 1892, p. 2 of typescript of original, in Francis J. Grimké Papers, Manuscript Division, The Moorland-Spingarn Research Center, Howard University; also J. C. McAdams, "The Mourning Preacher," in James T. Haley (ed.), *Sparkling Gems of Race Knowledge Worth Reading* (Nashville, 1897), 124. Quotations are from Andrew F. Hilyer, "Analysis of American Color-Prejudice and How to Suppress It," p. 15, ms. of talk presented before the Bethel Literary and Historical Association, March 23, 1892, in Andrew F. Hilyer Papers, Manuscript Division, The Moorland-Spingarn Research Center, Howard University; Victoria Earle Matthews to Frederick Douglass, August 3, 1894, in Douglass Papers. For a good discussion of the role of individuals of mixed race in black society at this time, see Joel Williamson, *New People: Miscegenation and Mulattoes in the United States* (New York, 1980), 82–84.

period, one sees such an orientation in the kinds of expectations about social behavior that middle-class black people had for themselves and for others. More formally, one sees their middle-class orientation in the kinds of institutions that contributed to middle-class life, not only in religious organizations but also in education. Black colleges, as well as white institutions, not only provided credentials for many of those who entered the middle class through such professions as ministry, teaching, and the law but also gave many young people a significant formative exposure to Victorian culture and ideals. This was especially true of the black institutions with strong liberal arts curricula—including Howard, Fisk, and Atlanta universities. The curricula at these schools were firmly grounded in the classics of Western civilization and gave graduates a strong background in the knowledge and ideas shared widely among middle-class Americans.

One may say something similar about one of the most significant institutions of middle-class social life in post-Reconstruction black communities, the literary society. Some of these societies—for example, the famous Bethel Literary and Historical Association of Washington, D.C.—were associated with churches; others were more secular. But all did much to bring about discussions of contemporary literary and intellectual issues among their members. Black writers themselves were often members of these organizations. In some cases, they used them as forums for readings of their own works.

In general, the activities of these literary societies allowed for a broad exposure to aspects of Western thought and culture, including material by and about blacks. In 1904, for example, the Book Lovers Club of Kansas City devoted a year to discussing W. E. B. Du Bois' *Souls of Black Folk*; in 1905, to Franklin Henry Giddings' works in sociology; in 1906, to Edward Tylor's anthropology and Alfred Lord Tennyson's *Idylls of the King*. In later years the group addressed such topics as history and art; the status of woman in America, England, France, and Germany; and Russian history and art.[10] Societies elsewhere had similarly diverse interests. All provided a significant and continuing familiarity with the mainstream of Victorian American life and with the main features and tendencies of middle-class culture.

But such a middle-class orientation was especially clear in the works of post-Reconstruction black writers. In regard to religion, they gave

10. Elizabeth L. Davis, *Lifting as They Climb: The History of the National Association of Colored Women* (Washington, D.C., 1933), 414.

expression to a middle-class piety that confirmed the pride in decorum one finds in other contexts. And they showed their devotion to other middle-class virtues—temperance, culture, and refinement—as well. This conclusion in itself will seem familiar to many readers, as other historians and critics—particularly those writing after Robert Bone's pioneering work on early black fiction appeared—have noted this characteristic. But few have examined it in any detail, instead viewing the middle-class orientation of the literature as an effort on the part of black writers to escape from the harsher realities of American racism or, to follow the view of critic Addison Gayle, Jr., as a surrendering of the right of self-definition to others.[11] There is certainly some truth to such views; however, they tend to deal with "middle-classness" as such a general characteristic that their authors fail to perceive significant aspects of the literature itself, particularly the specific role that dominant values played in the post-Reconstruction era in the creation of literary works, the organizing of ideas and images, and the structuring of intentions. When one begins to survey the literature, it becomes apparent that the uses black writers made of piety and of the virtues of refinement were more than superficial; they were essential to the portrayal of characters and situations and to the expression of moods and desires. In their works, these writers attached an importance to middle-class concerns—and showed a fluency with them—that suggests the concerns were taken quite seriously. Hence, they must occupy an important place in any analysis of the literature from this period.

In addition, the works by black authors published between 1877 and 1915 show a high level of agreement about the values of American middle-class culture. Students of black intellectual history, familiar with the divisions that existed among black thinkers and political leaders, may be surprised by the consensus among black writers of poetry and fiction about the meaning and importance of middle-class ideals. Indeed, one cannot fail to be impressed by the extent to which, in literature, even the protest against prejudice and racial injustice was framed in terms of more generally focused ideas and ideals. The middle-class orientation of these writers provided a defining background to the works they produced.

The commitment to middle-class ideals also defines much of the writers' significance. Just as the writers were unrepresentative of the

11. Robert A. Bone, *The Negro Novel in America* (Rev. ed.; New Haven, 1965); Addison Gayle, Jr., *The Way of the New World: The Black Novel in America* (New York, 1975), 11.

larger black community in such social characteristics as education and religion, so too were they probably unrepresentative in their appreciation for middle-class culture. One has to say "probably" because the available evidence makes such a generalization problematic. On the one hand, there is evidence that most blacks shared with other Americans, including white middle-class Americans, certain broad aspirations for economic independence and upward mobility. Historian Joel Williamson, among others, has seen this in the widespread black desire for land upon emancipation and throughout the late nineteenth century. On the other hand, as scholars such as Lawrence Levine and Sterling Stuckey have shown, there was a large community of rural southern blacks who expressed and used a culture that was, in crucial ways, very different from that of middle-class America—with a different system of ethics, for example, and a different understanding of the forces at work in the world. Like many of the prominent leaders discussed by Stuckey, the writers surveyed here definitely did not share in that tradition-based rural culture, at least not if their writings are any indication. Although it is possible to identify elements of that culture even in the earliest black literature, for most of the period before World War I the presence of such elements was far from common and, even then, was highly self-conscious, still framed by an orientation toward the literary and cultural styles of the larger society. For the most part, early black writers showed no unambiguous identification with the folk culture Levine and Stuckey have described. To the extent that such a culture was widely shared among black Americans—and one can speculate that it was, given the overwhelmingly rural character of the black population prior to World War I—black literature from this period further emphasizes the unusual social position of its creators.[12]

But significance can grow out of more than representativeness. In the case of the black writers surveyed here, it grows out of the extent to which they have allowed us to see the meanings of powerful, strongly held values in the difficult historical setting provided by an increasingly segregated and racist society. They have allowed us to see how a group of men and women with well-defined aspirations—aspirations that many had fulfilled educationally and professionally—tried to adapt,

---

12. Williamson, *Crucible of Race*, 45; Lawrence W. Levine, *Black Culture and Black Consciousness: Afro-American Folk Thought from Slavery to Freedom* (New York, 1977); Sterling Stuckey, *Slave Culture: Nationalist Theory and the Foundations of Black America* (New York, 1987).

modify, define, and redefine their ideals and values in the face of a society that was hostile to them.

Perhaps the most crucial force in black writing during this period was the interaction of racism and the writers' middle-class character. This interaction provided the chief dynamic in black literature in the post-Reconstruction era. It was the major source of tensions and ambiguities in that literature. Black writers produced works showing an awareness that, despite their own ideals and achievements, they had to confront increasingly rigid barriers to their participation in the American mainstream. Bell has recently noted ways in which early black novels—and more recent ones as well—have revealed the "shifting emotions" produced by the interaction of discrimination with concerns about class and culture.[13] What must also be stressed, however, is that, at least for the period before World War I, these shifting emotions, and the ways in which they were expressed, were part of a definite historical process, one in which the position of the black writer, as a black American, was growing more difficult.

Joel Williamson has discussed this issue in regard to the black middle class as a whole, showing how one impact of Jim Crow was to render increasingly difficult even minimal positive contacts between black people and the major sources and institutions of American culture.[14] It is compelling to read black literature in terms of the process Williamson has described, because, in fact, the literature does show not only shifting emotions but also patterns of adaptation and redefinition in ideals and values over time; Williamson's characterization of the processes of race relations in the late nineteenth century does much to illuminate those patterns. Above all, the literature shows an attempt to come to grips with dominant values in an increasingly bifurcated American world.

Looking at such historical and sociological factors is not intended to minimize the creative efforts of individual writers. These efforts must always stand at the center of any analysis of literary achievements. But historical and sociological factors provided a strong framework within which literary achievements took place—a framework so strong that one cannot understand the nature of those achievements without a thorough appreciation of it.

13. Bernard W. Bell, *the Afro-American Novel and Its Tradition* (Amherst, 1987), 14.
14. Williamson, *Crucible of Race*, 50–52. This point was also made by Ray Stannard Baker in *Following the Color Line: American Negro Citizenship in the Progressive Era* (1908; rpr. New York, 1964), 65.

I

Foundations of a Black American Literary Tradition, 1877–1896

The period from the late 1870s to the middle 1890s may be set apart as a time of laying foundations for later developments and changes in black literature. For the most part, the black poets and authors of this period labored in relative obscurity—at least so far as the larger American reading public was concerned. Not until the mid-1890s, marked by the 1896 recognition of Paul Laurence Dunbar by William Dean Howells and the regular appearance of Charles W. Chesnutt's writing in mainstream American magazines, would there be black writers with a large readership, white or black. Models had to be developed and discovered, and the years immediately after Reconstruction represented a fertile setting for such efforts. The appearance of Dunbar and Chesnutt would, however, turn these early efforts in strikingly new directions, marking an end to this first period of black writing.

Black writing itself, during the early post-Reconstruction years, had all the marks of an emerging literature. Although there was rapid growth in the amount of black literature published after Reconstruction, compared to the years before 1877, publication still took place on a modest scale. There were a few novels, two book-length works of poetry by Albery A. Whitman—*The Rape of Florida* and *Not a Man, and Yet a Man*—and a long verse-play by William Edgar Easton on the heroism of the Haitian Dessalines. The bulk of the literary work from this early period was poetry that appeared in black-edited newspapers and periodicals. Black writers turned, in particular, to the scholarly and sophisticated *A.M.E. Church Review*—founded in 1884 and edited first by Benjamin T. Tanner and then, beginning in 1888, by Levi J. Coppin— as the major outlet for creative work. Some writing was also collected in little volumes published by job printers. A very little—chiefly some early works by Chesnutt—appeared in more mainstream American publications.

For much of the post-Reconstruction period, black writers were conservative in the models they chose to work from. A great deal of their writing did little more than carry over antebellum themes and forms, particularly those of the antislavery tradition. Virtually all of it drew heavily on the most popular elements and sentimental models in mainstream, white-written American popular literature. One finds little in black literature of this early period that corresponds to the currents of regionalism and realism that had begun to take shape in other areas of American literature at this time; nor does one find anything like experimentation in forms of poetry or fiction. Instead, black writers closely adhered to the most common, and most polite, modes. In poetry, this meant that virtually all the work conformed to regular patterns of rhythm and rhyme and that much of it used the kind of imagery also found in the works of white poets appearing in popular American newspapers and magazines. In fiction, this meant that black writers worked in such widely popular forms as the melodrama and the romance, even where they used such forms to address racial themes.

As such conservatism indicates, black literature from this era was the most thoroughly middle-class of any written after 1877. It provides the base line in terms of which later shifts in stance toward dominant American ideals and values must be read. Such shifts began to be visible only in the 1890s, at the close of the early period.

This basic conservatism provided the framework for literary achievement and creativity on the part of black writers before the 1890s. There were no real technical innovators. The writers who labored in obscurity, and to whom one must give much attention in a survey of this early period, were highly conventional, with little to set them apart from one another. Such a major figure as Albery Whitman, whose work will be discussed in some detail, was distinguished chiefly by the level of his ambition, rather than by any efforts to produce genuinely innovative work. Toward the close of this period, such writers as Frances Ellen Watkins Harper and Victoria Earle Matthews did start to shift slightly away from more traditional themes and ideas; but they couched that shift in literary forms and language that should have shocked no one familiar with the black writing that had come before, or indeed with much of the writing by white writers from this era.

One can best account for the conservatism of post-Reconstruction black literature in terms of the dominant literary purposes black writers had during the years before the mid-1890s, purposes they defined mainly in terms of the racial situation they found themselves in. Black writers often talked about their reasons for writing: in prefaces to their books, in essays in such places as the *A.M.E. Church Review*, in reviews of one another's works. But as succinct a statement as any in this early period was made in 1892 by a group of black writers and intellectuals, including Frederick Douglass, Bishop Daniel Payne of the African Methodist Episcopal Church, I. Garland Penn, T. Thomas Fortune, and Alexander Crummell, who called a conference to discuss common concerns. They focused on the failure of black writing to "make its way among our white fellow-citizens to anything like a desirable extent, and not even to a degree which our literary merit deserves." They were also concerned about the need to increase "the interest of colored men in its circulation"; but at the center was a desire to produce a literature that would reach a broad, general audience, particularly a white reading public.[1] These writers and intellectuals wanted to reach such an audience because they believed that literature could make a difference in race relations. Specifically, they believed that literary works could provide the ideas and the record of achievement that could lead to a breaking down of racial barriers.

Implicit in such a view was what one might call literary assimilationism. I use the term *assimilationism* advisedly in this context. Critic Houston Baker has rightly scored other commentators for their treatment of this feature of early black writing. He says, "Certain periods and certain authors of Afro-American expression have simply been written off as 'assimilationist' "; and he decries the tendency in such treatments to categorize "assimilationist" works as "slavishly imitative and metaphorically impoverished occurrences."[2] The point in using the term here, however, is neither to write off the work produced in the post-Reconstruction era nor to treat it as simply imitative—built on what some might term white models. It is rather to suggest that this literature was created from a perspective very much like that summarized by Andrew Hilyer when he delineated the similarities of black and white middle-class Americans. This perspective stressed the extent to which black and white Americans were members of the same cultural commu-

1. "A Call for Afro-American Authors of America: To Meet with the American Association of Educators of Colored Youth, in Wilmington, N.C., December 27–30, 1892," pamphlet, in Frederick Douglass Papers, Manuscript Division, Library of Congress.

2. Houston A. Baker, Jr., *Blues, Ideology, and Afro-American Literature: A Vernacular Theory* (Chicago, 1984), 114–15.

nity, for whom the same literary models were common property, intrinsically neither black nor white.

Nor was such an approach somehow "accommodationist," in the sense that its proponents had made a peace with white American racism and discrimination. To the contrary, as we shall see, it was an approach that virtually demanded protest, as those who held it saw their proper place, with no ambiguity, to be one of full participation in American society, and saw the proper American society to be one in which distinctions based on color had become irrelevant.

This was the point of view embodied in the purposes of black literature during the period. It was to prove its writers' right to be recognized as mainstream Americans, by both its content and its character, even as it demonstrated the writers' cultural similarity to the larger American community.

So the purposes of these writers were far from imitative, however they might look to later generations. Those purposes led, nevertheless, to the thorough conservatism of black literary work during this time. Such aims militated against any great degree of technical innovation or experimentation by focusing on the creation of a literature that could gain a large and general audience. They implicitly recommended a literature based on the most widely accepted models. Such purposes also pointed toward a literature whose message was the desirability of conservativism, of entering into the mainstream dominated by "white fellow-citizens." Assimilationism was to dominate black writing well into the 1890s.

The strength of this assimilationism is important to note. Recent scholars, including George Levesque and Sterling Stuckey, have taken others to task for overstressing what appear to be assimilationist assumptions in black intellectual history and for ignoring evidence of significant separatist, even nationalist, thought going as far back as the late eighteenth and early nineteenth centuries.[3] Such criticism may be justified so far as political and social thought are concerned; but it does not apply to black literature, at least not in the first two decades after Reconstruction. Among black writers of fiction and poetry, there was a strong assimilationist consensus, as strong and as clear as the writers'

3. George Levesque, "Interpreting Early Black Ideology: A Reappraisal of Historical Consensus," *Journal of the Early Republic*, I (1981), 269–87; Sterling Stuckey, *Slave Culture: Nationalist Theory and the Foundations of Black America* (New York, 1987).

commitment to middle-class American ideals. One can find nothing of separatism or nationalism in black literature from this era.

But apart from questions of consensus, assimilationism could guide black literary purposes because, although racism was a powerful force in American life—as it had long been—the social and political processes that were to lead to a racial bifurcation of American society were just gathering momentum. As a result, although black writers were fully aware of the power of racism in their lives and of the need to address racism through their works, they did not yet clearly see the virtually complete disengagement from the dominant American society that ultimately would have profound effects on their middle-class life. These concerns were not very apparent in 1877 or even through the 1880s. Only as racism became stronger, in the 1890s, did black writers begin to raise strong questions about the meaning of assimilationist ideals and goals. But for most of the years up to the 1890s, assimilationist ideals and purposes played the key shaping role for black literature in the post-Reconstruction era.

The clearest measure of the assimilationism of black literature during this period is the approach black writers took in protesting against racism in American life. Protest was a central theme in post-Reconstruction black literature, as it long had been and as it continues to be. Collections of poetry inevitably included poems indicting racial injustice. Although a few works of fiction—notably Emma Dunham Kelley's religious novel *Megda* and James L. Young's "French Romance" *Helen Duval*—avoided racial questions altogether, most fiction also protested against the American racial order. Given the conditions black people faced in post-Reconstruction times, it is hardly surprising that black writers felt a need to protest. As assimilationists, they focused their protest mainly on their exclusion from the mainstream of American life.

Consistent with the 1892 remarks of Douglass and his colleagues, black writers of this period saw the main culprit in racial oppression as prejudice, the wrongheaded ideas whites had about the character and capabilities of blacks. The primarily assimilationist thrust of the literature these writers produced was plain in the kinds of cases they made against prejudice. A poem entitled "Of One Blood," by the South Carolina minister George Clinton Rowe, was typical. Rowe rhetorically asked the white man:

Who taught thee, man, thy brother to despise?
By nature art thou favored more, or wise
As gods? Art thou in untaught state beclothed
In strength of mind, with lofty thought endowed?

He answered his own question by declaring, "Then know that *all men are of God!*"[4] For Rowe, white people could make no special claim to superiority, because, as human beings, black men could make a claim on equality with no less strength.

The basic structure of Rowe's poem was a paradigm for post-Reconstruction black literature, and it was a model with roots in antebellum writing. Black writers in both eras commonly juxtaposed accounts of white prejudice with opposition to racism's main tenets. They did so, moreover, in a way that accorded with their assimilationist purposes. The opposition they offered was inevitably founded on what were supposed to be American ideals. How, they asked rhetorically, can white Americans claim any real devotion to their own best ideals and, at the same time, view blacks with prejudice? Thus Rowe, for example, asserted the irreconcilability of prejudice with widely professed Christian beliefs in human equality. Other works elaborated on this argument, showing that prejudice was contrary to facts as well as to principles. They did so by demonstrating that white ideas and efforts to the contrary, black people had every right to a place of equality in American life.

Black writers saw evidence for their claim on behalf of black Americans in many areas, one of which was history. A number of black historians began during this period to publish accounts of the role of blacks in the American past; George Washington Williams' 1883 two-volume *History of the Negro Race in America* is the most notable. Assimilationist in thrust, these accounts paid the greatest attention to the contributions black people had made to the creation and growth of the American nation, even as they detailed the prejudice black Americans had been forced to confront in order to contribute to American life. Black poets and writers of fiction followed these works in order to celebrate what blacks had accomplished and what they had contributed to American life in the face of oppression.

Alfred Stidum's 1890 poem "1620 to 1863" is a good example of a work taking such a historical focus. A long poem, it presents a virtual summary, in verse, of the historians' accounts of the role of black people

4. George Clinton Rowe, *Thoughts in Verse* (Charleston, S.C., 1887), 111.

in American history. The poem begins with an indictment of slavery that calls into question white America's devotion to its cherished principles of freedom and equality. It also takes this point in a more complex direction by calling up the spirits of the leaders of America's major slave revolts: "Deep within the smouldering embers of a crushed and beaten race, are stealing ever upward, through the fissures of some iron heart, avenging flames. / Ahead the noble Gabriel, Turner, Vassey [Vesey] forged, to wrest the chains that held them captive, ere joined the hero, Brown, the martyred trio of illustrious names."[5]

The language of Stidum's celebration of the slave revolutionaries is important, because paradoxically it supports the assimilationism of the period. These were not men, Stidum made clear, who were out to challenge American principles. Rather, they were men who were fired by those principles to fight against an institution that itself perverted the purposes of the nation. Stidum emphasized the point when he described the bravery of the black troops who fought against slavery in the Civil War. "In fierce encounter, shock-resisting shock, they met," Stidum wrote, "champions of their country's cause, and enemies of a people's right to the boon of human liberty."[6] As Rowe used principles of Christian equality, Stidum used principles of American freedom to indict prejudice in terms of the very ideals white Americans claimed to hold dear.

Other writers matched Stidum's historical pageantry, and still others focused on more specific themes drawn from history for indicting prejudice from a clearly American point of view. Such a perspective was apparent when poets, for example, praised black heroes. Rowe was only one of many who celebrated that "Afric's son" Crispus Attucks for helping ignite the fire of American liberty. The noted editor T. Thomas Fortune was close to Stidum in the form of his appreciation of Nat Turner, whose very life declared, according to Fortune, "I Will be free! I will be free! / Or, fighting, die a man!"[7]

The heroes and historical achievements celebrated by these early writers helped fill in the paradigm that structured the indictment of prejudice. Prejudice was wrong because black people not only could be

---

5. Alfred H. Stidum, "1620–1863: Poem," *A.M.E. Church Review*, VI (1890), 421.

6. *Ibid.*

7. George Clinton Rowe, *Our Heroes: Patriotic Poems on Men, Women and Savings of the Negro Race* (Charleston, S.C., 1890), 10; T. Thomas Fortune, "Nat Turner," *A.M.E. Church Review*, I (1884), 101.

but were good Americans, according to America's highest standards. This assertion was the key to the assimilationist case.

The model in terms of which this assertion was put was effective because there were a variety of ways to fill it in. Although principles and history were important, so were other accomplishments. Solomon G. Brown published an exemplary version of such a use of the assimilationist model for protest in a long 1891 poem, "He Is a Negro Still: The Uncompromising Prejudice Towards the Negro American":

> "Why don't the Negro keep his place,"
> Not force himself upon our race?
> It matters not what men may say,
> They are inferior in every way.
>
> Inferior to the meanest white,
> Are always hateful in our sight;
> We never will accept his race—
> 'Twould bring our children to disgrace.
>
> . . . .
>
> Suppose he be physician square,
> With practice large and charges fair?
> He cures disease with extra skill—
> He is a Negro doctor still.
>
> . . . .
>
> Suppose his wife has manners fine,
> Cultured, brilliant, splendid mind?
> And every rule she rightly fills—
> That woman is a Negress still.[8]

Brown's poem is an angry denunciation of the resistance of prejudice even to proven accomplishments by black men and women. In its presentation of the cynicism of the white racist, it recalls Frederick Douglass' antebellum characterization of prejudice as "no less than a *murderous, hell-born hatred* of every virtue which may adorn the character of a *black man*."[9] No matter what a black man or woman may achieve, the poet wrote, to the white man he or she remains an object of scorn.

Although the tone is angry, the poem does not stray either from the model black writers usually employed in attacking prejudice or from

8. Solomon G. Brown, "He Is a Negro Still: The Uncompromising Prejudice Towards the Negro American. A Reply," pamphlet, February, 1891, in Solomon G. Brown Papers, The Moorland-Spingarn Research Center, Howard University.

9. Philip S. Foner (ed.), *The Life and Writings of Frederick Douglass* (5 vols.; New York, 1950—75), II, 128.

assimilationist ideals. It even declares, in its closing stanzas, that conditions must improve. Black men, Brown concluded, are ultimately des-
tined for equality:

> Here is a fact you cannot hide,
> The Blackman is our country's pride;
> May twist and turn it as you will—
> The Negro is your brother still.

> This fact he loves above the rest.
> While it disturbs the white man's rest;
> Twist and turn it as you may,
> The Negro's here, HE'S HERE TO STAY![10]

Thus the anger should not obscure the poem's assimilationist message.
Brotherhood and equality are at its core, supporting the governing idea
that blacks are no different from whites—if only whites could recognize the truth. Brown predicted that whether they liked it or not, whites
would be compelled by the achievements of black men and women to
recognize the truth of black America's claim for a full share in the
nation's life. For all its anger, Brown's poem shared both the goals and
the optimism of assimilationist black writing in the post-Reconstruction
period.

The substance of literary assimilationism was established not only in
protest writing. It also presented a world that was fully in keeping with
the middle-class orientation of black writers. This was a world informed, above all, by ideas of gentility.

The Victorian world into which the black middle class emerged in
the late nineteenth century gave a crucial place to gentility, understood
as the development of inner virtue through the cultivation of proper
thoughts and feelings, or proper "sentiments." These sentiments were
to be fine and pure, noble and tender. Where they were present, they
would be reflected in every aspect of appearance and behavior, which
would themselves be refined and correct. Coarse language, coarse manners, and coarse ideas were to be avoided. So were the cruder passions
of lust and anger. Self-restraint, sincerity, and refinement were to mark
everything the genteel person did.

Gentility could be cultivated. It could be developed, for example, by
a studied appreciation of the arts and literature. As one developed a
faculty for aesthetic discrimination, one also learned to recognize the

10. Brown, "He Is a Negro Still."

kinds of emotions and ideas that led to virtue and refinement. Gentility could also be cultivated through a due attention to home and family, to religion, and to the kind of presentation one made of oneself in society. But at its center was a kind of moral sentimentalism founded on a Victorian assurance that both head and heart led to virtue and a confidence that, of the two, the heart was probably the surer guide.[11]

There was much to challenge this genteel ethos in the late nineteenth century. As historians such as T. Jackson Lears have shown, intellectual developments, urbanization, and industrialization were all undermining older notions of inner virtue and sentimental ideals. Moreover, in the works of such writers as William Dean Howells and Henry James, a kind of literary subversion of American middle-class gentility had come to play a prominent role. But the older ideas remained significant as conservative forces in middle-class life.[12] This was true for blacks as well as whites. Thus, just as literary gentility remained a mainstay in much of American popular writing, no subversive elements appeared in the works of black writers of this period. For them, the ideals of gentility remained wholly positive; and their literature remained wholly faithful to its tenets.

To see more clearly what gentility meant, and to see how it could apply to black as well as white middle-class life, it is useful to look at an appreciative description of a young black Bostonian in 1894 by a reporter for the Boston *Globe*. It is as good a summary as one could hope for of the general ideals of gentility in Victorian America. Looking about the young woman's home, the *Globe*'s reporter remarked on the tastefulness of the furnishings. The bookshelves, he wrote, "are lined with books that speak of a taste at once classic and scholastic. The pictures on the wall," he added, "are suggestions of the true and beautiful in life." The environment was perfectly suited for the young woman; "she is so thoroughly a lady and so thoroughly artistic, from the crown of her small, proud head to the tips of her slender, beautiful, brown fingers." The reporter's admiration was aroused particularly by "the

11. For a good, concise account, see Joan Shelley Rubin, "Self, Culture, and Self-Culture in Modern America: The Early History of the Book-of-the-Month Club," *Journal of American History*, LXXI (1985), 784–85. Much of this discussion is also based on Daniel Walker Howe, "American Victorianism as a Culture," *American Quarterly*, XXVII (1975), 529; and on Karen Halttunen, *Confidence Men and Painted Women: A Study of Middle-Class Culture in America, 1830–1870* (New Haven, 1982), 186–90.

12. For a thorough discussion of the changes taking place in late nineteenth century American culture, see T. Jackson Lears, *No Place of Grace: Antimodernism and the Transformation of American Culture, 1880–1920* (New York, 1981), especially Chap. 1.

rich, refined tones of her voice as she discusses warmly the world of arts and letters."[13] Here, personified, were the genteel virtues of high culture, refined taste, good manners, and lofty ideals—not to mention a physical appearance that in its delicacy reflected the genteel quality and character of the individual. And underlying all was a core of noble sentiments, a "warmth" that came from thinking of arts and letters but that did not overcome the "refined" tone of the young woman's voice. Refinement and proper feelings created a gentility revealed in every aspect of the woman's appearance before the world.

Contained in this description were the kinds of genteel ideals that, along with racial concerns, helped to inform the ideas black Americans had about literary work. As late as 1899, for example, Josephine Turpin Washington, a leader of black society—and a sometime poet—published a brief essay on literature and its functions. In this essay, she stressed the power of literature to improve the individual. "While sentiment, feeling, the cultivation of an inner, a soul life, does not directly contribute to the breadwinning process," she wrote, "it sweetens and strengthens man's whole nature, and so fits him for the better performance of any duty." She added: "Poetry is allied to our best affections. Home, wife, mother, country, are themes ever dear to the poet."[14] One can never know how many writers of her day were familiar with Mrs. Washington's remarks. But as a summary description of much of the writing done by black writers during the first two decades after Reconstruction, her comments were completely on the mark. In themes and images, black writers produced work designed to evoke the "best affections," with language that was refined and soft. Their poetry embodied such virtues. When they wrote fiction, they created characters who embodied the virtues of gentility. The heroines were chaste and delicate, the heroes pure and manly. Indeed, the young Bostonian described in the *Globe* could have been the model for a character in the fiction produced by black writers of the post-Reconstruction era.

It would be hard not to recognize the extent to which the writing of genteel literature fit in with the assimilationist purposes articulated by Douglass and his colleagues in 1892. When black writers created a literature that cohered with the ideals of conservative gentility, they

13. ". . . In Colored Society," Boston *Globe*, July 22, 1894, clipping, in Ruffin Family Papers, Manuscript Division, The Moorland-Spingarn Research Center, Howard University.

14. Josephine Turpin Washington, "The Province of Poetry," *A.M.E. Church Review*, VI (1889), 139, 141.

found a common ground with the larger American middle class and a basis on which to appeal to the larger reading public. Genteel poetry and fiction dominated popular writing among whites and blacks alike. The main themes and conventions of black genteel writing were those of white genteel writing as well.

Furthermore, in general terms, this genteel literature, by its very nature, fit into the paradigm for protest that governed post-Reconstruction black writing. Implicitly, such literature disproved racism by demonstrating the extent to which black people were capable of expressing fine thoughts and feelings. And as critic Jane Campbell has rightly reminded us, this may have been especially true in regard to the sentimental heroines of the era's black fiction, who provided an important and necessary counterstatement to ideas of black sexuality—ideas that played an important part in the racist ideology of the period.[15] But, again, the thoughts and sentiments of gentility as such should not get lost in more general considerations, because a more specific understanding of literary gentility helps to make more tangible the perspective from which middle-class black Americans approached a range of matters, including questions of race. There were a number of key themes in terms of which black writers expressed their own gentility, a number of themes through which they evoked their own "best affections."

Certainly the most important aspect of gentility for black writers of this era was religion. The kind of religion that dominated black literature in the second half of the nineteenth century was that of a thoroughly genteel piety. It was a religious expression of the genteel ideals of the age. Such a piety informed the works of one of the earliest black poets of this period, Islay Walden. Born in slavery and early recognized to have a talent for "reckoning," Walden had occupied a favored position as a slave. After the Civil War, he moved to Washington, D.C., relying on his wits to stay alive. He memorized several chapters of an anatomy textbook and traveled around giving lectures on the topic. At the same time, however, he also displayed a strong devotion to religion and set up Sunday schools in some of the city's toughest neighborhoods. In the course of his work, he met a Rutgers professor, who sponsored him at Howard University. He went on to a Reformed Church seminary in New Brunswick, New Jersey, and ultimately became a Presbyterian minister,

---

15. Jane Campbell, *Mythic Black Fiction: The Transformation of History* (Knoxville, 1986), 38–39.

working mainly in North Carolina. Walden published two volumes of poetry. The first, in 1873, was intended to help him raise funds for his expenses at Howard. The second, *Sacred Poems*, published in 1877, was written to help meet his seminary expenses. In both books, the poetry was heavily religious.[16]

At the center of Walden's poetry was a deep devotionalism. The poems focused on an emotional relationship between the believer and God and on the hope for a heavenly union. In "Evening Prayer for Children," Walden put forth in simple terms the kind of relationship one should have with God:

> Beneath the falling shades of night
> 　Dear Lord I bow and pray
> That Thou wilt keep me while I sleep
> 　As Thou dost through the day.
>
> I pray that harm may not appear
> 　Nor evil near my bed,
> Nor that I should be hurried hence
> 　And numbered with the dead.
>
> But that I may, O Lord, arise
> 　Refreshed from every care;
> That I may bow and pray again,
> 　And feel thee ever near.[17]

Walden's poem is reminiscent of the *New England Primer*'s familiar "Now I lay me down to sleep," but it avoids the Puritan's fearful surrender to God's power over life and death. Instead, Walden used his verses to express a deep affection for God and a complete confidence in His goodness.

Walden's other poems conveyed similar sentiments. In "Love for God's Name," Walden proclaimed: "Thy name is music sweet, / And every note's a charm; / Because creation is upheld by Thy Almighty arm."[18] The poem evoked God's power, but in language resembling what Mrs. Washington used to describe poetry itself, relying on such words as *sweet* and *charm* to describe the feelings the love of God

---

16. Islay Walden, *Walden's Sacred Poems, with a Sketch of His Life* (New Brunswick, N.J., 1877), 9; Joan R. Sherman, *Invisible Poets: Afro-Americans of the Nineteenth Century* (Urbana, 1974), 106; Islay Walden, *Walden's Miscellaneous Poems, Which the Author Desires to Dedicate to the Cause of Education and Humanity* (2d ed.; Washington, D.C.,1873), 9.

17. Walden, *Sacred Poems*, 14.

18. *Ibid.,* 23.

offered an individual. Through this kind of language, the power of God was domesticated and made gentle. The love Walden had for his God was a quiet, serene love; the power of Walden's God was a power in which he could feel joy and find tenderness.

The religious feelings of the kind evoked by Walden's poetry were widely portrayed by black writers and were in keeping with the genteel sentimentalism of the time. The belief that all relationships had an emotional core to be cultivated and that the most satisfying ties were those based on affection and tenderness was as much a part of the ideas about one's relationship with God as about one's relationships with others. Gentleness and tenderness on a cosmic scale were as meaningful as they were in everyday life.

The devotional writings of this period fit fully into the context of black middle-class life by portraying the basic elements of an essentially middle-class piety. American evangelicalism had been an evolving religious stance for most of the nineteenth century. From the individualistic, highly emotional religion of the Second Awakening, around 1800, through the psychologically oriented revivalism of Charles Grandison Finney in the 1820s and 1830s, to the sentimental preaching and singing of Dwight L. Moody and Ira Sankey in the second half of the nineteenth century, American evangelicalism had become increasingly personalistic and restrained. Evangelicalism still sought to convert sinners to God, but hard wrestling with the sin-sick soul and fear of God's wrath came to be replaced by a conversion that brought inner peace and friendship with a loving God.[19] Such a religion stood in sharp contrast with what the black writer John P. Green termed the "religious enthusiasm, exhibited in so many vigorous ways" of black folk religion.[20] It was, instead, closely governed by the ideals of refinement and self-restraint at the heart of gentility. And it became a central feature of black genteel writing in the years after 1877.

A more secular side of black genteel literature may be seen in the works of the poet Henriette Cordelia Ray, daughter of the noted black abolitionist Charles B. Ray. Miss Ray received a master's degree in peda-

19. Ann Douglas, *The Feminization of American Culture* (New York, 1977), provides a good account of this evolution. See also Clyde Griffen, "The Progressive Ethos," in Stanley Coben and Lorman Ratner (eds.), *The Development of an American Culture* (2d ed.; New York, 1983), 144–80.

20. John Patterson Green, *Recollections of the Inhabitants, Localities, Superstitions, and Ku Klux Outrages of the Carolinas, by a "Carpetbagger" Who Was Born and Lived There* (N.p., 1880), 122.

gogy from the City University of New York and worked for many years as a teacher in the city. She began her poetic career in 1876 and published frequently, particularly in the *A.M.E. Church Review*. She also published two volumes of collected poems.[21] The gentility of her verse is well shown in one of her 1893 sonnets, "The Poet's Ministrants":

> The smiling Dawn, with diadem of dew,
>> Brings sunrise odors to perfume his shrine;
>> Blithe Zephyr fans him, and soft moonbeams twine
> An aureole to crown him, of a hue
> Surpassing fair. The stately stars renew
>> Majestic measures, that he may incline
>> His soul unto their sweetness; whispers fine
> From spirit-nymphs allure him; not a few
> The gifts chaste Fancy and her sisters bring.
>> Rare is the lyre the Muses for him wrought,
> A different meaning thrills in ev'ry string,
>> With ev'ry changing mood of life so fraught.
> Invoked by him, when such the strains that flow,
> How can the poet e'er his song forego![22]

The sensibility conveyed in this poem is one fully in tune with a genteel age and with genteel ideas about literature. The treatment of nature in the poem is filled with gentleness and peace. Miss Ray wrote of a "smiling Dawn," of "soft moonbeams," and of a "diadem of dew." The poet inclines his soul toward the "sweetness" of the stars. The Muses sing to the poet, accompanied by the gentle sounds of a lyre. The "Fancy" that gives the poet his gift is "chaste." It would be hard to imagine a more genteel understanding of poetry than this, not even Mrs. Washington's.

The sensibility expressed in "The Poet's Ministrants" informed all of Miss Ray's work. In her optimistic poem "Aspiration," though she would have her reader "climb the slopes of life with throbbing heart," she would also have the journey accompanied by nightingales, through "dewy skies." A tribute to Beethoven evoked his "harmony, the sweetest," and an inspiration that arrived "on dainty pinions." Her own choices for inspiration and her reactions to the world around her were always informed by the most refined taste. The feelings she evoked could not have been finer or more restrained.[23]

Other black writers stayed within the main lines of gentility that Miss

---

21. Sherman, *Invisible Poets*, 130.
22. Henriette Cordelia Ray, *Sonnets* (New York, 1893), 21.
23. *Ibid.,* 11, 29.

Ray's work reveals. When they wrote of love, for example, they wrote of a relationship based on tenderness and propriety. The language of love was soft and gentle. New Orleans political and civic leader John Willis Menard wrote:

> Come to me fairy queen,
>   To these waiting arms;
> Thou'rt lovely, and I mean
>   To extol thy charms.
>
> Sweet charms, for ever dear—
>   Dear as dear can be;
> They are mine; love, come near,
>   You belong to me![24]

If the poetry is not as skillful, the vocabulary is virtually the same as Miss Ray's, not to mention Islay Walden's.

Genteel writing was thus a major element in black literature of the post-Reconstruction period. Its prominence and consistency point to the importance black writers gave to genteel ideals and values and to their meaning as standards for thought and behavior. If one can also say that genteel literature fit in with assimilationist purposes by proving that blacks were as capable as whites of expressing fine thoughts and feelings, it is even more important to say that because the elements of gentility were so well and fully understood, gentility gave content to assimilationist aims. When black writers wanted to portray the meaning of assimilation beyond the level of equality of opportunity and achievement—when they wanted to show what equality meant at the level of daily life—what they wrote was based fully on ideals of gentility.

One sees an example of this in Solomon Brown's poem "He Is a Negro Still," in which Brown held the image of a "cultured, brilliant" black woman with "manners fine" up against society's treatment of her as "a Negress still." In this example, Brown made the case against racism in terms of genteel ideals and conventions. They provided the measure of achievement and of oppression. Gentility thus became a tangible way of talking about black virtues and about the specific barriers that existed to assimilation.

Again, there was nothing here that could not have been found in popular white literature from this period. Drawing on themes such as these gave black writers an important way of producing work that met

---

24. John Willis Menard, *Lays in Summer Lands: Poems, with the Press Notices of His Speech and His Appearance in Congress* (Washington, D.C., 1879), 44.

assimilationist purposes even as it affirmed the writers' own gentility. But black writers had more strategic uses for genteel literature in making the case against racism. Gentility provided a set of conventions, with strong roots in American culture, that could be used to elaborate on the model of protest and achievement that shaped black writing during these years.

One sees something similar in the presentation of black heroism. Gentility dominated, for example, tributes to Frederick Douglass that appeared during this period. Douglass was easily the most admired black man of his time, and black writers celebrated his accomplishments in language that recalled the genteel virtues of the Victorian era. The characterization of Douglass by historian William Alexander was a fine summary of the usual perspective on the man by black writers. Describing Douglass' origins in slavery, Alexander wrote, "From this position, he has raised himself to the habits of mind, thought and life, of a cultivated gentleman."[25] The same may be said of another black hero whom writers of this generation greatly admired, François Dominique Toussaint L'Ouverture, the leader of the fight for Haitian independence. Robert C. O. Benjamin, an attorney and poet, described him in particularly ideal terms: "Splendid examples of some single qualification no doubt there are. Caesar was merciful; Hannibal was patient; Scipio was continent; Washington was serene; but it was reserved for Toussaint L'Ouverture to blend them all in one, and, like the lovely masterpiece of the Grecian artist, to exhibit in lone glow of associated beauty the pride of every model and the perfection of every master in one transcendent superiority. . . . A conqueror, he was untainted with the crime of blood."[26] For Benjamin, then, whatever Toussaint had done, gentility provided the language that gave summary content to Toussaint L'Ouverture's heroism.

Such character as that of Alexander's Douglass and Benjamin's Toussaint L'Ouverture was common in the genteel writing of this period, especially in the male figures that appeared in popular fiction. The gentleman in popular fiction was never one to shy away from confrontations with the evil of the world, but he was never a brigand. He was well mannered, refined, and as sensitive as Miss Ray's poet. He treated women with courtesy and respect. Although it was his manly duty to

25. William T. Alexander, *History of the Colored Race in America* (1887; rpr. New York, 1968), 391.

26. Robert C. O. Benjamin, *Life of Toussaint L'Ouverture, Warrior and Statesman* (Los Angeles, 1888), 95.

use his physical strength in defense of the right, the mark of his gentility lay in his ability to retain his virtuous self-restraint even in the face of provocation.

A prime example of such genteel heroism appeared in William Edgar Easton's 1893 verse-play about the Haitian emperor Dessalines, a play actually performed in 1902. Easton himself was northern-born and -educated and even spent some time in a Catholic seminary in French Canada. Forced to leave the seminary after other students objected to his presence on the ground of race, Easton lived for a time in Reconstruction Texas, where he became an influential figure in Republican politics, before finally settling in Los Angeles.[27] His play, along with a later one on the Haitian general Christophe, was a significant effort to bring together the themes of black heroism and genteel virtue.

On the face of it, Dessalines would not seem a very promising figure for a historical drama, at least not a drama in which he was to be a genteel hero. Dessalines, who succeeded Toussaint L'Ouverture, was distinguished by his cruelty and arrogance, instituting forced labor in the island empire even as he surrounded himself with the trappings of royalty. Easton was, however, serious in his efforts to make a hero of the emperor; and he drew heavily on genteel ideals in order to do so.

Easton's play focused on the violent antagonism between Dessalines and the mulatto leaders of early Haitian independence, particularly Rigaud and Lefebre, with much of the dramatic interest placed on a relationship between Dessalines and Rigaud's beautiful sister, Clarisse. Early in the play, Clarisse is kidnapped by a clownish pair, who hold her for ransom. Despite their clownishness, Clarisse's situation is desperate, especially when she ends up at a voodoo rite conducted by the ugly Mère Marguerite. She is to be a human sacrifice. Fortunately, Dessalines himself comes to her rescue, saving her from death.

Clarisse is the perfect sentimental heroine. Beautiful and refined, she is also a devout Christian. Upon her rescue, she not only begs mercy for her abductors but also begins a determined campaign to bring Dessalines to God. When Dessalines and Rigaud confront each other and fight, Clarisse intervenes to prove to her brother that although Dessalines is not yet a gentleman of culture and refinement, he is a gentleman by instinct. Dessalines, for his part, recognizes his need and love for

Clarisse. The play closes in a church. Dessalines has gone there to sack the building; but meeting Clarisse and coming under her influence, he changes his mind. He proclaims, " 'Tis well, then, that the religion which fostered in the slave the love of liberty and gave him the courage to contest the power of might—with the weapons of right, shall be hereafter—the proud heritage of every Haitien!"[28] Thus the proud general, intrinsically noble, is imaginatively tamed by the combination of virtue and piety with the principles of liberty and democracy.

Easton's play is a significant document in the literary work of post-Reconstruction black writers. Taking a major historical figure, a symbol of black courage and aspirations for freedom, Easton made an effort to fit that figure into the literary conventions of his day, and to do so without denying Dessalines' courage or strength. The heroism of Easton's Dessalines provides a bridge between the demands of fighting oppression and those of finding a place in the Victorian American world.

Gentility served not only as a standard for the positive portrayal of black heroism and black aspirations but also as a way of denouncing white oppression. At one level, this meant, as in Brown's poem, seeing racism as in part a refusal by whites to acknowledge black gentility. At another level, it meant condemning racism itself as contrary to gentility. Indeed, the value of genteel conventions for protesting racism was most clearly shown when black writers used them to play off black virtue against white venality. They did this by presenting black figures who clung to genteel ideals while whites were making no effort to live up to any of the demands of virtue.

This technique of juxtaposing black gentility with white venality figured strongly in *Bond and Free*, a novel by James H. W. Howard, published in 1886. *Bond and Free* is the story of a slave named Purcey, of her degradation in bondage and her escape to freedom in Canada. Purcey, the daughter of a slaveholder and a slave, was, like Easton's Clarisse, one of the many genteel heroines who appeared in black fiction during this period. A beautiful woman, "her features were as delicate and chaste as a lady bred in luxury and refinement . . . her carriage and bearing were characterized by both dignity and grace." But, Howard wrote, she was also "no more than a mere thing . . . with no protection for her virtue, and whose beauty only made her the more valuable in the eyes of some brute whose lust urged him to bid a higher price for her

28. William Edgar Easton, *Dessalines, a Dramatic Tale: A Single Chapter from Haiti's History* (N.p., 1893), 117.

possession."[29] The structural parallel of this novel to other protest writing is clear; American slavery was found wanting in terms of American ideals, and Purcey herself was seen to embody those ideals despite the forces working against her.

Much of the rest of the novel chronicles Purcey's resistance to degradation. When her father dies, she falls into the hands of her half-brother and his jealous wife. At one point, her young master tries to turn her into a breeder; at another, her mistress forces her to neglect her own children in order to care for the master's young son. Through it all, Howard shows Purcey to be devoted to her virtue and to her family. She refuses to let the degradations of slavery corrupt her soul. Purcey is separated from her family when her husband is lost in a card game. The mistress accepts the loss with a remark that emphasizes the contrast between the ever-virtuous Purcey and her white oppressors. Purcey is mourning her separation from her husband, but the mistress says: "She will soon get over that. You have plenty as good niggers upon the place as William. She will soon be in love with some of them."[30] The genteel Purcey is not, of course, that kind of woman. The novel closes with her escape from slavery and her reunion with William in Canada.

By placing the virtuous Purcey in a corrupt setting, Howard indicted whites for their failure to see virtue in black people, much as Solomon Brown bemoaned the white failure to understand black achievement. Using motifs connected with the ideals of gentility, however, Howard provided an important background of feelings and ideals to underlie his more specific charge of racial injustice. And it is a background that tied his protest in with significant concerns in American culture as a whole as well as with dominant aspirations among middle-class black Americans. He mobilized the sentiments at the heart of American gentility to make his readers feel the cruelty of racism.

Thus gentility provided standards in terms of which black writers could show the wrongs of prejudice. Using genteel motifs also allowed them to approach American history and society with a touch of irony. White America, they implied, in its quest to keep blacks in an inferior position, had made itself inferior to black America. One sees this in the novel *Bond and Free*. White men defended slavery on the ground of blacks' inferiority. Black people, they claimed, are incapable of independent virtue and thus must be controlled. The system of control they

29. James H. W. Howard, *Bond and Free: A True Tale of Slave Times* (1886; rpr. College Park, Md., 1969), 10.

30. *Ibid.,* 122.

created, however, so brutalized the white men that they lost the very virtues they claimed to defend. Compounding the irony was the superior ability of many slaves to live up to the virtues whites were unable to maintain in themselves.

This element of irony could be powerful. It was, for instance, used to great effect—if with great sentimentality—in a story from 1890, written by "Ettesor Yerg." The story concerns little Ethel, the only black girl in her school, who is cruelly insulted by the white children. The insults make her so angry that she tells her aunt, "I often get so slighted and insulted that my heart nearly chokes me, and sometimes I feel *so* wicked." It is especially maddening because, as she says, "I feel and act like other girls, and I am sure that I act better than many." Her aunt counsels holding to her virtue. The whites who insult black people, she tells Ethel, are "feeling their own inferiority and angered thereby," a point Ethel quickly grasps. She will not, she promises, forget herself in order to answer those who treat her contemptuously. Her own character and conduct will always be such as to "raise the standing of my race." Gentility, "Yerg" and other writers tried to show, was a double-edged weapon, one that by displaying the achievements of a black person put the character of white racists in a still worse light.[31]

The use of gentility by black writers did not originate in the post-Reconstruction period. It was, in fact, one of those legacies from the antebellum period, especially from antislavery writing. Abolitionist fiction relied heavily on stock characters and situations similar to those found in post-Reconstruction writing. *Bond and Free*, for example, was little more than an abolitionist novel published after the Civil War. One of the main emphases in such writing, from before and after the war, was the potential gentility of those in bondage and the corruption of the slaveholders in the light of genteel standards. Characters such as Harriet Beecher Stowe's "Emmeline," William Wells Brown's "Clotel," and Harriet E. Wilson's "Frado" were typical genteel heroines cast into the shadows of slavery or prejudice, as were Purcey and little Ethel.[32]

31. "Ettesor Yerg," "My Resolutions for 1890," *Afro-American Budget*, I (1890), 220–21.
32. Sterling A. Brown, *Negro Poetry and Drama* (1937; rpr. New York, 1978), 32; Mary-Emma Graham, "The Shaping of a Cause: American Romanticism and the Black Writer," *CLA Journal*, XXIV (1980), 22; Ronald G. Walters, *The Antislavery Appeal: American Abolitionism After 1830* (Baltimore, 1976), 95; Harriet Beecher Stowe, *Uncle Tom's Cabin* (1852; rpr. New York, 1962); William Wells Brown, *Clotel; or, The President's Daughter: A Narrative of Slave Life in the United States* (1853; rpr. Upper Saddle River,

Nevertheless, the combination of gentility with protest was especially well suited to the post-Reconstruction period. In 1877, and well into the 1880s, there was still much to be hopeful about in race relations. If, from the perspective of hindsight, the catastrophes of the 1890s seem to have been inevitable, they were not so clearly comprehensible at the time. After all, in the 1870s and 1880s, black men continued to vote and to hold public office, especially in the South. Public accommodations were still integrated in some places. The fight for equality was not by any means viewed as a losing battle; worsening conditions appeared to be nothing more than a temporary setback. The early black historian William Alexander caught something of this mood in 1887; in reviewing recent difficulties, he suggested that such problems should simply inspire black Americans to "renewed exertion," arguing that "the possibilities for them, as a race, are boundless."[33]

The genteel literature produced by post-Reconstruction black writers was a measure of their optimism about possibilities for the future. There was nothing evasive about observing genteel themes and conventions. Racial barriers were not seen as impregnable. Given this point of view, genteel literature conveyed the fully assimilationist message at the heart of black middle-class racial ideas during the post-Reconstruction era, as black writers claimed their right to and their desire for recognition as Americans.

Still, the conservatism of early black literature and its devotion to gentility reveal a certain measure of uncertainty on the part of these black writers. In fact, middle-class aspirations and literary purposes fed on each other to produce an orientation toward literature whose conservatism posed severe limits on black writers. Seeking to create a literature that established their credentials as artists while, at the same time, appealing to a wide audience, post-Reconstruction writers took an approach to their work that can appropriately be described as "safe"; they did nothing that might undermine the appearance they hoped to give as literary artists—and as men and women—wholly within the American mainstream.

It is against this background that one can begin to assess the significance of one of the more prominent writers of this period—at least among

---

N.J., 1969); Harriet E. Wilson, *Our Nig; or, Sketches from the Life of a Free Black* (1859; rpr. New York, 1983).

33. Alexander, *History of the Colored Race*, 20.

black readers—Albery A. Whitman. Of all the black writers who produced genteel protest literature, none was more self-conscious about his craft and its meaning than Whitman. And no one's work more clearly revealed gentility's key implications for black literature and thought.

Whitman was born a slave in Kentucky in 1851. He was orphaned at an early age and spent the next several years of his life as a laborer. During this period, he was able to obtain some schooling and became a teacher in Ohio. Around 1870, he entered Wilberforce University. There, he studied for about six months with the legendary Bishop Daniel Payne, though he never graduated. By 1877, he had become an elder in the A. M. E. Church, the "stationed pastor" of the Springfield, Ohio, church, and general financial agent for Wilberforce University. In 1878, he resigned his post at Wilberforce; and he spent the rest of his life in the ministry, working in Ohio, Kansas, Texas, and, finally, Atlanta. He died in 1901. His name lived on through his daughters, who, playing as the Whitman Sisters, led one of the most important black companies in vaudeville between about 1910 and 1930.[34]

Whitman's reputation as a poet rests primarily on his two book-length works: *Not a Man, and Yet a Man*, published in 1877, and *The Rape of Florida*, published in 1884 and reissued as *Twasinta's Seminoles* in 1885 and 1890. These two had been preceded by an 1873 volume entitled *Leelah Misled*, a drama of seduction set in white society.[35] They were followed in 1901 by *An Idyl of the South*, another book-length work. Whitman also produced a fair amount of magazine verse and a few poems published as pamphlets.

Whitman was well respected as a writer during his lifetime. William J. Simmons included a sketch of Whitman in his 1887 biographical dictionary, *Men of Mark*, quoting a great deal of Whitman's poetry. As late as 1900, John E. Bruce described Whitman as "one of the greatest, if not the greatest of living Negro poets—the Dean of the profession." A reviewer of *The Rape of Florida* described that volume as "beyond question, the finest poetical effusion of the race," adding that it would "favorably compare with the average of the best of the whites." Accord-

34. Biographical information on Whitman comes from Sherman, *Invisible Poets*, 112, 115; Richard Bardolph, *The Negro Vanguard* (1959; rpr. Westport, Conn., 1971), 93–94; William Johnson Simmons, *Men of Mark: Eminent, Progressive, and Rising* (1887; rpr. Chicago, 1970), 1122–23; Albery A. Whitman, *Not a Man, and Yet a Man* (1877; rpr. Upper Saddle River, N.J., 1970), 5. On Whitman's daughters, see Marshall Stearns and Jean Stearns, *Jazz Dance: The Story of American Vernacular Dance* (New York, 1968), 85–91.

35. Sherman, *Invisible Poets*, 113.

ing to this reviewer, "such poets as Longfellow and Bryant recognized in Whitman a brother poet." College student James Weldon Johnson, developing his poetic techniques, clipped Whitman's work for his scrapbook, apparently using it as a model for his own efforts.[36]

Whitman's self-consciousness as a poet was well shown in his introduction to *The Rape of Florida*, where he discussed his ideas about poetry, about his role as a poet, and about racial questions. Whitman stoutly defended the importance of poetry and poets, to a great extent in ways that were compatible with others' genteel ideas about literature. He argued that poetry had a special connection with truth, and that truth itself was founded on beauty, goodness, and sentiment. And he saw the poet's mission as one of setting forth the proper feelings—what Mrs. Washington called the "best affections."[37]

But Whitman went beyond sentimental ideals in his understanding of literature, and even beyond the ideological directions outlined by Douglass and his colleagues. Whitman's understanding of the function of literature grew out of his more general perceptions of himself as an individual. One gets a sense of these perceptions from an autobiographical passage in the introduction. "I was in bondage," Whitman wrote. "*I never was a slave*,—the infamous laws of a savage despotism took my substance—what of that? Many a man has lost all he had, except his manhood." Whitman was deeply concerned with freedom and manhood and with what might be considered a psychological resistance to racism. At one point in the poem itself, he has one of his characters declare: "The good, the great, and the true, are, if so, born, / And so with slaves, *chains could not make the slave.*" Whitman believed that poetry could allow the poet to make a similar psychological stand against oppression. "Poesy is free," he wrote, "and not for hire." From his point of view, writing poetry provided an individual with an opportunity to experience psychological freedom, even in the face of the worst racial oppression.[38]

No one else in this period came to terms with the psychological dimension of literary work so clearly as Whitman. No one else so fully

36. John Edward Bruce, "A New Negro Poet," *Howard's American Magazine*, IV (1900), 368; Review of Albery A. Whitman's *The Rape of Florida*, in *A.M.E. Church Review*, I (1884), 76; James Weldon Johnson, "Scrapbook Made While Attending Atlanta University," in James Weldon Johnson Collection, Collection of American Literature, Beinecke Rare Book and Manuscript Library, Yale University.

37. Albery A. Whitman, *Twasinta's Seminoles; or, The Rape of Florida* (Rev. ed., 1885; rpr. Upper Saddle River, N.J., 1970), 9–10.

38. *Ibid.*, 8, 19, 10.

described literature as a way to achieve at least a momentary transcendence over a racist society. But Whitman's view of poetry was a psychological complement to the ideological orientation of virtually all black writing from this perod. Producing literature was generally seen as a way of fighting prejudice by proving black character. In his remarks, Whitman added a level of meaning that was implied by more ideological views of what literature could do—pointing to a satisfaction that other writers may have felt but never put into words.

His great self-consciousness makes all the more significant the fact that Whitman was, in most ways, as conservative as other black writers of his era. It is hard to quarrel with the modern assessment that, as a poet, Whitman was an excellent craftsman who admired good poetry and sought to equal it himself rather than to create much that was new. Sterling Brown, in 1939, described him as one of the "mocking-bird school of poets."[39] On the whole, this meant that Whitman did not depart far from the main poetic fashions of his day in either form or theme. His newspaper and magazine pieces tended to deal with such familiar topics as evangelical piety and the sentimental beauties of nature. His shorter works on racial questions were no less carefully circumscribed. His 1893 poem "The Freedmen's Triumphant Song" extolled the patriotism of black Amerians and celebrated their contributions to American life and history. Indulging in some ugly anti-immigrant sentiment, Whitman concluded the poem with an optimistically voiced plea to white America to recognize "One land: the best by mortals ever trod; / One flag, one people, and one father—God."[40]

Even in his longer epic works, Whitman strayed little from the themes and conventions of black genteel writing. The first poem, *Not a Man*, is the story of the progress of a black man, Rodney, from slavery to freedom. In neoabolitionist style, the poem moves from the Mississippi frontier—where Rodney saves a white village—to the depths of southern bondage, where he falls in love with the genteel Leeona. It follows him to Canada, where he and Leeona escape slavery, and on into the Union army, as he fights to hasten slavery's death. The poem concludes with Whitman's optimistic prediction of racial equality. *The Rape of*

39. Sterling A. Brown, *Negro Poetry and Drama*, 11–12. See also Blyden Jackson and Louis D. Rubin, *Black Poetry in America: Two Essays in Historical Interpretation* (Baton Rouge, 1974), 11; Jean Wagner, *Black Poets of the United States from Paul Laurence Dunbar to Langston Hughes*, trans. Kenneth Douglas (Urbana, 1973), 25.

40. Albery A. Whitman, *World's Fair Poem, Read in Memorial Art Palace, Chicago, Illinois, September 22nd, 1893* (Atlanta, [1893]), 6.

Florida is based on the Seminole wars and, like *Not a Man*, describes white perfidy and black—and Indian—virtue. Its characters were taken from Victorian types—the pure maiden, her defender, and the villains, whose sexual corruption matches their thievery. In plot and character-ization, Whitman broke no new ground in his epics.

What set Whitman apart from other black writers of his day was ambition rather than innovation. Pushed, perhaps, by the psychological imperatives he described in discussing his art, Whitman wanted to write in ways that matched those of the major works of Western literary tradition and that would place him clearly in the literary world. This was especially true in his epics. The first, *Not a Man*, was over two hundred pages long. In it, he followed several models of versification, using them according to the dramatic situations he wanted to create. When, for example, he described events in the lives of his main characters, he relied mainly on heroic couplets. A long passage on the Indians of the Mississippi frontier was written in the strongly rhythmic trochaic tetrameter used by Longfellow—whom Whitman greatly admired—in "Hiawatha."

The Rape of Florida was still more ambitious. This work was written in what Whitman called the "stately verse" of Spenserian stanza. The form consists of eight iambic pentameters and an alexandrine—an iam-bic hexameter. Each stanza rhymes *a b a b b c b c c*. Whitman handled the form skillfully in over 257 stanzas. Certainly no other black poet of Whitman's time took on the kind of challenge he attempted in his second epic. Few enough white poets had done it.

These efforts are revealing, because they help indicate the implica-tions and limitations of literary assimilationism in the post-Reconstruc-tion era. There is no doubt about Whitman's own assimilationist ideals. He made them clear in his introduction to *The Rape of Florida*. This poem was, he wrote, an attempt at "essaying the 'stately verse,' *mas-tered* by *only* Spenser, Byron, and a very few other great poets." And, he said, there was reason for doing this. "Some one of my race is sure to do everything that any one else has ever done, and as none of my race have ever executed a poem in the 'stately verse,' I simply *venture in*."[41] The point for Whitman, as this passage makes clear, lay in proving himself in terms of those models of achievement known to be widely accepted by the larger society; the same point was made by other writers' celebra-tions of black heroism and black gentility.

41. Whitman, *Twasinta's Seminoles*, 10.

But as Whitman's efforts also indicate, assimilationism raised sharp literary boundaries for the writer. Because it seemed to demand formal and thematic conservatism, even ambitious writers stayed within received forms, concentrating on technical skill rather than on thematic or formal development. How much of this Whitman was aware of is hard to say. Given his great self-consciousness as a poet as well as his effort to define a kind of freedom for himself through the act of writing, it is possible that Whitman had a sense of the limits under which he was operating. In any event, the kind of work he created helps emphasize the constraints placed on black literature by its ideological foundations.

When one looks at Whitman's poetry, one is looking at work that reached the limits on ambition in the black literary community during the period between the close of Reconstruction and the mid-1890s, when Paul Laurence Dunbar's writing, in particular, would change the course of black literature. Whitman reached these limits with his ambitious scope and his self-conscious stress on technique. But he remained within them by never moving beyond what, in polite circles, would be considered good poetry.

As Whitman's work reveals, then, the creative energies of black writers could be channeled in only a few directions. In terms of form, they could go only toward existing forms, or at most in the direction of the ambitious use of received forms, as in Whitman's poetry. Thematically, the constraints were still tighter. There were approved ways of talking about racial questions, a point emphasized by the extent to which the self-conscious, ambitious Whitman, no less than other black writers, stuck with them.

But the kinds of limitations represented by Whitman's poetry were not the only problems raised for black writers by their attachment to assimilationist purposes and literary gentility. There was one other issue that at least some black writers addressed during this period and that also helps show the difficulties hidden in the literary focuses of this generation of writers. This was the issue of racial identity. Given the force of white racial thought, black Americans had long had to confront what it meant to be black and to be identified as such within the larger society. The dominance of genteel ideals meant, however, that for the most part these writers could talk about themselves, their hopes, their aspirations, only in the language of mainstream America. There was no vocabulary for dealing with a black identity as anything distinctive. This was a serious dilemma for black writers in the post-Reconstruction period.

The problem took on significance because, despite the overwhelmingly assimilationist character of black writing in the post-Reconstruction era, racial pride and solidarity were widely held values among black thinkers during this period. August Meier has documented the important role of such ideas in black political and social thought, particularly in the recognition that solidarity was essential if black people were to wage any kind of effective campaign for racial justice. Such rhetoric was far from new; it may be easily traced back as far as the early national period in American history, when the language of racial identity and racial solidarity emerged with some force. In the years after Reconstruction, these ideas remained powerful. There was even some protonationalist rhetoric intended to encourage solidarity. Rev. H. Edward Bryant, writing in the *A. M. E. Church Review* in 1885, specifically attacked those whose thoughts and actions declared, "*Look here, sir, I am an American, and my race are Americans, not Negroes.*" Bryant went on to say, "I readily admit we are Americans in nationality, but raceologically I am willing to be called a negro, and I shall labor to make that word honorable." In these sentiments, he echoed historian George Washington Williams, who urged that the word "Negro . . . is a good, strong, and healthy word, and ought to live. It should be covered with glory: let Negroes do it."[42]

Such rhetoric seems, on the surface, to counterbalance the kind of assimilationism that dominated genteel and protest writing in the post-Reconstruction era; but a more accurate approach to it is one that recognizes that the rhetoric took place within an assimilationist consensus, a consensus that determined both its meaning and its power. Although one might, for example, interpret the words of Bryant and of Williams as calls for a greater appreciation of a black community with its own distinctive virtues and characteristics, in the context of assimilationist ideals, those words had far more to do with allegiance to a cause than allegiance to a culture. In 1881, John P. Sampson summarized the prevailing view when he wrote, "The colored people stand together on the subject of rights by a natural sympathy, through the prejudice against them." He added, "When these rights are no longer an issue, they will disband and unite on subjects of similar tastes and interests, with-

42. August Meier, *Negro Thought in America, 1880–1915: Racial Ideologies in the Age of Booker T. Washington* (Ann Arbor, 1963), 55–58; Levesque, "Interpreting Early Black Ideology," 280ff.; Rev. H. Edward Bryant, "Our Duties, Responsibilities: Negro Literature," *A.M.E. Church Review*, I (1885), 262; George Washington Williams, *History of the Negro Race in America, 1619–1880* (2 vols.; 1883; rpr. New York, 1968), I, 14n.

out regard to race identity." One may recall, as well, Andrew F. Hilyer's remarks stressing the cultural identity of black and white Americans, at least those of the middle class. From this point of view, there was no contradiction between assimilationism and identification with one's race, because it was more a political than a cultural matter. As August Meier has suggested, racial solidarity as a goal originated mainly in the need for unity in the face of white opposition to black interests. Racial identity was understood mainly in terms of the fight for racial justice. And this was the form the issue of identity took in virtually all black literature from this period. No black author of the period eschewed an identification with the race. Most proclaimed it proudly. But all did so within the framework of the fight for racial justice and the assimilationist purposes of their work.[43]

One sees a measure of this characteristic of ideas about identity in, for example, the understanding of black history. The evocation of black heroism was clearly intended to encourage racial pride and, with it, a reason to identify with the race; but the heroism these writers celebrated was conceived in fully assimilationist terms. The blacks who became heroes were those who, in one way or another, were particularly "American." One sees more complex assimilationist underpinnings of early efforts to encourage identity in the ways in which black thinkers of this period treated Africa. They saw the African heritage as something to take pride in, but they ignored or even condemned modern Africa when they talked about that heritage. They preferred to focus instead on ancient Egypt and Ethiopia, and they took pride in that heritage precisely because of its direct connection with modern Western civilization.[44]

This assimilationist framework also determined the focus on racial identity that informed black writers' ideas about creative work as such. Whitman, for instance, was typical of writers of the time, asserting in his prefaces his identification with his race and his desire to use poetry to advance racial pride as well as racial justice. But this identification did not make him consider that racial identity should lead him to poetry that was, somehow, peculiarly black. Other writers felt the same way. In the introduction to *Dessalines*, Easton wrote of the need to turn the

43. John Patterson Sampson, *Mixed Races: Their Environment, Heredity, and Phrenology* (Hampton, Va., 1881), 26; Meier, *Negro Thought*, 24. See also Stuckey, *Slave Culture*, 231–44.

44. See Dickson D. Bruce, Jr., "Ancient Africa and the Early Black American Historians, 1883–1915," *American Quarterly*, XXXVI (1984), 684–99.

attention of "the literati of the race to the rich fields of dramatic and narrative art, which by every right are distinctively the property of the Negro."[45] A literature written by blacks on subjects drawn from black history and life, Easton went on to argue, was essential if writers were to encourage an identification with the race. But Easton's own work shows how assimilationist such an identity could be, as it was informed by literary ambitions similar in nature—if not in degree—to Whitman's.

Some difficult literary problems were posed by the prevailing assimilationist approach to racial identity. The problems grew out of the lack of substance in notions of racial identity—out of the fact that, to paraphrase Sampson, racial identity was understood to have more to do with a common oppression than a common culture. They took shape in literature chiefly in the difficulties black writers faced in putting notions of racial solidarity and identity into satisfying dramatic and literary terms and in seeing what those notions might really mean. The demands of literature, that is, exposed deeper problems in black thought during the era, so far as racial identity was concerned.

The problems were readily apparent in a novel from this period, W. H. Stowers and W. H. Anderson's *Appointed*, published under the pseudonym "Sanda" in 1894.[46] This novel has a white protagonist named Seth Stanley, and it traces his friendship with a young mulatto man named John Saunders, who is working as a steward when the two meet. The novel is ultimately the account of the racial education of Stanley, who becomes a champion of black people. Saunders, a graduate of the University of Michigan in civil engineering, is the means of this education. Through dialogue that is sentimental and preachy, Stanley learns of the heritage of black Americans and of black accomplishments in American life, as well as of such black and American heroes as Crispus Attucks. And he learns of the racial barriers that have precluded Saunders' pursuit of his chosen career. In this, the book follows the familiar model for black protest of the era. Stanley's eager listening to Saunders' stories, one might add, dramatizes black literary hopes.

The book also deals, however, with issues of identity and solidarity, chiefly by setting forth Saunders' own strong sense of being black. This identification with the race takes an exemplary form as Saunders develops a determination to go to the South to help his people, a determination he fulfills by the book's close.

45. Easton, *Dessalines*, v.
46. "Sanda" (W. H. Stowers and W. H. Anderson), *Appointed: An American Novel* (Detroit, 1894).

The novel ends ambiguously, however. If Saunders' racial identity is positively affirmed by his determination to use his education and expertise for the good of his people, it is also affirmed by his ultimate fate. Arrested on trumped-up charges, Saunders is lynched by a white mob. Stowers and Anderson did not let this interfere with a conclusion that captured the prevailing literary optimism. Stanley, in reaction to the lynching, pledges to devote his life to the cause of racial justice. He is, in other words, "appointed"; and the book optimistically notes the possibilities for future progress. But it is not hard to see that there are problems with such an ambiguous conclusion.

For one thing, despite the important role that Saunders' recounting of black achievements plays in making Stanley a friend, Stanley's conversion really takes place when, Christlike, Saunders surrenders his life to the brutality of a mob. For another, Stowers and Anderson implied that when change came, it would do so mainly as a result of white rather than black efforts. Despite Saunders' ability to enumerate black achievements, his own contribution to racial justice was ultimately far more passive than active, far more a matter of winning sympathy through victimhood than of making a positive contribution to social change.

The ambiguity of the novel is directly related to the difficulties growing out of trying to create notions of racial identity in an assimilationist framework—out of the lack of substance those notions had and out of the extent to which they were formed on the basis of a desire to gain whites' respect. In a way that dramatizes Sampson's comment about a natural sympathy among blacks on questions of rights, Stowers and Anderson seem to have felt that the only thing that both united blacks and appealed to whites was black victimhood. Such a view renders racial identity a negative commodity, Saunders' expressed appreciation for his black heritage notwithstanding. But the thrust of assimilationist ideals made such a negative approach to identity questions unavoidable.

Appointed was, to be sure, unusual in the kind of role it gave to its white protagonist and, by extension, to white people generally. But the importance of the novel lies not so much in whether it should be seen as typical as in the way it condensed the key issues raised by assimilationist approaches to racial identity. It epitomized and took to a logical extreme what assimilationism implied—namely that however valuable racial identity might be, it rested on a negative base. Stowers and Anderson may not have written a typical story, but they did not misrepresent the issues that were raised for all black writers by assimilationist ideals of racial identity.

The real complexity of the kinds of issues raised by *Appointed* was especially striking in the ways in which black writers used one of the most significant motifs in black literature from this period, the motif of racial mixture. Mixed-race protagonists dominated black fiction from this period, and their physical characteristics served as a metaphor for the ideological issues raised by questions of racial identity. The way black writers handled such characters reveals much about the problems these writers faced in trying to talk about racial identity within their assimilationist literary framework.

The metaphorical power of racial mixture for black writers grew, to a great extent, out of historical and social sources. A substantial number of "black" Americans—and an even greater proportion of the middle class, from which most writers came—were not completely black. Somewhere, and often not too far back, was a white ancestor.

Black writers could turn this fact to literary purposes in several ways. First, it was an important symbol of the victimization of black people, going back to slavery. The roots of racial mixture, in most cases, were in slavery; the mixture itself was usually the product of the victimization of female slaves by white slave owners and overseers. The fact of racial mixture, like the facts of racism, was a major symptom of what white society had done to black people.

Given the origins of most people of mixed race, it was also an issue that related powerfully to concerns about gentility. The fact that many blacks could point to white ancestors, but ancestors who had, in fact, been guilty of rape or adultery, provided yet another occasion for an ironic comment on the white man's devotion to his own ideals. This was especially important in an era when black men were being lynched for allegedly desiring white women. Alexander Crummell captured this irony when he remarked, in 1889, that "the negro in this land has ever been the truest of men, in marital allegiance, to his own race."[47]

Because black writers could use this aspect of racial mixture to telling effect in ways that supported the general thrust of genteel pro- test literature, the main character in a substantial proportion of the short fiction and in most of the novels was of mixed race. This, too, was not an innovation of the post-Reconstruction era. Such heroes and hero- ines, as a type, went back to antislavery fiction, to the literature pro- duced by white and black exponents of abolition. The use of such characters could take several forms. Widely popular, for example, was

47. Alexander Crummell, *The Race Problem in America* (Washington, D.C., 1889), 8.

the story of the "tragic mulatto." Given special fame as a result of Dion Boucicault's 1859 drama, *The Octoroon*, the tragic mulatto story can be dated even earlier, and figured in such a pioneering black novel as William Wells Brown's *Clotel*, published in 1853. Usually focusing on a nearly white heroine, it was a tale of unrequited love across the color line, in which romantic ideals were frustrated by racial barriers, and the heroine's virtue was threatened by the evils of slavery. Often the tragedy was increased by the suicide of the heroine, although in the London version of Boucicault's play, at least, tragedy was averted when the heroine and her lover chose to escape both slave society and racism by going abroad.[48] Less elaborately developed than the tragic mulatto, but no less important, were those many characters, such as Eliza or Emmeline in Harriet Beecher Stowe's *Uncle Tom's Cabin*, who, though slaves, were virtually white in appearance and Victorian in characteristics.

The function of such characters for antislavery fiction was clear. Addressed mainly to whites, antislavery writing had to have a central character with whom white readers could identify. Looking like a typical figure in mainstream sentimental literature made the main character one who fit the white audience's literary expectations, and it made the evils of slavery all the more impressive. The mixed-race character played a similar role in such post-Reconstruction revivals of abolitionist fiction as James Howard's *Bond and Free* (where Purcey's light complexion enhances the author's portrayal of her as simply a young Victorian American woman thrust into the crucible of slavery) and Albery Whitman's two major epics.

But a message about racial identity was also implicit in literature of this sort. The mixed-race works helped emphasize the notion of a common black victimhood that underlay Sampson's comments on racial unity and "Sanda's" novel by showing that complexion was no protection against injustice. The complexity emerges when one realizes that what this implies, above all, is the real absence of choice confronting black people of whatever complexion—or level of culture—in late nineteenth century America. This, too, gave a negative content to racial identity, as black writers tried to give it literary shape. Identity became,

48. See Arlene A. Elder, *The "Hindered Hand": Cultural Implications of Early African-American American Fiction* (Westport, Conn., 1978), 6–7; Werner Sollors, *Beyond Ethnicity: Consent and Descent in American Culture* (New York, 1986), 225. On Boucicault's play, see the discussion in Philip Butcher, ed., *The Minority Presence in American Literature, 1600–1900* (2 vols. Washington, D.C., 1977), II, 71.

again, a matter based on victimhood rather than achievement, whatever the public rhetoric may have been.

The literature on racial mixture also raises ambiguities deeper than those in "Sanda's" novel, because there are, in fact, two very different ways to read the message about identity that the literature conveys. On the one hand, and in light of Sampson's comments and of the purposes of Stowers and Anderson's novel, one may see such literature as an effort to encourage solidarity by bringing home the fact that all black people, regardless of color or character, share a common oppression. But on the other hand, one may see it as making a special case for nearly white middle-class individuals. According to this second reading, the attributes of a Purcey or a Rodney—enhanced by their complexions—make it especially scandalous that they should be the recipients of injustice. Racism is seen as especially heinous because racists make no allowances for differences among black people, treating even the physically or culturally "white" with the same contempt used for the least refined.

Such a reading is not without foundation. The existence of color consciousness among black Americans of mixed origins in post-Reconstruction America has been documented by historians and social critics alike. Although such recent historians as Joel Williamson and Howard Rabinowitz have shown that wealth and culture were the real keys to gaining status in black society during this period, they have also noted areas in which an internal color line was of great significance. Rabinowitz, for example, has shown how, in the major southern cities of Richmond, Raleigh, Atlanta, Montgomery, and Nashville, people in the census categories "black" and "mulatto" tended overwhelmingly to marry in their own group. Nashville had a formally constituted "Blue Vein Society," so called because membership was restricted to individuals who were so light that their blue veins were visible.[49] Their own light complexions meant a great deal to the men and women who would join a "blue vein society"; and characters such as Purcey, Rodney, and any of the other light-skinned protagonists would easily have captured the resentment of those who were nearly, but not quite, white.

This latter reading is not, one suspects, a reading of which the authors themselves would have approved, since their stated purposes precluded any open repudiation of race. But it certainly lies between

49. Joel Williamson, *New People: Miscegenation and Mulattoes in the United States* (New York, 1980), 82; Howard N. Rabinowitz, *Race Relations in the Urban South, 1865–1890* (New York, 1978), 248–49.

the lines of their works, and the fact that it does emphasizes the complexity of the problems black writers faced in trying to create literary portrayals of the racial solidarity they held so dear. In their assimilationism, they could not come up with an unambiguous approach to what it meant to be black. The problems this created could not be solved until the writers could find a basis for formulating more positive approaches to the issue of identity.

Perhaps one reason the issue of identity remained problematic in so much black writing from this period is that identity questions were subordinated, for most writers, to purposes of protest. Hence, black writers were, for the most part, unaware of the difficulties about identity they revealed when they tried to give dramatic shape to racial questions. During the early 1890s, however, identity issues did take on added urgency for a few black writers, who perceived a need for a more positive understanding of what it meant to be black in America.

One evidence of changing focuses and concerns was the growth of relatively new ways of dealing with stories involving racial mixture. Above all, black writers began to pick up more clearly on the issue of identity as it figured in such stories, and even to indicate more positive bases for the identification as black that their mixed-race protagonists made. A major example of such a change in focus was Frances Ellen Watkins Harper's 1892 novel, *Iola Leroy; or, Shadows Uplifted*.

Harper herself was a major writer of this period, one of its most noted poets. Born in 1825, she was the child of free parents in Baltimore. She received some formal schooling, published her first collection of poetry in 1845, and for a brief time taught school in Ohio and Pennsylvania. She joined the antislavery movement in 1854 and was active in the movement as both a writer and a lecturer. After the Civil War, she continued to use her talents in support of racial justice, women's rights, and temperance. In addition to *Iola Leroy*, Harper published several volumes of poetry—all well within the assimilationist tradition—including *Poems on Miscellaneous Subjects*, first published in 1854 but going through several editions; *Moses: A Story of the Nile*, first published in 1869; an 1871 volume entitled *Poems*; and an 1872 volume entitled *Sketches of Southern Life*. She remained an active figure in social reform, especially temperance, until her death, in 1911.

That she did lead such an active life is significant, because Harper sought to find avenues for combining genteel ideals with an activist imagination. One sees this clearly in an 1885 essay in which she offered her own prescription for dealing with racial difficulties: "Trust in God and be patient." Her prescription was not a call for accommodation:

> By patience, I do not mean a servile submission to wrong; an idle folding of hands and going to sleep, waiting, for the good time coming, but that patience which, realizing that between the white and colored people of the country there is a community of interests, will base its action, not on the old animosities of the past, but on the new conditions of the present and go earnestly to work and develop self-reliance, self-control, and self-respect in the race; and so build up worthy characters by planting the roots of progress under the hearthstone. By faith in God, I do not mean an unreasoning waiting for God to do for us what we can do for ourselves, but that faith which teaches us to work on the same line with him, with the assurance that the only true safety for a race or nation is to live in harmony with God's laws of moral and spiritual life.[50]

Religion was at the core of Harper's thought, as it was for many black writers; but the degree to which she stressed the activist side of religion and of life was a distinguishing feature of her creative work. Scholar Cheryl Walker, comparing Harper with other women poets of the time, has noted in her a strength and lack of "ambivalence toward power" quite unlike what one reads in white women poets of the period.[51] One may contrast her with other black writers from her time on much the same grounds.

Iola Leroy captured Harper's spirit, and it was recognized as an important book when it appeared. Mrs. N. F. Mossell, a prominent civic leader and activist, wrote, "All of the open and settled questions of the so-called Negro problem are brought out in this little volume." She added that, at points, "Mrs. Harper has risen to a height of eloquent pleading for the right that must win for the race many strong friends." The distinguished black former abolitionist William Still, who remained active in the black community, described the novel in a private letter as an "excellent work" with "much in it that is calculated to do great benefit to the race." Still also wrote an introduction to the novel. Time has not been wholly kind to Harper's novel. More recent critics have stressed, in particular, that the characters are a bit too perfect, a bit too

50. Frances Ellen Watkins Harper, "The Democratic Return to Power," *A.M.E. Church Review*, I (1884), 223–24.

51. Cheryl Walker, *The Nightingale's Burden: Women Poets and American Culture Before 1900* (Bloomington, Ind., 1982), 85–86.

angelic. But in its day, *Iola Leroy* was acknowledged to be an important book by a major writer.[52]

The central figure in Harper's novel is her title character, Iola Leroy. The story follows her from slavery to freedom and to her life in the North, where she becomes a valuable member of the black community. Along the way, Harper uses Iola's life to comment on the central issues of race relations and black identity.

Iola is also the epitome of the light-skinned sentimental heroine. Her character, in this regard, emerges early in the novel. Released from slavery by the advancing Union army, Iola is taken to the headquarters of the victorious general, who is "much impressed by her modest demeanor, and surprised to see the refinement and beauty she possessed." Put to work in a field hospital, she eagerly applies herself to nursing the wounded: "The beautiful, girlish face was full of tender earnestness. The fresh, young voice was strangely sympathetic, as if some great sorrow had bound her heart in loving compassion to every sufferer who needed her gentle ministrations."[53] Beautiful, compassionate, and utterly feminine, Iola Leroy is all a sentimental heroine could be.

Much of the early part of Harper's novel describes the Civil War itself, stressing the bravery of black troops under Union command as well as the desire of the southern slaves for freedom. One episode during the war helps define the rest of the novel. The central male character, Robert Johnson, is a slave who has fled his mistress in order to join the Union troops. He proves to be an excellent soldier and is offered a chance for a promotion by a young white officer. There is, however, a catch. Robert is light enough to pass for white, and he must do so if he is to become an officer. Robert refuses. He wants to be where he is "most needed." Beyond that, he argues, bravery has nothing to do with the color of a man's skin; and he cites a heroic fellow soldier, "just as black as black can be," to prove that this is so. The white officer agrees.[54]

The element of choice in this episode—as Johnson refuses to pass for white—is paradigmatic for the novel. Whatever else racial mixture implies, Harper used it in *Iola Leroy* to address a central theme of

52. Mrs. N. F. Mossell, *The Work of the Afro-American Woman* (1894; rpr. Freeport, N.Y., 1971), 61; William Still to John E. Bruce, August 1, 1893, John E. Bruce Collection, Schomburg Center for Research in Black Culture, New York Public Library; Sterling A. Brown, *Negro Poetry and Drama*, 76–77.

53. Frances Ellen Watkins Harper, *Iola Leroy; or, Shadows Uplifted* (Philadelphia, 1892), 39–40.

54. *Ibid.,* 43–44.

identity and courage, of choosing to remain with one's own people, even if one need not. Harper was not unaware of older treatments of racial mixture, and there were even elements of the tragic mulatto tradition in the novel, especially in the portrayal of Iola herself. But Harper used such more conventional elements primarily to highlight the questions of identity and choice, as her characters continuously confront opportunities to pass for white, and consistently refuse to do so. Iola's first opportunity to pass occurs in the field hospital, and in a way that consciously evokes the tradition of the tragic mulatto. A young white physician, not knowing her race, proposes marriage. When she tells him of her Negro blood, he asserts that she need only pass as white and they can still be married. However, Iola, unlike earlier heroines, refuses, in part to save him from potential embarrassment, and in part so she can look for her mother, from whom she was separated by slavery. Willingly, she accepts her black identity.

Harper similarly used the tragic mulatto tradition in a recounting of Iola's life prior to the Civil War. As was common in tragic mulatto stories, Harper gives Iola a past in which she grew up knowing nothing of her black ancestry. Her father married her mother, Marie, knowing full well Marie's status—prior to marriage, Marie had been a slave. Iola, her sister, Gracie, and her brother, Henry, were raised in the South as white and were attending northern schools when the war broke out. Iola, knowing no better, even defended the southern way of life against the aspersions of her classmates. Early in the war, however, Iola's father died, and his unscrupulous cousin managed to have Marie, Gracie, and Iola remanded to slavery. Henry, protected at his northern school, learned of this and immediately enlisted in the Union army—like Robert Johnson, refusing to join any but a black regiment. Gracie died of the shock. But for Iola and Marie, slavery was to become their lot; and Iola was to learn what it meant to be black. It is this identity she accepts in refusing the young doctor's proposal. She will have an opportunity to make the same choice at several points as the novel progresses.

Indeed, the rest of the novel is structured around such opportunities. Iola ultimately takes up with Robert Johnson, as both travel through the South in search of the mothers from whom they have been separated, searches that end in success. Iola also takes up a career as a teacher among the freedmen of the South, though her school is destroyed by a white mob. And she learns that she is, in fact, Johnson's niece, he being the brother of Marie. The family is reunited; even Harry—as her brother is now known—returns to the fold. After some discussion, Robert and Iola decide to go to the North, to live as a black family.

The choice is not an easy one. Iola needs work if she is to survive, but it soon becomes clear that the jobs most suitable for ladies of refinement are available only to white women. Iola clearly could pass and could hold such a job, but she refuses to do so. Her honesty inevitably costs her employment opportunities and even stands in the way of her ability to find a way to live. The issue is raised in other ways as well; from this point on, the novel becomes more a series of instructive vignettes than a story. Iola's wartime physician suitor remains ardent in his love for her; she maintains her identity by remaining adamant in her refusal to become white. Harper also introduces a black doctor, Frank Latimer, a friend of Iola's suitor, who is, like Iola, light enough to pass for white. He, too, refuses to renounce his race. And Harper even moves away from the focus on mixed-race characters through the presentation of Miss Lucille Delany, a cultured and highly educated young woman of unmixed parentage who is very dark in color. Miss Delany has worked closely with Harry in the uplifting of southern Negroes; indeed, they are in love and are to be wed. Her presence in the novel indicates clearly that culture and refinement know no color line.

The introduction of these characters leads to a fitting conclusion for Harper's novel. Iola chooses the brilliant Dr. Latimer as her husband, and the two of them move back to the South to work among their people. Harry marries Lucille, and they too return to the South. Their marriage allows Harper one more comment on questions of identity, when Lucille expresses a fear that Harry's mother "may not prefer me for a daughter. You know, Harry, complexional prejudices are not confined to white people." Harry replies that his mother is "too noble to indulge in such sentiments," adding that his sister approves as well.[55]

The passage provides a major clue to *Iola Leroy*'s significance. In her presentation of Lucille Delany and her deliberate rejection of an internal color line, Harper posits and celebrates the existence of a black community wherein one can both maintain genteel ideals and find a satisfying way of life. She sees an identification with that community not merely as a matter of common victimage but as a matter of conscious choice and moral principle. Her references to the tragic mulatto tradition help to emphasize this message. Harper's novel raises the tradition's

55. *Ibid.,* 278.

conventions in a way that strikingly turns them upside down, as Iola accepts her identity, not with tragic melancholy, nor even resignation, but with strength and pride.

For Harper, then, the central theme is neither tragedy nor victimage—though she recognizes the roles both have played in the black experience—but, rather, choice. As Jane Campbell has noted, one compelling feature of Harper's novel is its encouragement of black women to "view themselves as actors in, rather than victims of, history."[56] This changing perspective on self and identity is clear in the case of Iola Leroy, and it is no less so in regard to other characters—particularly on the issue of racial identity. Harper's characters are frequently given the choice of passing for white, in situations where they can do so with virtually no fear of exposure or even with the willing complicity of whites. They choose, however, to identify themselves as black and, having done so, to devote their lives to working among their own people for racial justice. Unlike her contemporaries, Harper dramatized the meaning of a black identity in a way that made being black a positive act as well as a social ascription.

To be sure, Iola, Robert, and Latimer all choose their black identity mainly on the basis of love and family loyalty. Iola and Robert reject passing in order to search for and remain with their mothers after the war. Latimer is offered great opportunities for success by his white grandmother but refuses to renounce his mother. Harry refuses to give credence to the internal color line and thus makes an unambiguous choice to live as black. Although one might argue that the bases of these decisions really have little to do with racial loyalty,[57] one must also recognize that in framing their choices this way, Harper maintained the grounding of her story in sentimental genteel ideals. Indeed, given the literary and religious frameworks within which Harper worked, no other basis for deciding on a black identity would have made sense. Family loyalty was not a selfish reason for identifying with all black people. It was, rather, the best reason of all in a sentimental, pietistic world. It is no accident that Alexander Crummell, one of the foremost ideologists of black solidarity, once characterized that solidarity as something based on a kind of "family feeling."[58]

56. Campbell, *Mythic Black Fiction*, 25.

57. Richard Alan Yarborough, "The Depiction of Blacks in the Early Afro-American Novel" (Ph.D. dissertation, Stanford University, 1980), 228.

58. Crummell, *Race Problem*, 10.

Certainly Harper did not offer a radical alternative to assimilationist ideals in *Iola Leroy*. Nor would she have wanted to. There is no doubt that, as critic Robert Bone and others have suggested, Harper was like other writers of this era in accepting a kind of "Anglo-Saxonism" that left unquestioned the belief that blacks should aspire to Victorian middle-class lives.[59] In that, Harper was a fully assimilationist writer.

But Harper at least moved in new directions, asserting the possibility of a black identity that, being less a matter of necessity and more a matter of choice, could be seen as a positive fact. Certainly, Harper's conception of a black identity was itself limited. But it was positive and showed, by implication, an awareness that a satisfactory sense of identity had to be given some kind of positive base. It was an awareness that many others of her day could not yet share.

One who did, however, was Victoria Earle Matthews, a prominent New York clubwoman and writer. Like Harper, Matthews was one of the first black writers to address identity issues directly. Her 1892 short story "Eugenie's Mistake" was, like *Iola Leroy*, centered on a character who must confront the discovery that she has a trace of Negro "blood." In this story, the beautiful Adele Van Arsden of Louisiana, daughter of a wealthy planter originally from the West Indies, becomes engaged to Royal Clifford. As we have come to expect, Adele herself is the epitome of gentility—sensitive, refined, French educated.

When her father dies, Adele inherits his wealth. She is befriended by Eugenie St. Noir, the daughter of her father's lawyer. Eugenie also loves Royal; and when Adele and he are wed, she resolves revenge. A document appears, indicating that Adele is Negro. Upon reading it and discovering her racial background, Adele declares, with all the self-sacrificing virtue of any sentimental heroine: "O my father! your fatal kindness has wrecked my life. Had I known the truth, my darling should have been spared." Fearing for Royal's reputation, she leaves him. Royal is crushed. Eugenie, mortified, also flees. But all works out. Royal later finds the document and seeks out Adele. He travels to France and discovers her at the home of her teacher. Declaring, tellingly, that "I had been to America and knew that purity and goodness were of no account when placed in the balance with the despised taint," the teacher brings the couple back together. As it turns out, not only was Adele's mother not white but Royal's mother also had the "despised taint." They are a

59. Robert A. Bone, *The Negro Novel in America* (Rev. ed.; New Haven, 1965), 19.

black couple whose marriage is no longer threatened by issues of race.[60]

At one level, the story offers an indictment of the arbitrariness of racial categories. The French teacher's words emphasize that point. It is also a story of vulnerability. Adele is the perfect sentimental heroine; and her character, like Purcey's, makes it all the sadder that she should be so vulnerable to the cruelties of a racist society. Her color serves the same rhetorical purpose as that of other writers' light-skinned protagonists. That she suffers despite her complexion raises the same points about racial identity that one finds in *Bond and Free* and similar works, and the tale of unrequited love also recalls the tragic mulatto tradition.

But Matthews' story differs significantly from others that use mixed-race protagonists in the degree to which the problems characterizing assimilationist works are counterbalanced by a happy ending that involves not an opposition to racism but, rather, a satisfaction found in settling with one's own people within the confines of a racist society. One could interpret such an ending as an acquiescence to racism. However, in the context of the early 1890s and of the kinds of concerns about identity and solidarity that were beginning to develop, it is more likely that Matthews' story shows the possibility of finding happiness while accepting one's race. There is an inward turning implied in Matthews' story that is very different from the protest motifs at the heart of other works and from the implications for identity that those motifs raise.

Matthews still does not escape from the problems of dealing with identity from an assimilationist point of view. The story ends happily not because of any achievement on the part of either Adele or Royal, but because the two discover their racial kinship. Neither had lived as black, in any positive sense, prior to that discovery. But as in *Iola Leroy*, Matthews' characters do find love a sufficient reason for accepting their identity; and in turning her gaze inward, Matthews adopted a perspective on identity questions that departed from older points of view on the meaning of race.

Far more significant in literary terms, however, is Matthews' noted short story "Aunt Lindy." This story, first published in the *A.M.E. Church*

---

60. Victoria Earle [Matthews], "Eugenie's Mistake: A Story," *A.M.E. Church Review*, VIII (1892), 262, 267.

Review in 1891, was reprinted in pamphlet form in 1893.[61] It is based, Matthews wrote, "on real life." The story is set in her own hometown, Fort Valley, Georgia, after the Civil War; it begins with an account of a great fire that burns out much of the town. Many people are injured, and the local doctor goes to an old black woman, Aunt Lindy, to ask her aid as a nurse. He particularly needs help with one difficult case, a victim he wishes her to take into her cabin. She agrees: "De cabin is pore, but Joel ner me ain't heathins; fetch him right along, my han's ain't afeered of wuk when trubble comes."[62]

The man, in very bad shape, is brought in. Lindy and Joel testify to their Christian spirit and seek to make him as comfortable as possible. Then, a light is put on the man's face. "Great Gawd!" Lindy exclaims, "it's Marse Jeems!" A flame leaps in her eyes; and as the man begins to babble, Aunt Lindy screams, "Whar's my chil'en?" She answers her own question: "To de fo win's ob de earfh, yo ole debbil yo." He had been her master and had sold off her children. Vengeance is hers for the taking. Just then, however, she begins to hear singing from a nearby church. "'Vengeance is mine, ses de Lawd,' came from within; her anger died away; quickly her steps she retraced. 'Mi'ty Gawd, stren'fin my arm, an pur'fy my heart,' was all she said." She nurses the man back to health. In gratitude, he provides for Joel and Lindy for the rest of their days and even sees to it that their firstborn, now an adult, is restored to them. The others have died but are at least accounted for.[63]

Although the story seems straightforward, in the context of the early 1890s it is a complex work. For one thing, its making a central figure out of a rural "folk" character, and one who speaks in dialect, sets the story apart from other works of its time. To be sure, dialect writing by black authors was not unknown at this time. It had been used in theatrical productions, including minstrelsy; and other black writers, even going back to antebellum times, had created dialect-speaking characters. They appeared, for example, in William Wells Brown's *Clotel*, published in 1853. But again, such uses of dialect and folk elements were far from common and, in earlier works, such a character as "Aunt Lindy" had never served as a focus for a serious piece. Usually, folk characters

---

61. Victoria Earle Matthews, "Aunt Lindy (A Story Founded on Real Life)," *A.M.E. Church Review*, V (1889), 246–250; Matthews, *Aunt Lindy: A Story Founded on Real Life* (New York, 1893).
62. Matthews, "Aunt Lindy," 247.
63. *Ibid.,* 249.

served mainly to provide a contrast with more genteel protagonists, however sympathetically they might be portrayed. Harper herself did this in *Iola Leroy*. The only possible exception might be some of Charles Chesnutt's stories, which gave central place to dialect-speaking figures, and which had appeared by 1889. But Chesnutt was not at that time widely known to be a black writer. He had not really entered into black literary tradition. Matthews' story, appearing in the *A.M.E. Church Review*, was published in what was then the central organ of that tradition.

This open appreciation of such a character points to an understanding of racial identity that was new, in that it involved a celebration of character traits and a way of life that were clearly black but not entirely in the realm of middle-class gentility. Although it might be argued that Aunt Lindy was in some sense prefigured by Harriet Beecher Stowe's Uncle Tom and by what historian George Fredrickson has described as the "romantic racialist" view in antislavery—the view that blacks were somehow naturally given to Christian virtue[64]—that character type had never really been part of the assimilationist black tradition, because it tended to stress submissiveness as well as piety. Indeed, black writers even in the 1870s and 1880s—notably Albery Whitman and the historian George Washington Williams—were openly hostile to Stowe's protagonist for precisely that reason. Aunt Lindy herself, in the temptation she feels to get revenge on her former master, was not entirely in the "romantic racialist" tradition. Thus Matthews' story represented a significant departure.

It was, to be sure, a qualified departure. There was much to tie "Aunt Lindy" in with more traditional forms of black fiction. Aunt Lindy was not genteel, but the folk virtues Matthews celebrated had much in common with genteel virtues as well. Aunt Lindy was pious, caring, and devoted to her family, traits that were widely prized by all Americans, however important they were in black folk culture. Matthews was willing to celebrate the rural, folk way of life, but she did so by portraying folk-based characters who shared at least some mainstream virtues.

Still, there was a departure from certain key features of gentility, especially from its class and cultural bases, in "Aunt Lindy." In her sympathetic portrayal of the uncultivated Aunt Lindy and in the fact that she used Aunt Lindy, rather than some dewy-eyed ingenue, as her central figure, Matthews made at least a tentative approach to seriously portray-

64. George M. Fredrickson, *The Black Image in the White Mind: The Debate on Afro-American Character and Destiny, 1817–1914* (New York, 1971), 103.

ing a black experience not fully within the norms of middle-class America. In this respect, then, Matthews was among the first of the black writers who, capturing some of the main themes and images of other American regionalist writers, focused on the question of identity in a way that stressed sources for identity outside the American mainstream. In doing so, she moved away—however tentatively—from the older assimilationist consensus. She saw at least the possibility of celebrating a distinctive black way of life—of describing a black experience that had to do with more than victimization by whites, although it included that as well. Thus she pointed toward new directions for black literature.

II

Identity and Ambiguity: The Literary Career of Paul Laurence Dunbar, 1892– 1906

The mid-1890s saw two events that would have a major impact on black literature for the next decade and beyond. The first occurred in 1895. It was Booker T. Washington's notable speech before the Cotton States and International Exposition in Atlanta, Georgia. Washington proposed a truce between black people and white in the South through a compromise in regard to prejudice and segregation. Peace between the races, he urged, could be based on a recognition by blacks and whites of their mutual interest in the progress of the region and on a retreat by blacks from agitation for immediate equality. Progress, he declared, "must be the result of severe and constant struggle rather than of artificial forcing." In the most quoted line of the speech, Washington asserted, "In all things that are purely social we can be as separate as the fingers, yet one as the hand in all things essential to mutual progress."[1] An accommodation to segregation, Washington's speech signaled the intentional withdrawal of many blacks from a confrontation with white-dominated American society, particularly in the South, as they sought to set up independent black institutions and to create an independent social and economic base.

The second event, though of more limited impact, was the appearance in *Harper's Weekly*, June 27, 1896, of a column by William Dean Howells that discussed an obscure volume of poems by an obscure twenty-four-year-old black man, Paul Laurence Dunbar. Subsequently, Howells helped to publish, and wrote the introduction to, Dunbar's first major collection of verse, *Lyrics of Lowly Life*, issued by Dodd, Mead

1. Booker T. Washington, *Up from Slavery* (1901; rpr. New York, 1986), 221–22, 223. See Louis R. Harlan, *Booker T. Washington: The Making of a Black Leader, 1856–1901* (New York, 1972), Chap. 11.

later that year. It was the first collection by a black poet to be published by a major American publishing house. In that introduction, Howells, the era's leading critic, at first professed indifference to the poet's race. "I should scarcely trouble the reader with a special appeal in behalf of this book," he wrote, "if it had not specially appealed to me for reasons apart from the author's race, origin, and condition." But it had indeed appealed to him, and he could not quite forget the author's race after all. He wrote, "Here was the first instance of an American negro who had evinced innate distinction in literature." And he added, "So far as I could remember, Paul Dunbar was the only man of pure African blood and of American civilization to feel the negro life aesthetically and express it lyrically." Dunbar was, for Howells, a major literary discovery. Howells was only too happy to promote Dunbar's work to the public and to aid the young man in other ways as well.[2]

Despite Howells' claim, Dunbar was not, of course, the first black American of some literary ability. But as a result of that claim, he was the first black American writer to acquire a broad national following. Indeed, one could justifiably argue that for the ten years after Howells' tribute, Dunbar was the most *popular* poet—black or white—in the United States. His work appeared in all the major periodicals, including *Century*, *Atlantic*, *Outlook*, and *Saturday Evening Post*. His readings drew large white and black audiences and received enthusiastic responses. He was certainly America's first black literary celebrity. Because of this, he was a writer no other black author could easily ignore. Especially in the realm of poetry, his influence was strong and unmistakable. For black writers, Dunbar was as important in his way as Washington was for black Americans in general because Dunbar's writing was an important measure of the difficult tensions created by the forced withdrawal of blacks from the American mainstream that Washington had signaled by his Atlanta speech. Dunbar was one of the first writers to reveal the difficulties of holding to the middle-class ethos that had earlier given substance to literary portrayals of black aspirations and achievements.

Dunbar's fame and his impact on black writers grew mainly out of his poetry, especially out of the large body of work written in what was intended to be black dialect. To be sure, Dunbar was not simply a black

2. Described and quoted in Lida Keck Wiggins, *The Life and Works of Paul Laurence Dunbar* (1907; rpr. New York, 1971), 13–15. See also Edwin H. Cady (ed.), *W. D. Howells as Critic* (London, 1973), 243–55.

dialect poet. He also did a great deal of work in standard English—and a few pieces in the dialect of the white Midwest. Moreover, in addition to his poetry, he produced four collections of short stories and four novels, as well as a number of miscellaneous works. With Will Marion Cook, he wrote a musical comedy, *Clorindy*, which was presented in New York City and was quite successful. But, again, it was Dunbar's poetry, especially his dialect poetry, that first got him noticed and that served as the basis for his impact on black writing. Put simply, for years after Dunbar emerged, very few black writers failed to follow him into the realm of dialect. This was to be a major development in black literary life.

Dunbar's dialect poetry and his ideas about it have long been subjects of controversy among literary historians. The poems themselves were quite varied in tone and content. Some dealt with love on the plantation, others with simple folk customs. A few were well within the confines of the white plantation tradition; others used dialect subtly to counter that tradition.

The sources for Dunbar's dialect writing were also varied, but a key source undoubtedly was the plantation tradition itself. Dialect poetry was a major part of the plantation tradition developed by the white writers Thomas Nelson Page and Irwin Russell, along with a host of other popular white writers. The contention of critic Michael Flusche that Dunbar came along at just the right time, that a market primed by Page and others was ready for the real thing—a Negro writing in dialect—is probably correct, at least so far as Dunbar's popularity is concerned.[3] In addition, Dunbar was strongly influenced by the kind of popular regional writing produced by James Whitcomb Riley—a poet whose work Dunbar greatly admired and who liked Dunbar's work. Indeed, Dunbar's dialect work can be viewed as American regionalist and "local color" writing—much as Matthews' "Aunt Lindy" was—incorporating and elaborating what was already a significant form in American literature.

To view Dunbar's work this way is not to minimize its importance for black literary tradition, even though Dunbar was not alone as a pioneering black dialect writer. Not only was Matthews' "Aunt Lindy" already distinguished by its use of dialect when Dunbar came on the scene, but James Edwin Campbell and Daniel Webster Davis were Dunbar's exact contemporaries as dialect poets. However, none of these writers gained

3. Michael Flusche, "Paul Laurence Dunbar and the Burden of Race," *Southern Humanities Review*, XI (1977), 49–50.

Dunbar's level of general recognition. Similarly, although Charles Chesnutt had published the first of a number of folktale-like stories, with much of the writing in dialect, in the late 1880s—and Chesnutt's stories had even appeared in *Atlantic*, giving his work, like Dunbar's, a prominence unmatched by most black writing—Chesnutt's racial identity was not widely known at the time, and this minimized his impact on other black writers. To some extent, perhaps, the more general turning to dialect writing may be seen as part of the continuing effort by black writers to produce works that would gain them a large general audience. All those who produced dialect writing sought such an audience; Dunbar and Chesnutt in particular hoped for an audience large enough to enable them to support themselves solely by their literary efforts. That they should have turned to such a popular form as dialect writing is not, therefore, surprising. Still, Dunbar's impact was undoubtedly great; it can be measured in the increase in black dialect writing that followed his success.

However, Dunbar himself was, at best, ambivalent toward his own dialect work. He believed there were limitations in dialect writing. In conversations with James Weldon Johnson, Dunbar lamented his reputation as a dialect poet and what that reputation had done to his career: "You know, of course, that I didn't start as a dialect poet. I simply came to the conclusion that I could write it as well, if not better, than anybody else I knew of, and that by doing so I should gain a hearing. I gained the hearing, and now they don't want me to write anything but dialect." Dunbar's widow, Alice, reinforced Dunbar's comments. "Say what you will, or what Mr. Howells wills, about the 'feeling the Negro life esthetically and expressing it lyrically,'" she remembered, "it was in the pure English poems that the poet expressed *himself*. He may have expressed his race in the dialect poems; they were to him the side issues of his work, the overflowing of a life apart from his dearest dreams." Indeed, Dunbar stated his frustrations with his identity as a dialect poet in one of his most famous standard English poems, one entitled, appropriately, "The Poet"; he lamented that, for all his ambition, he had been recognized only for his ability to write "a jingle in a broken tongue."[4]

Despite his ambivalence, however, Dunbar did not identify his dialect poetry with the excesses of the white plantation tradition. In a

4. James Weldon Johnson, *Along This Way* (New York, 1933), 160–61; Alice M. Dunbar, "The Poet and His Song," *A.M.E. Church Review*, XXXI (1914), 124; Paul Laurence Dunbar, *The Complete Poems of Paul Laurence Dunbar* (New York, 1913), 191.

letter to Frederick Douglass' widow, Helen, Dunbar defended his writing, saying rather contentiously of those who charged him with demeaning black people, "I am sorry to find among intelligent people those who are unable to differentiate dialect as a philological branch from the burlesque of Negro minstrelsy"—thereby implying a clear distinction between his own work and that of the plantation tradition. Most of Dunbar's black contemporaries agreed. Certainly, there were a few who did not like Dunbar's dialect poetry. Alexander Crummell was not happy with Howells' identifying it as Dunbar's best work. An anonymous critic for the New York *Age* cited the inaccuracy of the dialect itself and asserted, "Fifty years hence it will be a jargon without a key." Most, however, agreed with Howells' assessment that it was Dunbar's best work and that it was good writing. Archibald Grimké, in a 1909 talk on Dunbar before the Bethel Literary and Historical Association, quoted from one of Dunbar's works in standard English but noted, "As for me I like him best when he sang not in regulation English but in Negro dialect instead. In Negro dialect he is at his very best, and produced his finest work as a poet." Grimké went on to quote appreciatively from several of the dialect poems. Even Alice Dunbar, although recognizing her husband's frustration, believed that his dialect poems were far better than those in standard English: "Love of nature was there, but the power to express this love was not. Instead he harked back to the feeling of the race, and intuitively put their aspirations into song." Perhaps some of the poet's frustration came from a recognition that he was much better at his sideline than at the work he really wanted to do.[5]

But Dunbar's ambivalences and frustrations had deeper sources than matters of literary concern. Dunbar connected his own dialect writing with issues of personal and racial identity, more profoundly than any writer had done before. One may most profitably look at Dunbar as a poet who, whatever his motives for doing dialect work, recognized that such work was intimately tied to the direction that ideas about racial identity were taking in a segregated society. His dialect work reveals the kinds of tensions, at an emotional level, that such a society could produce.

5. Paul Laurence Dunbar to Helen Douglass, October 22, 1896, in Paul Laurence Dunbar Papers, Ohio Historical Society (microfilm ed.); Alexander Crummell to John Edward Bruce, December 24, 1896, in John E. Bruce Collection, Schomburg Center for Research in Black Culture, New York Public Library; New York *Age*, February 15, 1906; Archibald H. Grimké, "Paul Laurence Dunbar: The Poet," p. 7, ms. essay in Archibald H. Grimké Papers, Manuscript Division, The Moorland-Spingarn Research Center, Howard University; Alice Dunbar, "The Poet and His Song," 123.

At its most positive, Dunbar's dialect writing celebrated a black heritage revealed by black folk life and used it as a basis for molding a distinctive black identity, going beyond what even Victoria Earle Matthews had done. Dunbar's dialect poems, at their best, fully evoked that life and celebrated its characteristics.

A seminal poetic statement of Dunbar's understanding of what black folk life could mean was one of his most famous early dialect pieces, "When Malindy Sings," a poem whose significance has also been noted by critic Trudier Harris. Published in Dunbar's first major collection, the poem takes the form of a slave's address to his young mistress, describing the beautiful voice of the black woman Malindy. It quickly turns into a celebration of black folk music as such, contrasting the natural beauty of that music with the artificiality of white song:

> G'way an' quit dat noise, Miss Lucy—
> Put dat music book away;

the narrator urges his mistress. He tells her:

> You ain't got de nachel o'gans
> Fu' to make de soun' come right,
> You ain't got de tu'ns an' twistin's
> Fu' to make it sweet an' light.

Later, he describes Malindy's music as

> sweetah dan de music
> Of an edicated band

and refers specifically to the power of "Sing Low, Sweet Chariot." Humble, natural, and deeply felt, the music of the folk, as presented in this poem, had unparalleled power. Citing such properties of black folk music as "tu'ns an' twistin's" and such a noted black song as "Swing Low, Sweet Chariot," Dunbar also called attention to black distinctiveness as revealed in the uncultivated talents of the people.[6]

For all its roots in white and black dialect literature and popular art, much of Dunbar's dialect poetry looked directly to the folk tradition, as did "When Malindy Sings." Actually, this was not as true of the dialect itself—despite Dunbar's defense of its "philological" roots. The dialect of Dunbar's poetry seems to have had far more to do with literary traditions than with folk speech. It was based on many of the conven-

6. Trudier Harris, *Exorcising Blackness: Historical and Literary Lynching and Burning Rituals* (Bloomington, Ind., 1984), 31; Dunbar, *Complete Poems*, 82–83.

tions that informed the works of both white and black dialect poets.[7] The ties between Dunbar's poetry and folk tradition existed in the elements of theme and performance. Dunbar himself seems to have felt that such ties were important. Although he had been raised in a virtually white environment in his hometown of Dayton, Ohio, Dunbar as a child had been regularly exposed to elements of the tradition through his parents, both of whom had been slaves. He maintained his associations with former slaves even as his career progressed. During a period when he lived in Washington, D.C., he invited old friends in for beer so they could tell him "before the war" stories, some of which he converted into poetry.[8] Even though he himself did not speak dialect, and even though he never lived in the South for any length of time, Dunbar was not out of touch with people who knew rural southern ways intimately; and he learned from them.

What he believed he learned, above all, was a black distinctiveness manifested in an approach to life that was natural, spontaneous, and honest. In a 1901 *Saturday Evening Post* essay, "Negro Society in Washington," Dunbar decried the "commonly accepted belief" that since emancipation "the colored people of the country . . . have gone around being busy and looking serious." Instead, he asserted, "The people who had the capacity for great and genuine enjoyment before emancipation have not suddenly grown into grave and reverend philosophers," but still know how to have fun. "Indeed," he said, "as a race, we have never been a people to let the pleasures of the moment pass"; and this, he added, was true even of the most important leaders of the people. Negro society was characterized from top to bottom by an appreciation for joy and "gayety."[9] This characterization of black people was not entirely Dunbar's creation; it was instead one aspect of the tradition of "romantic racialism" going back to antislavery writings. Dunbar, however, did much to fix this view in black literary tradition and to give life to a literary form in which it could be expressed.

As Dunbar gave shape to such ideas of black distinctiveness in his poetry, several themes stood out. In addition to the naturalness praised in "When Malindy Sings," there was the joyous gayety of "The Party," an

7. Myron Simon, "Dunbar and Dialect Poetry," in Jay Martin (ed.), *A Singer in the Dawn: Reinterpretations of Paul Laurence Dunbar* (New York, 1975).

8. Edward F. Arnold, "Some Personal Reminiscences of Paul Laurence Dunbar," *Journal of Negro History*, XVII (1932), 401.

9. Paul Laurence Dunbar, "Negro Society in Washington," *Saturday Evening Post*, 1901, clipping in Dunbar Papers.

account of a plantation party at which even the preacher, "Eldah Thompson," " got so tickled dat he lak to los' his grace, / Had to tek bofe feet an' hold dem so's to keep 'em in deir place."[10] There were also the simple but honest emotions of Dunbar's love poetry in dialect. In "Lover's Lane," Dunbar evoked such emotions in the affection between two country lovers:

> Bush it ben' an' nod an' sway,
>   Down in lovah's lane,
> Try'n' to hyeah me whut I say
>   'Long de lovah's lane.
> But I whispahs low lak dis,
> An' my 'Mandy smile huh bliss—
> Mistah Bush he shek his fis',
>   Down in lovah's lane.

The popular "Little Brown Baby" described a family scene of similar simplicity and authenticity.

> Little brown baby wif spa'klin' eyes,
>   Come to yo' pappy an' set on his knee.
> What you been doin', suh—makin' san' pies?
>   Look at dat bib—you's ez du'ty ez me.
> Look at dat mouf—dat's merlasses, I bet;
>   Come hyeah, Maria, an' wipe off his han's.
> Bees gwine to ketch you an' eat you up yit,
>   Bein' so sticky an' sweet—goodness lan's![11]

The folksy, affectionate humor was wholly in keeping with Dunbar's ideas about black distinctiveness.

So, too, was one of Dunbar's few protest works in dialect, "An Ante-Bellum Sermon," first published in *Lyrics of Lowly Life*. The poem, which is supposed to be a sermon by an antebellum slave preacher, is a thinly disguised articulation of the slaves' hope for freedom, expressed in the story of Moses and the pharoah.[12] The focus of the poem—a focus with a real basis in history—is the slaves' need to keep under wraps anything other than the religion imposed upon them by the plantation owners. What slave religion was and what the masters thought it to be were two very different things. The slaves were supposed to receive

---

10. Dunbar, *Complete Poems*, 86.

11. *Ibid.*, 132, 134.

12. Much of this discussion is taken from Dickson D. Bruce, Jr., "On Dunbar's 'Jingles in a Broken Tongue': Dunbar's Dialect Poetry and the Afro-American Folk Tradition," in Martin (ed.), *A Singer in the Dawn*, 94–113.

their religious instruction from approved preachers, white or black, who preached that freedom was to be found in heaven and awaited only those who had been submissive and obedient in life. But for most slaves, as is well enough known, such religion was no religion at all; and the slaves worshiped, more hopefully, a God who could bring freedom on earth. Dunbar captured that reality in his poem.

"Ante-Bellum Sermon" is filled with prophecy. Set in a rustic church, it shows a slave preacher trying to say what the whites expect him to say, but never quite able to do so. Like any good preacher, he applies the lessons of the Bible to his congregation's own experiences, at the center of which is slavery:

> An' yo' enemies may 'sail you
> In de back an' in de front;
> But de Lawd is all aroun' you,
> Fu' to ba' de battle's brunt.
> Dey kin fo'ge yo' chains an' shackles
> F'om de mountains to de sea;
> But de Lawd will sen' some Moses
> Fu' to set his chillen free.

At this point, Dunbar's preacher knows he is on dangerous ground. In the next stanza, he warns his people to be sure they understand "Dat I'm still a-preachin' ancient, / I ain't talkin' 'bout to-day." Later, he will add the caution "Dat I'm talkin' 'bout ouah freedom / In a Bibleistic way." The counterpoint runs through the rest of the poem, to its triumphant conclusion:

> But when Moses wif his powah
> Comes an' sets us chillum free,
> We will praise de gracious Mastah
> Dat has gin us liberty;
> An' we'll shout ouah halleluyahs,
> On dat mighty reck'nin' day,
> When we'se reconised ez citiz'—
> Huh uh! Chillun, let us pray!

The Moses motif was widely known in black folklore, even to whites; but in evoking the life of the "invisible institution" of the slave church, Dunbar displayed an awareness of slave life and community that went beyond what plantation-tradition writers were willing, or able, to display.[13]

13. Dunbar, *Complete Poems*, 14–15.

One should not be too solemn, however, about this treatment of slave religion and its deliberate use of the double entendre. The poem is funny, a joke on white people played by a clever black preacher. It reveals, for all the seriousness of its ultimate message, a playfulness that fits in well with Dunbar's notions of black distinctiveness. It is a willingness to find pleasure in hard times, even to mock the hard times themselves, that characterizes the language of Dunbar's preacher, who is like the well-known tricksters of black folklore—the clever slave John or the cunning rabbit—taking pleasure in manipulating, to the extent possible, those who try to oppress him.

Still, the persevering lightheartedness and simplicity that characterize folk Negroes in Dunbar's dialect poetry illuminate the ambivalences Dunbar felt about that poetry and the ambivalences that underlay his use of the form. James Weldon Johnson's considered judgment that dialect writing is limited to humor and pathos and, hence, is unsuited to expressing either deep or ambiguous human feelings has often been noted in connection with Dunbar's poetry.[14] So far as his work is concerned, the judgment is accurate. But it was less a matter of limitations inherent in the literary use of dialect—as future generations of black writers have demonstrated—than of limitations in the conception of black identity that informed Dunbar's work. Whatever his ties with other American local color writers, and as had been the case for Matthews in "Aunt Lindy," Dunbar was not willing to go too far in his views of black distinctiveness. He kept his own ideas grounded in the mainstream of American culture, trying to square them with assimilationist ideals.

Dunbar did this, in part, as Matthews had done, by creating a concept of black distinctiveness that drew on a mixture of elements of black folk life and middle-class gentility. "Little Brown Baby" compares with "Aunt Lindy," for example, in locating sentimental affections in the hearts of the oppressed, with all the irony that implies. Indeed, Dunbar took pains to specify such irony in the last stanza of "Little Brown Baby":

> Come to you' pallet now—go to yo' rest;
>   Wisht you could allus know ease an' cleah skies;
> Wisht you could stay jes' a chile on my breas'—
>   Little brown baby wif spa'klin' eyes![15]

14. James Weldon Johnson (ed.), *The Book of American Negro Poetry* (Rev. ed.; New York, 1931), 4.

15. Dunbar, *Complete Poems*, 135.

Ease and clear skies were the lot of no black person in America, and the lines play off that fact against the tenderness of a black father's love for his child.

In addition, and in significant ways, Dunbar's appreciation for black distinctiveness was not entirely comfortable. For one thing, despite Dunbar's professed interest in folk life, the folk Negroes whose lives his dialect poems evoked were not the black people he most admired. One sees this in his 1901 *Saturday Evening Post* essay, the one in which he praised the black elite's distinctive love of pleasure. Pointing out that black society in Washington, D.C., boasted graduates of "nearly every prominent college in the country," Dunbar stressed the sophistication of the city's leading Negro citizens. He also stressed the restricted nature of the elite. Describing the major balls conducted by society, he urged, "Do not think that these are the affairs which the comic papers and cartoonists have made you familiar with; the waiters' and coach-men's balls of which you know." These were exclusive affairs: "The people who come there to dance together are people of similar educa-tion, training, and habits of thought." Invitations were hard to come by. Hence, the conclusion was clear: "In the light of all this, it is hardly to be wondered at that some of us wince a wee bit when we are all thrown into the lump as the peasant or serving class. In aims and hopes for our race, it is true, we are all at one, but it must be understood, when we come to consider the social life, that the girls who cook in your kitchens and the men who serve in your dining-rooms do not dance in our parlors." Echoing John P. Sampson's words from two decades before, Dunbar asserted that black distinctiveness was tempered by education and refinement and that assimilation was more relevant than difference in understanding the lives of the black middle class.[16]

Balancing his literary ambitions with his ambivalent view of folk life was, in fact, a hard act for Dunbar to keep going. His most important folk-based dialect poems were written during his early years as a poet. They found renewed life in elegant, illustrated brief volumes—reprint-ings of popular material—published regularly by Dodd, Mead in the early years of the twentieth century. Although Dunbar continued to produce some interesting dialect work in his later years, it was joined by material that crossed the line into plantation-tradition sentimentality and burlesque.

16. Dunbar, "Negro Society."

Dunbar was never one to eschew popularity; and when his ambition got the upper hand, he could create characters who were as loyal and docile as any created by Russell or Page and who were unredeemed by any of the cleverness that marked his best dialect figures. Moreover, despite his defensive comments to Helen Douglass, Dunbar could, and did, dip into minstrelsy. His successful *Clorindy* was filled with minstrel bits. Apparently, Dunbar even faced marital problems as a result of his wife's anger over a second theatrical venture, *Uncle Eph's Christmas.* Alice Dunbar could not stand her husband's growing reputation as the "prince of coon song writers."[17] A glance at the plot for a proposed collaboration with James Weldon Johnson and Will Marion Cook for a musical entitled "The Cannibal King" indicates just how far Dunbar could go. This musical tells the story of one Pompous Johnson, head-waiter in a Florida hotel. Johnson has sent his beautiful quadroon daughter, Parthenia, to Vassar, from which she has graduated with honors, keeping her Negro background a secret. Upon returning home, she expresses a desire to marry Jerry Jenkins, a young underwaiter. Pompous is opposed, wanting his daughter to marry at least a headwaiter.

From this premise, the plot descends to slapstick as Pompous, accidentally receiving great wealth, comes to believe that his daughter can marry nobility. The nobleman turns out to be "Eat 'Em All," the cannibal king. The king is all one would expect, full of pride and not too bright, a fitting complement to Pompous himself. He does not, of course, get to marry Parthenia, who in the end marries Jerry. There is an interesting similarity between Parthenia and the heroines of black sentimental fiction; and her presence dramatizes the views Dunbar expressed in his 1901 essay concerning the existence of a genuine black elite, as well as an attachment to sentimental norms that would never have allowed the ingenue to be made a buffoon. But otherwise, the story is filled with buffoonery. There is very little to separate "The Cannibal King" from the excesses of minstrelsy.[18]

Buffoonery did not represent the norm for Dunbar's work in dialect. But Dunbar's willingness to engage in it points to a basic flaw in the foundation of his ideas of black distinctiveness—a real ambivalence

17. Jean Wagner, *Black Poets of the United States from Paul Laurence Dunbar to Langston Hughes,* trans. Kenneth Douglas (Urbana, 1973), 78.
18. New York *Journal,* October 20, 1901, in James Weldon Johnson, Scrapbook, 1905–1910, in James Weldon Johnson Collection, Collection of American Literature, Beinecke Rare Book and Manuscript Library, Yale University.

about a distinctiveness that could be both celebrated and ridiculed, that could be both a source of creativity and an embarrassment to people of education and culture.

Dunbar's ambivalent approach to folk Negro life through dialect writing was not confined to poetry. Dunbar also produced a great deal of short fiction, the bulk of which consisted of plantation stories with folk Negro characters. These stories further indicate the ambivalence Dunbar felt about such characters.

Some of Dunbar's plantation stories were as positive about the folk past as was much of the poetry. "The Case of 'Ca'line,'" from his 1900 volume *The Strength of Gideon*, was a story well within the trickster tradition; it was about a bad cook who fools her employer—who is on the verge of firing her—into giving her a raise. "Supper by Proxy," from the 1903 *In Old Plantation Days*, was a skillful retelling of the traditional tale "Master's Gone to Philly-Me-York."[19] Like much of his dialect poetry, some of Dunbar's fiction showed a familiarity with and a respect for folk traditions that indicated a genuine appreciation of them.

Still, as critic Arlene Elder has pointed out, much of Dunbar's plantation fiction shows real "uncertainties about his people." This is because Dunbar wrote many of his stories in a way that indicated his desire to keep his distance from the folk Negroes who were his subjects; that is, he treated the characters with paternalism and a detached amusement.[20] A good example appears in the "Brother Parker" stories published in the collection *In Old Plantation Days*. Brother Parker is a peculiarly human man of God. He is jealous of his position and finds personal holiness a difficult state to maintain. In "The Walls of Jericho," he is aided by the slave owner's son and one of the young man's friends in keeping his place among the slaves. A new preacher has moved into the neighborhood, and this new man is especially attractive to Brother Parker's flock. The two young white men, seeing the situation, remind Brother Parker of his position and, at the same time, concoct a plan to sabotage the new man's growing strength. They hide in the woods; and just as the congregation is beginning to "march around the walls of Jericho" at the close of a service, they loudly blow a horn and send

19. Paul Laurence Dunbar, *The Strength of Gideon and Other Stories* (1900; rpr. Miami, 1969), 105–12; Dunbar, *In Old Plantation Days* (1903; rpr. New York, 1969), 71–82 (a version of the tale itself appears in Richard Dorson, *American Negro Folktales* [Greenwich, Conn., 1967], 151–52).

20. Arlene A. Elder, *The "Hindered Hand": Cultural Implications of Early African-American Fiction* (Westport, Conn., 1978), 119, 125.

several trees crashing down. Everyone flees, including the new minister; but Brother Parker, guessing what is afoot, stands his ground, shouting, "Stan' still, stan' still, I say, an' see de salvation." Brother Parker is not above participating in a little chicanery if it keeps his position secure, and it does. Seeing his devotion, the flock returns.[21]

Dunbar's treatment of the plantation preacher was, in some ways, similar to that found in the black folk tradition. A large body of mostly comic tales had grown up about the character of the preacher, most of which stressed his fallibility. J. Mason Brewer, tracing the stories back to slavery time, has shown that these "preacher tales" played an important role in the black community. Those that Brewer and others have collected seek to lampoon the preacher by showing him to be easily caught up in the power he possesses in his community—and willing to do almost anything to retain that power.[22] Dunbar clearly drew on the tradition of preacher tales in his characterization of Brother Parker.

At the same time, one cannot ignore the extent to which Dunbar ridiculed the religion of the rural folk; nor can one ignore the role of whites in "The Walls of Jericho"—whites who have fun at the congregation's expense and who have little real sympathy for the crisis in status that Brother Parker experiences. Dunbar's story makes clear that the two white boys see Brother Parker's dilemma as funny. They are more concerned with finding an opportunity for horseplay than with helping the troubled minister. There is no conspiracy among equals in the help they give to Brother Parker. This is quite unlike anything in the tradition of the preacher tales, and it takes the story very close to the white plantation tradition.

In stories of this sort, Dunbar could play on the most patronizing stereotypes; and he did. "Aunt Tempe's Triumph," another story in *Old Plantation Days*, portrays the character of an old "mammy," a slave who appears to run her white folks' lives and whose "rule" is treated by the whites with a kind of amused tolerance. The slave, Aunt Tempe, wants to give her master's daughter away at the young woman's wedding, because she has brought up the child. When she bursts in on the ceremony at the moment the minister asks, "Who giveth this woman," and shouts, "I does! Dat's who! I gins my baby erway!" there is more amusement than anger among the assembled guests.[23] Although one might read

21. Dunbar, *In Old Plantation Days*, 27–38.
22. J. Mason Brewer, *The Word on the Brazos: Negro Preacher Tales from the Brazos Bottoms of Texas* (Austin, 1953), 2–3.
23. Dunbar, *In Old Plantation Days*, 10.

into the story an assertion of the right of possession—Aunt Tempe had, after all, raised the bride—the story's tone is too patronizing and the white characters are too tolerant to support such a reading. There is, in Aunt Tempe, nothing of the simple dignity of an Aunt Lindy. She is instead simplistically devoted to her white family, as clearly so as any character from white plantation-tradition writing.

These stories may be taken as strong evidence of Dunbar's commercial instincts. They represent the sort of thing a white press was accustomed to buying, and Dunbar had to sell his work to live. But they go beyond the most plantation-tradition-oriented dialect poems, even as they dramatize the most hostile of Dunbar's scattered comments on folk Negro characters. The characters Dunbar wrote about in such stories were inhabitants of a kind of cultural backwash and were unrepresentative of the best that the race could offer.

This view was especially prominent in a story that evoked the cultural conflict between a tradition-bound rural folk and the middle-class urban black community. The story, "Old Abe's Conversion," tells of a country preacher who must come to terms with a son who has been educated in college and trained in a seminary. As the story opens, the son has become pastor of an urban church and is visiting his father in the country. Abe is mightily disappointed in the young man, whose return home for a visit is a disaster that reveals the gap between the urban and rural cultures. Above all, the son does not fulfill Abe's expectations of what a preacher should be. The younger man's literate urbanity has no fit with Abe's more traditional, highly emotional folk religious style. When Abe goes to the city, however, his estimation of his son is quickly raised by a glimpse of the kind of work the young man does in improving the lot of urban black people. The love of father for son is rekindled as Abe comes to see the value of his son's approach to religion.[24] The story ends happily, and Abe is treated sympathetically throughout; but the situation is a virtual dramatization of Dunbar's *Saturday Evening Post* article. Not all black people are folk Negroes, and Dunbar did not identify the best in black life with folkways and traditions.

Dunbar also showed his ambivalence toward folk Negro life by the tone of most of his plantation stories. Like American local color writers harking back to the early nineteenth century, Dunbar tended to use two voices in a story. One was that of the omniscient narrator, an outsider

24. Paul Laurence Dunbar, *The Heart of Happy Hollow* (1904; rpr. Miami, 1969), 105–21.

who was always an individual of taste and refinement observing folk society. One effect of this was to distance the author from his subjects— a structural parallel to the attitudes toward folk Negroes that Dunbar expressed in other contexts. Dunbar was writing about interesting people. This writing did not make him one of them.[25]

So one sees in Dunbar's plantation stories the same tension that marked his dialect poetry. On the one hand, he tried to distance himself from folk Negroes, a people with whom he had no wish to identify personally. On the other, he made an effort to conserve the black folk heritage, putting it to literary use while tying it to certain distinctive virtues he saw in Negro life.

In betraying such an ambivalence toward the life of rural folk, Dunbar was not, to be sure, entirely unlike other American local color writers during this period. As already noted, his tendency to speak in two voices was not unprecedented. Other writers, too, moved well beyond nostalgia to record the narrowness and despair of the communities whose lives they evoked. One need think only of Hamlin Garland's Midwest or even of Sarah Orne Jewett's New England—for all its virtues—to see that this was so.[26] But for no other writer was the ambiguity created not only by the evoked community but also by the literary work as such and by the identification of the author with that work. Dunbar's ambivalence was more than social commentary or social criticism; it was a matter of the artist's sense of himself and of his place in the larger society.

Above all, Dunbar's ambivalence was an important sign of the extent to which his ideas of black distinctiveness ran up against assimilationist ideals in his thinking. Dunbar's literary ambitions forced him to confront that conflict in ideas and ideals. He could, and did, make a career out of black distinctiveness, as a black poet who wrote about black life using a literary form that emphasized that distinctiveness. But in a sense, this meant that he let the literary form define the meaning of blackness for him; and it was a definition—with its roots in the racist plantation tradition—that made him uncomfortable.

25. In several of his stories, Dunbar actually let his dialect-speaking characters speak for themselves. In "A Family Feud," for instance, the story of a conflict between members of a slaveholding family is told in the voice of a former slave. In dialect, she tells how one of her fellow slaves entered into the conflict and resolved it. The story appears in *Folks from Dixie* (1898; rpr. Upper Saddle River, N.J., 1968), 137–56.

26. Larzer Ziff, *The American 1890s: Life and Times of a Lost Generation* (New York, 1966), 93; Jay Martin, *Harvests of Change: American Literature, 1865–1914* (Englewood Cliffs, N.J., 1967), 147.

William Edgar Easton and his son, in Los Angeles, *ca.* 1910.
Courtesy of Mrs. Athenaise Hill.

Albery A. Whitman.

Frontispiece from *Not a Man, Yet a Man* (Springfield, Ohio, 1877).

Frances Ellen Watkins Harper.

Frontispiece from *Iola Leroy, or Shadows Uplifted* (Philadelphia, 1892).

Victoria Earle Matthews.

From Monroe A. Majors, *Noted Negro Women*
(Chicago, 1893).

Paul Laurence Dunbar.
Courtesy of Moorland-Spingarn
Research Center, Howard University.

Elliott Blaine Henderson.
Frontispiece from *Darky Meditations*
(Springfield, Ohio, 1910).

Daniel Webster Davis.

Frontispiece from *Idle Moments* (Baltimore, 1895).

James D. Corrothers.

Frontispiece from *In Spite of Handicap* (New York, 1916).

William Stanley Braithwaite.
Courtesy of Moorland-Spingarn Research Center, Howard University.

Alice Dunbar.
From *Crisis,* VII (April, 1914), 307.

There is no doubt that pursuing his career the way he did cost Dunbar psychologically. Throughout his career as a poet, rumors of drunkenness haunted him; they had begun to spring up as early as 1893, even before Howells' review. And drinking was a problem for him. His marriage to Alice was always stormy, and there was even talk that he physically abused her. In any case, he was often nasty to her, even in public.[27] He spent virtually all his adult life in poor health. He was never a happy man, and his frustrations were obvious and debilitating.

But one cannot fully understand Dunbar's ambivalence about his work and his career from looking only at his dialect poetry. The real significance of his frustrations and tensions becomes clear only when one places the issues raised by his dialect poetry in the context of his other literary work, including his poetry in standard English and his fiction on subjects other than plantation life. When one does, it becomes apparent how deep his concerns about identity were and how those concerns were complicated by, above all, the racial world that was coming to exist in America in the 1890s.

Such a view of Dunbar's ambivalence receives an important illumination from his standard English poetry. Dunbar's dialect work, with its persistent lightheartedness and its evocation of simple emotions, never came fully to grips with the changing conditions to which it responded and that it portrayed. But these were not conditions with which a man of Dunbar's leanings would be eager to come to grips. Dunbar, like Albery Whitman before him, wanted to be known as a poet. He was not ready to admit openly that he was excluded in crucial ways from such recognition. His dialect poetry portrayed anxieties that he was unable to articulate directly. So did his work in standard English, but at a uniquely profound level.

Dunbar was the first pessimistic poet in the black literary tradition. His pessimism did not enter much into his dialect poetry, at least not on the surface; but it was a powerful element in his standard English poetry and set him significantly apart from other black writers of his era.

To be sure, Dunbar's poetry in standard English was mostly sentimental; and his versification in standard English remained conservative throughout his career. The story is widely told of his introduction to

27. Paul Laurence Dunbar to Frederick Douglass, December 30, 1893, in Frederick Douglass Papers, Manuscript Division, Library of Congress; and Alice Dunbar to Matilda Dunbar, June 17, 1902, in Dunbar Papers.

Walt Whitman's work by James Weldon Johnson in 1901. According to Johnson, he himself had begun to be inspired by Walt Whitman and had written a few lines under his "sudden influence." Dunbar reacted to those Whitmanesque lines of Johnson's with a "queer smile," saying, "I don't like them, and I don't see what you're driving at." When Johnson read from some of Whitman's own works, Dunbar remained unimpressed.[28] Not surprisingly, one finds little experimentation in Dunbar's own standard English poetry.

Nevertheless, his best poems were distinguished by their pessimism and by a sense of ambiguity that was equally uncommon in black writing. Both appear in his poem "Promise," published in *Lyrics of Lowly Life*:

> I grew a rose within a garden fair,
> And, tending it with more than loving care,
> I thought how, with the glory of its bloom,
> I should the darkness of my life illume;
> And, watching, ever smiled to see the lusty bud
> Drink freely in the summer sun to tinct its blood.
>
> My rose began to open, and its hue
> Was sweet to me as to it sun and dew;
> I watched it taking on its ruddy flame
> Until the day of perfect blooming came,
> Then hasted I with smiles to find it blushing red—
> Too late! Some thoughtless child had plucked my rose and fled.

In the second section, the poet again cultivates the bloom, giving it extra protection from harm. When it opens, however, "a worm was at its heart!" Such a recounting of nature's own ambiguities, in a poem reminiscent of William Blake's "The Sick Rose," was rarely found in the works of earlier black writers; but Dunbar often stressed this aspect of human life. In another poem from the same period, "If," Dunbar made this view clear with his evocation of "the human's higher right, / To suffer and to love."[29]

It is likely that as his career progressed, Dunbar's personal problems influenced his mood. His stormy marriage to Alice ultimately ended in separation, and this was reflected in several poems that appeared at about the same time. In one, "Night, Dim Night," from his 1903 collection *Lyrics of Love and Laughter*, he declared, "My love goes surging

28. Johnson, *Along This Way*, 161.
29. Dunbar, *Complete Poems*, 12–13, 76.

like a river, / Shall its tide bear naught save pain?" In another, "Parted,"
published in his 1905 *Lyrics of Sunshine and Shadow*, he spoke with
bitter humor of an unhappy marriage:

> She wrapped her soul in a lace of lies,
>   With a prime deceit to pin it;
> And I thought I was gaining a fearsome prize,
>   So I staked my soul to win it.
>
> We wed and parted on her complaint,
>   And both were a bit of barter,
> Tho' I'll confess that I'm no saint,
>   I'll swear that she's no martyr.[30]

But whatever the influence of personal problems, Dunbar departed
from traditions in black writing in ways that showed more extensive
concerns on his part. For one thing, as the literary historian Jean Wagner
has rightly pointed out, Dunbar was the first black poet to present
heterodox views on religion. To be sure, Dunbar could write poems of
great piety, such as his extremely popular early poem, "A Hymn," which
reads:

> Lead gently, Lord, and slow,
>   For oh, my steps are weak,
> And ever as I go,
>   Some soothing sentence speak.

In many of his poems, however, scepticism is stronger than piety; this
skepticism began to appear in his earliest published verse. "Behind the
Arras," also from his first major volume, is a good example. The poet
declares:

> Poor fooled and foolish soul!
>   Know now that death
> Is but a blind, false door that nowhere leads,
>   And gives no hope of exit final, free.

Such a rejection of future hopes was to be found in no other black poet
of Dunbar's time.[31]

Indeed, Dunbar took occasion to criticize, through his poetry, the
religion of genteel piety. In "Religion" he declared:

30. *Ibid.,* 227, 240.
31. Wagner, *Black Poets*, 125; Dunbar, *Complete Poems*, 98, 95.

> I am no priest of crooks nor creeds,
> For human wants and human needs
> Are more to me than prophets' deeds;
> And human tears and human cares
> Affect me more than human prayers.

He concluded the poem with a plea for a militant religion of humanity rather than one focused on a comforting love of God or a hope of a world to come:

> Take up your arms, come out with me,
> Let Heav'n alone; humanity
> Needs more and Heaven less from thee.
> With pity for mankind look 'round;
> Help them to rise—and Heaven is found.[32]

Although Dunbar was, in many ways, a sentimental poet in standard English, his writings often showed a studied rejection of the bases for sentiment found in earlier black writing.

What caused Dunbar to write such skeptical poetry—poetry that, in fact, attacked the genteel traditions of black writing up to his time? Among his later poems, some of his skepticism can be traced to his unhappy marriage and his ongoing physical problems. But many of his most important and most skeptical verses antedate both those problems by some years.

One may argue that Dunbar's iconoclasm in his standard English writing—an iconoclasm within the framework of the black literary tradition—can be related to the deteriorating race relations of the late nineteenth century. Gentility in black writing had been an expression of optimism about the integration of blacks into American society. The production of genteel literature had been a proof that integration was possible and natural. But when Dunbar began his literary career, much of the basis for any integrationist optimism had started to wane, as Dunbar himself understood.

Although there is an image of Dunbar as a man little concerned with American racial politics, he was never entirely silent about racial issues; and the direction of his thinking was fairly clear. As a teenager, Dunbar edited a newspaper for blacks—the Dayton (Ohio) *Tattler*—and his editorializing there, from about 1890, indicates not only his awareness of racial problems but also his sharing in the assimilationist optimism of

32. Dunbar, *Complete Poems*, 38.

the age.[33] Subsequent years, however, showed real changes in Dunbar's perceptions of America's racial prospects. In the period just before the turn of the century, Dunbar's language became militant and defiant. In an 1899 essay written for the Chicago *Record*, for instance, Dunbar took issue with Booker T. Washington's programs, urging, in particular, unceasing demands for the right to vote: "Let these suffering people relinquish one single right that has been given them, and the rapacity of the other race, encouraged by yielding, will ravage from them every privilege that they possess. Passion and prejudice are not sated by concession, but grow by what they feed on." And, he warned, the growing "manliness" of the race would not allow its being denied.[34] Dunbar had, by this time, come to see race relations as based, in essence, on cutthroat competition—a view that would have made assimilationist optimism hard to maintain, despite the apparent optimism of the speech's defiant conclusion.

As time went on, Dunbar would find even his defiance hard to sustain. In a 1903 Fourth of July address, reprinted in the New York *Times*, Dunbar roundly condemned southern peonage, lynching, and disfranchisement. But he went further than this to stress what he felt should be the ambivalence of any responsible black American in a time of national self-celebration. "Not even the Jews and the Chinamen have been able to outdo us in the display of loyalty," Dunbar declared. "And we have done it all because we have not stopped to think just how little it means to us." Here was not celebration of black American patriotism such as earlier writers had frequently offered. Dunbar encouraged a radical shift in the attitude of black people toward their country. And his concluding lines offered one reason for this change; in them he thoroughly rejected the optimism of the past: "Aye, there be some who on this festal day kneel in their private closets and with hands upraised and bleeding hearts cry out to God, if there still lives a God, 'How long, O God, How long?'" Drawing on the language of the spirituals, Dunbar took a point of view that earlier writers would have found indefensible. Although there was no accommodationism of Washington's sort in his words, there was a view that segregation was to be a fact of life for some time to come.[35]

Dunbar's rejection of the trappings of gentility in such early works as "Religion" and "Promise" foreshadowed his later gloominess on racial

33. Peter Revell, *Paul Laurence Dunbar* (Boston, 1979), 48.
34. Paul Laurence Dunbar, "Negro and White Man," [1899], clipping in Dunbar Papers.
35. New York *Times*, July 10, 1903.

questions. At the time he was producing these early skeptical poems, however, he was writing hopefully and conventionally on racial matters. Indeed, he was producing poetry on racial themes that was indistinguishable from the works of other black poets in its assimilationist optimism. In his popular "Ode to Ethiopia," for instance, Dunbar wrote: "On every hand in this fair land, / Proud Ethiope's swarthy children stand / Beside their fairer neighbor."[36] Expressing hope for the future still appealed to the young Dunbar.

Nonetheless, Dunbar's conventional optimism was framed by events that showed a worsening oppression of blacks, events of which he was aware. There was reason for skepticism about the future, and Dunbar's ambivalence about gentility was one way of expressing that skepticism in a manner less threatening, less troubling than a treatment of racial issues as such would have been. Rather than confronting racial difficulties directly, Dunbar gave expression to repressed fears by questioning the genteel verities traditionally tied by black writers to hopes for imminent integration. Thus much of Dunbar's early poetry, though not directly related to racial matters, represented an uncontroversial but nevertheless significant emergence of what the critic Raymond Williams called a "structure of feelings"[37] in response to the undermining of an old optimism with a vague but well-founded fear for the future of black people in America.

Dunbar's awareness of the full import of this structure of feelings began to surface near the turn of the century, as he became increasingly outspoken on racial matters and increasingly bitter in his views. One sees this especially well in the poetry he wrote on specifically racial themes. If his earliest works were optimistic, his later racial poems showed a very different point of view. "The Unsung Heroes," from his 1903 collection, told the familiar story of the accomplishments of black soldiers who fought for emancipation and the Union during the Civil War. But rather than simply celebrating their heroism, Dunbar chose to use the poem as an occasion to lament their lack of recognition by the nation at large. "To the South, on Its New Slavery," from the same volume, was an early indictment of the convict lease system. It took the form of a review of black history from slavery to freedom; but rather than chronicling the birth of a new race, phoenixlike, from bondage into prosperity, it placed that familiar transformation in a different light.

36. Dunbar, *Complete Poems*, 15.
37. Raymond Williams, *Marxism and Literature* (Oxford, 1977), 132.

Dunbar asked: "Did sanctioned slavery bow its conquered head / That this unsanctioned crime might rise instead?" Indeed, the entire rhetoric of the poem was built on turning the conventional view of black history upside down:

> There was a time when even slavery's chain
> Held in some joys to alternate with pain,
> Some little light to give the night relief,
> Some little smiles to take the place of grief.

Here was not a plantation-tradition claim that blacks were better off under slavery. Rather, it was a conscious reversal of convention, as shown in a stanza that might have been addressed directly to other black poets:

> Till then, no more, no more the gladsome song,
> Strike only deeper chords, the notes of wrong;
> Till then, the sight, the tear, the oath, the moan,
> Till thou, oh, South, and thine, come to thine own.

Such lines marked a powerful change in mood from the hopeful works of the previous generation of poets.[38]

The same may be said of another poem from this collection, "The Haunted Oak," a graphic piece on lynching. Using personification, Dunbar gave voice to a permanently dead tree limb, the limb from which an innocent man accused of "the old, old crime" was hanged. Dunbar evoked the suffering of the victim and the treachery and brutality of a mob that could laugh as it went about its work. There is a kind of justice portrayed in the poem. The lynchers, it says, must be troubled by their guilt. But it is an angry and, in a sense, hopeless justice, involving not vindication and triumph of the oppressed but only the uneasiness of the oppressors.[39] The Dunbar who, after about 1900, observed and wrote poetry on racial conditions was not an optimistic poet; and the pessimism was foreshadowed by his earlier departure from gentility.

It may also have been foreshadowed by Dunbar's early turn to dialect and his sustained career in and ambivalence toward it. Regardless what his motives were initially, however, his pursuit of dialect poetry may have represented a recognition on his part that, whatever his desire, he was to be foremost a *black* poet and—with the weakening of grounds for optimism about an assimilationist future—would have to base his

---

38. Dunbar, *Complete Poems*, 196–98, 217–18.
39. *Ibid.,* 219–20.

career on that fact. Again, his growing awareness of the direction of American racial life was clear in his remarks on racial questions. His early literary focus on dialect, like the early departure from gentility, may have been a way of expressing that loss of optimism without having to confront its implications directly in the early days of his career.

In any case, Dunbar provides an instructive contrast with Booker T. Washington in his response to a constantly advancing white racism. However much both men evoked a racial identity, Dunbar's was not an evocation that tended toward even strategic withdrawal from the larger society. Rather, Dunbar's work points to what could be—and was for him—a weakness in the emotional underpinnings of Washington's strategy. Dunbar knew that the strategy of withdrawal was based on rejection, not choice, as was any call for racial solidarity in those days. Pushed in that direction by circumstances, Dunbar could never react toward an identity based on race with anything other than the deepest misgivings.

One reason Dunbar could be so strongly torn by questions of identity and race relations was that he saw a spiritual side to them that practical people such as Washington were unable to appreciate. For Dunbar, all issues of identity and social relations were intimately tied to questions of human freedom and authenticity. He saw freedom as something that, even under the best of circumstances, was hard to find. The peculiarities of American race relations only made the task more difficult. And he went beyond Albery Whitman in his understanding that freedom involved not simply an ability to choose one's place in the social order but, more, a finding of a self that was not constrained by the artificial demands of any social order.

As in his poetry, Dunbar revealed the depth of his concern profoundly in his novels and stories on nonracial themes; the structure of feelings that would evolve into a naturalistic perspective first emerged in a less controversial and troubling form than the confrontation of race. The concern appeared in his first novel, *The Uncalled* (1898), published the same year as his first collection of plantation stories, *Folks from Dixie*. The tale of a young midwesterner's search for independence, *The Uncalled* was not nearly as popular as the short story collection, leading one reviewer to urge Dunbar to "write about Negroes." But it was an important book in Dunbar's career, not only because it was his first novel but because, as most critics now accept, it served as a kind of testimonial for Dunbar himself, expressing his own ambitions and frustrations as a writer.[40]

The central theme of *The Uncalled* has been identified by critics as a protest against the kinds of constraints that inhibit self-expression and self-realization. It is the story of a young man, Freddie Brent, who, having been born of a woman of questionable character, is adopted by a strict, pious woman named Hester Prime; she conceives her main duty as a guardian to lie in crushing the young boy's spirit. Targeting him for the ministry, Miss Prime pushes him toward an adulthood against which his every instinct rebels. And, indeed, though he does become a minister, he is unable to fill the role, especially in the rigid, hypocritical environment of his hometown. Only when he leaves its structured setting—moving to Cincinnati and associating with the liberal religion of Congregationalism—does he seem able to give his own meaning to his life.

The parallels between Freddie Brent's life and Dunbar's are not hard to find. Like Hester Prime, Dunbar's mother had wanted her son to enter the ministry, an act that would have been very much against his will—as his own skepticism makes clear. Moreover, as Addison Gayle has argued, Dunbar was also an artist beset by restrictions, not the least of which were caused by his reputation as a dialect poet.[41] In looking for a real freedom, for an ability to escape roles others had laid out for him, Brent spoke for Dunbar's own frustrations. Too much in society limited the search for self, for identity; and Dunbar was inhibited in his own ambitions by both literary stereotypes and American racism.

In *The Uncalled* he dramatized these concerns and his own frustrations through Freddie's search for a freedom unconstrained by strict traditions and social conventions. As Dunbar declared in a passage near the center of the book: "Poor, blind, conceited humanity! Interpreters of God, indeed! We reduce the Deity to vulgar fractions. We place our own little ambitions and inclinations before a shrine, and label them 'divine messages.' . . . We make God the eternal a puppet. We measure infinity with a foot-rule."[42] The passage is important. Not only does it

40. Kenny Jackson Williams, "The Masking of the Novelist," in Martin (ed.), *A Singer in the Dawn*, 174; Addison Gayle, Jr., "Literature as Catharsis: The Novels of Paul Laurence Dunbar," in Martin (ed.), *A Singer in the Dawn*, 70.

41. Addison Gayle, Jr., *Oak and Ivy: A Biography of Paul Laurence Dunbar* (Garden City, N.Y., 1971), 90–99.

42. Paul Laurence Dunbar, *The Uncalled* (1898; rpr. Upper Saddle River, N.J., 1970), 123.

express Dunbar's own chafing against the restrictions of society, but it also ties *The Uncalled* in with the skepticism and even the pessimism of "Religion" and "Promise"—those two early iconoclastic poems—by condemning the tendency of people to confuse their own ideas with eternal truths. It helps establish links between *The Uncalled* and the corpus of Dunbar's work.

These links are important, and they have not often been noted by critics. They show *The Uncalled* to be a novel that, however important its autobiographical character, also fits in with and helps portray Dunbar's larger vision of self and society. This vision is not founded on the acceptance of traditional verities but, rather, openly questions even the value of holding to the forms of virtue and propriety put forth by the larger society. In an early passage of the novel, celebrating Freddie's rebelliousness, Dunbar wrote: "In life it is sometimes God and sometimes the devil that comes to the aid of oppressed humanity. From the means, it is often hard to tell whose handiwork are the results."[43] These words powerfully question the received truths of evangelical piety and go to the heart of Dunbar's notions of freedom and authenticity: finding one's truths for oneself.

They also help emphasize the great break Dunbar made with much of earlier black writing. In openly rejecting evangelical piety, as he did in *The Uncalled*, Dunbar sought a depth and detachment that earlier writers had avoided. Here was no simple acceptance of American middle-class culture; here was no protest firmly embedded in that culture. Here was, instead, an effort to question the power of culture as such and a recognition that prejudices of any sort were products of cultural settings. Such a fierce independence was introduced into black writing by Dunbar, subtly in his poems but openly and bitterly in *The Uncalled*. The novel represents an important document in the literary history of black America.

The issues raised by *The Uncalled* clearly went beyond questions of race. The concern for authenticity tied Dunbar to white naturalist writers. It was not far removed from the quest for authentic experience that T. Jackson Lears has found in the lives of many prominent American intellectuals at the turn of the century.[44] Nor was it unconnected from the picture of rural narrowness that at least a few American regionalists

43. *Ibid.,* 70.
44. T. Jackson Lears, *No Place of Grace: Antimodernism and the Transformation of American Culture, 1880–1920* (New York, 1981).

drew. But if the issues went beyond questions of race, they were also heightened and intensified by those questions. *The Uncalled* is important because it reveals the general frame of reference from which Dunbar confronted his career and his society. But that frame itself heightened Dunbar's awareness of the cruelty of racism and helps explain both his ambivalence about racial identity and his pessimism about the future.

The applicability of themes from *The Uncalled* to racial concerns is not difficult to see. The novel exposed not only the role of tradition—prejudice—in limiting individual freedom and authenticity but also the ways in which prejudices were deeply embedded in culture and society. As Dunbar treated them in *The Uncalled*, they were peculiarly uncontemplated—and strongly held—parts of people's lives. Hence they were not so easily attacked as past generations had believed. Such a view of prejudice is compatible with Dunbar's own evolving views of race relations and underlines much that characterized his poetry and fiction.

Dunbar dramatized the foundations for his views of race relations in several of his more somber works with racial themes. These views clearly informed, for instance, two short stories on lynching—"The Tragedy at Three Forks," printed in *The Strength of Gideon*, and "The Lynching of Jube Benson," printed in the later *Heart of Happy Hollow*. Both stories are about the lynching of innocent men, a motif Dunbar treated poetically in "The Haunted Oak."[45] In both, the account of the lynching is related through white eyes. In "Tragedy," Dunbar focused on the young white girl who had committed the crime for which innocent Negroes were lynched. In "Jube Benson," he told the story in the words of a remorseful judge who had participated in the mob and who vowed never to attend another such event after learning of the victim's innocence. The culprit in this case had been a white man who had blackened his face.

Dunbar considered such stories, along with "The Haunted Oak," to be important statements for racial justice and to make their point in a way peculiar to literature. He was at one time criticized for using the device of mob violence against the innocent, since, it was argued, lynching had to be protested whether the victim were innocent or guilty. Dunbar replied that such criticism was valid morally but that he felt the victim's innocence was important dramatically: "Our feeling at a crime

45. Dunbar, *Strength of Gideon*, 267–83; Dunbar, *Heart of Happy Hollow*, 223–40.

committed against a criminal is never as deep as that at an injustice done
to an innocent man."[46] The artist's function was to reach the feelings of
his readers and from there to work on the readers' ideas and beliefs. But
these feelings were bound up, Dunbar also understood, in the frighten-
ing racial culture of American society.

Trudier Harris has pointed the way to appreciating how Dunbar used
his feelings about the dangers of a closed society in her perceptive
analysis of "The Lynching of Jube Benson." Both Benson and his
lynchers were victims of custom, she has noted. Dunbar stressed his
white narrator's guilt over the lynching, as he did in "The Haunted Oak."
But once the lynching is under way, Dunbar showed, the roles of
lyncher and victim are "predetermined." The violent ritual is well established, and it precludes any analysis of what one is doing once it has
begun. As members of a cruel social order, all are tragically trapped.[47]
Harris' analysis is apt and, in its emphasis on determinism, coheres fully
with the central concern in Dunbar's fiction—as well as with the
sources of his frustration as a writer. It also helps account for much of
Dunbar's pessimism about race relations. Individual white people could
be educated to the humanity of individual blacks, perhaps; but Dunbar
recognized that the matter went beyond individual conscience to the
level of deep-seated traditional notions and values. These notions and
values were powerfully resistant to change, because they were, for the
most part, unanalyzed elements in traditions followed without thought.
Where these traditions were especially strong—and white racism was
gaining strength—even the very limited kind of heroism Dunbar had
celebrated in the case of Freddie Brent reached its boundaries. Here,
too, was where Dunbar's optimism reached its limits.

This understanding of racial matters was conveyed both subtly and
profoundly in another of Dunbar's novels, *The Fanatics* (1901). Set in
the Civil War, this novel, like "The Lynching of Jube Benson," features
white protagonists. Specifically, it portrays the tensions in a border state
community brought on by what was, from the white point of view, a
conflict of brother against brother. The only black featured character,
"Nigger Ed," serves to provide comic relief for most of the book. Little
separates Ed from plantation tradition stereotypes. He begins the book
as a good-natured, dependent clown; and he remains that way until the
end. He does earn the gratitude of the town's whites at the end—

46. Paul Laurence Dunbar to Brand Whitlock, December 26, 1900, in Dunbar Papers.
47. Harris, *Exorcising Blackness*, 85–86.

because of his loyalty to one of the town's young white men during the war. But he remains a child, happy to have been given "a place for life and everything he wanted, and from being despised he was much petted and spoiled." And yet, Dunbar added a phrase to the description, a phrase that prevents one from seeing Ed as simply one more plantation-tradition character. The black man was petted and spoiled, Dunbar added, "for they were all fanatics." The phrase indicates that, throughout the novel, Dunbar really was writing about the forces that made Ed so clownish. "Nigger Ed" provides a touchstone that helps reveal the character of American race relations.[48]

The Fanatics is set in the Ohio village of Dorbury and focuses on two families, that of Stephen Van Doren and that of Bradford Waters. Van Doren is a Democrat with southern roots, and Waters is a staunch Republican. For years they have entertained the village with their political disagreements. Their two children, Bob Van Doren and Mary Waters, are, like Romeo and Juliet, in love. With the onset of the Civil War, however, political disputes are no longer entertaining; and the two old friendly enemies no longer look with tolerance on their differences. The coming of the war means the end of cordial relations, and the two fathers separate the young lovers.

None of this happens quickly. The town is plagued by mob violence, and many young men must make the hard choice between loyalty to home and friends in Dorbury and loyalty to roots, North or South. And, of course, friends and families alike are divided as choices are made. Tom Waters, Mary's brother, chooses to fight for the North; Bob Van Doren, after much soul-searching, chooses the South. "Nigger Ed," for his part, goes with the Union troops as servant to a militia captain.

The effect on the townsfolk of these divisions is striking. Waters and Van Doren become bitter enemies. Here is one form of fanaticism, and Dunbar condemned it. "Both affectionate fathers," he wrote, "similarly bereft of sons and similarly alone, they might have been a comfort to each other, but that their passions forbade their fraternizing."[49] The war has done to them, one may suggest, what religion did to Hester Prime. For Waters, the northerner, the force of fanaticism is especially strong; Mary's continuing love for Bob Van Doren causes him to drive her from her home.

48. Paul Laurence Dunbar, *The Fanatics* (1901; rpr. Miami, 1969), 312; Robert A. Bone, *The Negro Novel in America* (Rev. ed.; New Haven, 1965), 41. My own interpretation does not, however, fully agree with Bone's.

49. Dunbar, *Fanatics*, 101.

More generally, the townspeople become increasingly fanatical in their hatred of southerners and blacks—both of whom they consider to be responsible for the war. In a lengthy section of the book, Dunbar shows both the evils of northern racism and the problems of racial unity. Dorbury is "invaded" by a group of black refugees from the fighting in the South. The refugees have come North to find their people; but one local demagogue, Stothard, forms a mob to drive them out. Van Doren, the paternalistic southerner, does what he can to aid the refugees; but Stothard ultimately engages the blacks—both locals and refugees—in a violent confrontation that results in the ousting of all black people from the community.

The episode is related with bitterness. Black writers had long expressed an awareness of the irony of northern racism during the Civil War. Alfred Stidum had made much of it in his poem "1620 to 1863," for example. Dunbar enhanced that irony by making a white southern character stand for decency in the face of a racist mob. Dorbury's native black population is, initially, as resentful of the black "invasion" as is the white mob. Things are peaceful, they argue, but an influx of southern rural Negroes is likely to change the situation. As in so many of Dunbar's works, it takes something traumatic to shake complacency. When the refugees are threatened, the blacks in Dorbury—native and outsider alike—understand that they must stand together.

At the same time, in a telling episode, Dunbar commented on the motivations of the blacks. Only one white man, Stothard, loses his life in the confrontation; and he is killed by one of the refugees, a "wild-eyed boy." But, wrote Dunbar, the boy did his deed, "not because he was fighting for a principle, but because the white man had made his mother cry the day before." Dunbar remarked, "His ideas were still primitive." There are two ways to interpret this passage. The more common is to see it as another example of Dunbar's misgivings about the black masses.[50] But the other, which puts the boy's action more fully in the frame of the novel, is to read the passage ironically. Whatever the boy's action is, it is not the product of fanaticism. Rather, it is based on a decent human sympathy, familial affection. In this, it contrasts sharply with the actions of Bradford Waters in casting out his daughter because of her love for Bob Van Doren. It contrasts, too, with the actions of another family appearing in the novel, the Stewarts. They have southern

---

50. See, for example, Richard Alan Yarborough, "The Depiction of Blacks in the Early American Novel" (Ph.D. dissertation, Stanford University, 1980), 341.

roots and disown their son because of his loyalty to Ohio, growing out of a loyalty to his friends. Here, too, the irony is clear; and in this case, it connects Dunbar's novel to traditional modes of black writing.

The war runs its course, touching the lives of everyone in Dorbury. Tom Waters dies in battle; "Nigger Ed" accompanies the body home. Bob Van Doren is wounded and loses an arm; his wound comes not in battle, however, but in an effort to protect Mary from danger. The old enemies are reconciled, and Bradford Waters even rescues young Van Doren from an antisouthern mob that has learned of his return to Dorbury. Ed resumes his place as a town favorite, petted and spoiled by those who, during the war, had run every other black person out of Dorbury.

And here, finally, was Dunbar's point, a point he had also made in *The Uncalled*. Ed, treated as a buffoon, was no more seen as a man after the war than he had been on its eve. Even his participation in the war had not brought him real freedom, had not allowed him to become a man— certainly not as Dunbar had defined these qualities at the conclusion of *The Uncalled*, as a recognition of the human right to grow, to love, and to be happy. Ed remained a clown for the same reason Dorbury had been torn apart by the Civil War, because everyone in Dorbury re- mained, in Dunbar's sense, a fanatic—so greatly attached to one per- spective on the world as to be unable to move beyond it to some greater reality.

This element of protest was, as Robert Bone has said, oblique, be- cause—as Bone and other critics have noted—Dunbar did not do as effective a job as he might have in drawing Ed's character.[51] But from another perspective, that may have been just the point. Ed remained a clown because neither he nor the whites could transcend what Dunbar showed fanaticism to be, both here and in *The Uncalled*—letting ideas take the place of reality and failing to appreciate the frail foundations of the ideas themselves. Here, for Dunbar, was the strongest barrier to achieving real humanity; and Ed's persistent clownishness proved that he had succumbed to fanaticism as much as he was its victim (a problem not unknown to Dunbar himself). An indictment of racism, the novel was also a delineation of racism's psychological threat, of the danger it posed to achieving human as well as social fulfillment. In it, Dunbar applied the basic perspective of *The Uncalled* directly to the issue of race. But this later novel shows a far less hopeful writer.

51. Bone, *Negro Novel*, 41.

And, indeed, Dunbar's concerns about human fulfillment and the difficulties of achieving freedom in society came to a head in his final novel, *The Sport of the Gods*. Like *The Fanatics*, it offered an oblique protest against a culture that made unnatural demands on black Americans. The novel has sometimes been read as a Washingtonian paean to the superiority of rural life—a pessimistic warning against the dangers of urbanization for blacks;[52] but such a reading ignores major elements of the novel's plot and structure and major thrusts of Dunbar's other fiction. The novel is pessimistic, but its pessimism runs deeper than the level of public policy.

Rather, the pessimism of Dunbar's final novel grows out of Dunbar's pervasive concerns about the problem of human freedom and self-realization. *The Sport of the Gods* has long been recognized as Dunbar's most important novel. Critics have seen it as making Dunbar a pioneer American naturalist—a brother to such writers as Stephen Crane, Theodore Dreiser, and Frank Norris—and the first black writer to adopt such a perspective in his fiction. Like other naturalists, Dunbar, in *The Sport of the Gods*, tries to show what critic Arlene Elder has termed "the helplessness of all individuals in the face of fate."[53] Here, indeed, is one source of pessimism in Dunbar's novel; and it connects this novel closely with other naturalistic works. But *fate* can be a vague word, or at least one with many meanings; and Dunbar here, as elsewhere, had a fairly clear notion of the forces that victimized human beings. For Dunbar, fate was far from impersonal. Rather, it grew out of the kind of indifference—an indifference born of ignorance—that marked too much of human relationships. It grew out of the human failure to take seriously the significance and reality of others. Indeed, it may be less important to stress the novel's naturalism than to stress its mode of voicing Dunbar's concerns about the nature of society.

The Sport of the Gods is the story of a southern black family, the Hamiltons; it traces their decay and dissolution in the face of the forces they must confront. The ending of the story is one of futility and resignation, born of the Hamiltons' inability to give any shape of their own to the world in which they live.

The story begins in the southern home of Berry Hamilton and his family. Berry has served as butler and his wife, Fanny, as cook in the

52. *Ibid.,* 42; Charles R. Larson, "The Novels of Paul Laurence Dunbar," *Phylon*, XXIX (1968), 266.

53. Elder, *"Hindered Hand,"* 141.

household of Maurice Oakley since before emancipation. When freedom came, the Hamiltons stayed on as trusted servants. The Hamiltons have also raised two children of their own, Joe and Kit, neither of whom is as well adjusted to southern rural ways as their parents, but each of whom contributes to the family. Life is not all peaceful for the Hamiltons. Berry has done well financially, so there is plenty of backbiting and jealousy within the black community over his success. But the Hamiltons lead a comfortable life.

Their comfort is not to last. At a dinner in the Oakley home, Maurice's brother, Francis, discovers that some of his money is missing; blame immediately falls on Berry, despite his years of service to the family. Berry is arrested, convicted, and imprisoned. Fanny and the two young people are driven from their home and, despite their past prominence in the black community, find themselves friendless.

Here, as in *The Fanatics*, Dunbar treated racism as a product of the inability of whites to see beyond stereotypes, a problem Dunbar had dealt with all his life. Maurice's quickness in wanting Berry imprisoned for the theft of Francis' money shows that although Berry had lived and worked with the white man all his life, the relationship had never been other than master to servant, and black servant at that. Berry was no "Nigger Ed," but he might as well have been, for all Maurice knew of him. Here, again, was the tragic human inability to escape from the familiar, the tragic human unwillingness to look for truth and reality.

Something similar may be said of the Hamiltons' treatment by the black community. This time, however, it was not racism but jealousy and the sort of petty moralism Dunbar condemned in his early poem "Religion" as well as in *The Uncalled* that helped demean the Hamiltons. If there was no sympathy for them, the novel declared, it was because, imprisoned by their own ideas and beliefs, the people with whom the Hamiltons dealt were cut off from humanity. In the Hamiltons' situation, Dunbar conveyed a sense of the evil built into the social order that cohered fully with much that he had portrayed of life and society in his earlier work.

Where Dunbar went further in *The Sport of the Gods* was in his portrayal of the inability of the victims to resist the inexorable processes of dehumanization. There was something of such a portrayal in the figure of "Nigger Ed," and one might even see a precursor to this point of view in Dunbar's lynching stories; but nowhere did Dunbar as fully develop this pessimistic assessment of human prospects, particularly black American prospects, than in *The Sport of the Gods*. He did this by transferring the action of the novel to New York City, to a world more fluid and less clearly defined than that of the rural South.

In order to escape the problems caused by Berry's imprisonment, the Hamiltons move to New York and, finding lodgings with a Mrs. Jones, quickly learn what the city has to offer. Joe, in particular, succumbs to the lure of urban life, seeking almost immediately to cast off the moral "baggage" of a rural upbringing. He takes up with the young men of the city and is soon introduced to all the low-life experiences an urban world has to offer. The center of this action is the "Banner Club," where Joe is eagerly welcomed by a set of young men who have learned to sponge off any naïve, rural immigrant. At the club, Joe also meets the strongest character in the novel, Hattie Sterling, an entertainer. She becomes a major figure in the rest of the story.

At first, Hattie seems as much of a sponger as any of the other New Yorkers Joe will meet; but she also comes to the Hamiltons' aid. When the story of Berry's crime catches up to the family—leading to their eviction from their New York home—Hattie stands up for Joe, convincingly humiliating the woman who has spread the news. When the family is in the direst financial straits, Hattie learns that Kit has real talent as a singer and helps her find a job on the stage—much to the chagrin of the pious Mrs. Hamilton. But Hattie's relationship with the family culminates in a tragedy greater than Mrs. Hamilton's displeasure. Disappointed in Joe and his failure to work, Hattie leaves him. Joe, in a drunken rage, kills her. He is sentenced to the penitentiary, to the great despair of his mother. Mrs. Hamilton suffers further as Kit becomes a success on the stage and adopts the theatrical life. To her, both the children are as good as lost.

It was in this New York setting that Dunbar created a naturalistic world, one in which human hopes and plans come to nothing. The Hamiltons' efforts to find a refuge from the "shame" of Berry's imprisonment were unsuccessful, and Hattie's efforts to help the family resulted in her death and Kit's corruption. As Elder has stressed, Kit's corruption was all the more significant because Kit began the novel with notably high ideals, resembling the usual heroines of black genteel fiction.[54] And here may be the core of Dunbar's pessimism in the novel and of the novel's naturalism—the element that sets it apart from, say, *The Fanatics*. Dunbar often wrote of people blinded by their prejudices and of the victims of those prejudices. But here was the only novel in which he

54. *Ibid.,* 146.

portrayed his victims struggling unsuccessfully with the world that prejudices create.

This portrait of futility continues to the end of the novel. Through a series of spectacular coincidences, Berry's innocence is established; and he is released from jail. Immediately, he goes to New York. But when he rejoins Fanny, he learns how degraded his children have become; and his hopelessness becomes profound. The two older people decide to return to the South—indeed, they return to work for the Oakleys. But as Dunbar made clear, they were returning to no southern idyll: "It was not a happy life, but it was all that was left to them, and they took it up without complaint, for they knew they were powerless against some Will infinitely stronger than their own."[55] The city had been degrading, and Dunbar spoke often and powerfully of the naïve rural southerner's lack of preparation for the complexity of urban life. But there was nothing desirable or easy about the rural South either. Will, not sociology, was Dunbar's concern in his conclusion to *The Sport of the Gods*; and the tone of his conclusion was overwhelmingly fatalistic.

What are we to make of the fatalism with which *The Sport of the Gods* concludes? Houston Baker, in his cogent reading of the novel, has sought to give this fatalism what he terms a "mythic" reading. He calls attention to the derivation of the title from Shakespeare's *King Lear*; and describing Dunbar's characters as mere toys "in the ludic world of the gods," he argues that the novel reveals Dunbar's view that, given the nature of human thought, everyone is "his own Lear." There is much to recommend Baker's reading; but in an effort to give what he calls a "non-historical" as well as a mythic reading of the novel, Baker may have missed some of the significance of the fatalism—both in regard to Dunbar's own career and in regard to the novel's place in the larger tradition of black American writing.[56]

Up to the writing of *The Sport of the Gods*, there was a sense in which Dunbar was a pessimistic but not a fatalistic writer. The contrast with *The Fanatics* is instructive. In both these works, Dunbar condemned what Baker has termed the "fallibility of human habits of thought," treating the ends his characters suffer as the "logical outcome of their misguided modes of apprehending the world."[57] But Dunbar's stance toward those characters in the earlier work was decidedly moralistic.

55. Paul Laurence Dunbar, *The Sport of the Gods* (1902; rpr. Miami, 1969), 255.
56. Houston A. Baker, Jr., *Blues, Ideology, and Afro-American Literature: A Vernacular Theory* (Chicago, 1984), 123, 124, 136.
57. *Ibid.,* 125, 129.

The very word he used to describe them, *fanatics*, indicated that their moral failure was what interested him.

Such moralism is absent from *The Sport of the Gods*, because in this novel, human beings are presented as misguided by nature, despite their best efforts. Human fallibility is presented as the essence of human existence, unavoidable and unavoidably tragic. That is to say, when the novel is read in the context of Dunbar's other work, its fatalism becomes all the more impressive, all the more distinctive. It is the culmination of a progression from the hope Dunbar placed, in *The Uncalled*, in the possibilities of individual rebellion against the tyranny of the mind—a hope in individual freedom—to a sense, in his final novel, that the prison house of mind and culture permits no escape.

And here it is tempting to read history and biography into Dunbar's message. The progress of Dunbar's novels mirrors the progress of his career, from that of a hopeful young poet to that of a writer trapped by society's labels. It also mirrors the changing conditions of his time (in much the way I argued in regard to his poetry), but more deeply and more thoroughly. The decay of hope that can be traced from *The Uncalled* through *The Sport of the Gods* calls attention to what must have been Dunbar's perception of the deteriorating racial situation of turn-of-the-century America. From Dunbar's point of view, one tragic consequence of that situation must have been the loss of even the smallest openings through which black Americans could realize their dreams and goals. Dunbar had always recognized the restraining power of the forms of society—the way in which society could stand as a barrier to self-realization. And he had seen the way in which society made that self-realization infinitely harder for black Americans. But by the time he wrote *The Sport of the Gods*, he had come to see those forms as impossible to resist. It is difficult to believe, given Dunbar's awareness of American racial life, that whatever other dimensions his last novel might have—mythic, naturalistic, universal—it was not also very much a work of history: a sensitive man's inner history of the triumph of racism in American society.

Thus *The Sport of the Gods* fits well into the broader frame provided by Dunbar's other fiction and by his more general ideas. But it also shows the final toll the poet's frustrations took on his outlook. Just as Dunbar rejected the evangelical piety and gentility of earlier black writing, so too did he move away from its optimism. Unable to find a popular literary voice that suited him, and witness to the worsening conditions of late nineteenth century race relations, Dunbar was unable to identify a satisfying strategy for either personal or racial advancement. Whereas earlier writers had expressed at least implicit faith that their own gentility would win them a place in American society, Dunbar seemed convinced that even the strongest efforts of blacks to present their American character would have little influence on white America. Dunbar himself had, after all, done about as much as any black man in this regard but had fallen short of his ambitions. At the simplest level, he sought to be a poet; but in the popular mind, he remained little more than a minstrel, despite his own protestations.

At the same time, a thorough skeptic, he had also departed from black writers' prevailing acceptance of American culture. Indeed, even as early as *The Uncalled*, he proclaimed his recognition of the limits imposed by being part of any culture. In that novel, he decried the restrictions of traditional rural society. He continued to do so, even though, by the time he wrote *The Sport of the Gods*, he seemed to have despaired of ever achieving any real independence and authenticity.

Here was the real paradox of Dunbar's writing. Known as a poet of joy and simplicity and as one of the first poets to make a conscious effort to explore the black rural folk heritage, he was also the first black writer to create a literature of pessimism and despair. These themes appeared in his poetry and his short stories, and they dominated his novels. In this creation, he made an important break from the middle-class black literary tradition that had preceded him; and he became a powerful influence on the black writers who began to emerge when his name was, for many people, synonymous with black literature in America.

III

Black Literature in Transition in the Age of Dunbar, 1896–1906

Paul Laurence Dunbar's impact on black literature during his lifetime was strong. The strength may be measured by the extent to which, despite other, scattered precedents for dialect writing, black writers moved rapidly into dialect work, and especially into dialect poetry, only after his early literary success. After the mid-1890s, virtually every black poet—with a few notable exceptions—did some dialect work. Few volumes of poetry by black poets from this period lacked examples of dialect work. Dialect also appeared with increasing frequency in fiction. Most of the dialect literature focused on similar themes and, significantly, displayed characteristics similar to those of Dunbar's work.

At the same time, Dunbar's impact was problematic, because of his severe psychological ambivalence about dialect writing. Few black writers shared Dunbar's unhappiness about dialect literature. The best evidence indicates that black authors and audiences liked dialect literature. Thus the key thrusts of that work, so far as black literary tradition was concerned, must be understood not in terms of the kinds of psychological ambiguities that dominated Dunbar's approach to dialect literature but rather in terms of the emergence of dialect as the basis for a popular literary form. Dunbar may have defined that literary form for black writers as a result of his own success with dialect. He did not define the attitudes other writers would have toward the form.

Dunbar's influence during this period, measured in the rise of dialect writing, is not the only factor to be taken into account in efforts to appreciate the characteristics and tendencies of black writing. Even black writers working outside the dialect tradition showed a changing awareness of their roles and needs in the years around the turn of the century. Although they remained fairly conservative in their approach to literature, both stylistically and thematically, they also began to look in directions that were quite different from those reflected in the works of their predecessors. If these directions did not indicate a new sense of purpose, they certainly indicated a reexamination of literary ideas and ideals and, particularly, a rethinking of the meaning and significance of gentility as a foundation for black literary work.

Finally, the sociology of black literature changed at about the turn of the century. In particular, the late nineteenth and early twentieth centuries saw the development of new publication outlets for black writers. Not only did some writers follow Dunbar and Charles Chesnutt into the major general-circulation magazines of this period, including *Century* and *Atlantic*, but they also found some possibilities for publication through major book publishers. No less significantly, however, this era also saw the birth of two important black-edited magazines, *Colored American Magazine* (1900–1909) and *Voice of the Negro* (1904–1907); both were imaginatively run, and both provided outlets for a broader range of writing than could appear in, for example, the older *A.M.E. Church Review*. The two new magazines, along with a few other, shorter-lived publications, encouraged black writing of all sorts.

The pursuits of the two major black periodicals of this era were themselves symptomatic of major racial concerns in turn-of-the-century America. Both were deeply involved in the ongoing debate over the propriety of Booker T. Washington's policies and leadership; in fact, *Colored American* was directly controlled by Washington after about 1904. This general-circulation magazine was devoted to encouraging Negro writers and to promoting racial progress. It was founded in Boston by three Virginians: Walter Wallace, a former medical student; Jesse Watkins; and Harper S. Fortune, who was a musician as well as a journalist. Among those involved in the venture from fairly early on were Pauline Hopkins, who became literary editor in 1903 and who was one of the more important black literary figures around the turn of the century; and William Stanley Braithwaite, a cultured New Englander and genteel poet who was to be a major figure on the black literary stage until the time of the Harlem Renaissance.[1]

The fortunes of the magazine were never easy. Funds were chronically short, and the venture almost went under several times. It was this situation that made the magazine vulnerable to the 1904 take-

1. Penelope L. Bullock, *The Afro-American Periodical Press, 1838–1909* (Baton Rouge, 1981), 106–108; R. S. Elliott, "The Story of Our Magazine," *Colored American Magazine*, III (1901), 43–77.

over by Washington, who sought to use it as a forum for combating the views of his opponents. Indeed, under the editorship of Fred R. Moore, this was precisely what it became. As such, *Colored American* lost much of its literary importance. Fiction and poetry appeared a great deal less frequently after about 1904. The magazine also lost the services of Pauline Hopkins, who, at the time of the takeover, was fired because of pressure from Washington's white supporters, who were offended by her outspoken opposition to his accommodationist ideas.[2]

Voice of the Negro was started in Atlanta under white auspices but with two black men, J. W. E. Bowen and J. Max Barbour, as editors. Bowen was a professor at Gammon Theological Seminary; Barber, a native South Carolinian, was a recent graduate of Virginia Union University. Barber was a vociferous opponent of Washington's ideas, and *Voice* became a major forum for writers opposed to Washington. Pauline Hopkins, after leaving *Colored American*, did some writing for *Voice*. Braithwaite, W. E. B. Du Bois, and other distinguished young black writers found *Voice* to be a major outlet for their works, and they were eagerly encouraged by Barber. Following the Atlanta riots of 1906, however, Barber and the magazine were forced out of the city; and despite an effort to reestablish *Voice* in Chicago, the magazine ceased publication in 1907. Barber moved to Philadelphia and took up a career as a dentist.[3]

These magazines and such others as *Alexander's Magazine* and *Howard's American Magazine* provided an important and relatively independent means for black writers to come before the public. Even the writers who published in mainstream magazines—including Dunbar, Chesnutt, and James D. Corrothers—appeared also in the independent black publications. The circulation of these periodicals was never large. Despite *Colored American*'s claim, for instance, of reaching "one hundred thousand readers," its circulation was never more than about eighteen thousand, a figure that also held for *Voice*. The circulation of other magazines was considerably smaller.[4] But their role as outlets for

2. See August Meier, "Booker T. Washington and the Negro Press: With Special Reference to the *Colored American Magazine*," *Journal of Negro History*, XXXVIII (1953), 67–90; Abby Arthur Johnson and Ronald M. Johnson, "Away from Accommodation: Radical Editors and Protest Journalism," *Journal of Negro History*, LXII (1977), 327–28.

3. Bullock, *Afro-American Periodical Press*, 118–25.

4. Elliott, "Story of Our Magazine," 43; Bullock, *Afro-American Periodical Press*, 236, 275.

black creative writing was large. Especially for the amateur writers who continued to dominate black literary activity, these magazines were the main outlets for publication and thus the chief arbiters of taste in black literary life.

These magazines also emphasized the acceptability of dialect literature for black writers, confirming both the strength and the problematic character of Dunbar's influence. There is no indication that they accepted such writing with any less eagerness than did their mainstream counterparts. For a time, *Colored American* even had a regular column devoted to dialect material—which did not preclude its printing such work elsewhere in the magazine. Taken together with the significant place of dialect work in volumes by black poets, and even in longer forms of fiction, the appearance of such work in these magazines stresses the extent to which dialect itself stood as the major distinguishing feature of black literature during the period around the turn of the century.

The dialect work produced by Dunbar's contemporaries and followers varied greatly in quality and character. Few other writers were as skilled as Dunbar with the form, although James Edwin Campbell and James D. Corrothers come close. Stylistically, even the renditions of dialect varied greatly, from thickly written efforts by Campbell to versions that involved little more than evocative misspellings of a few words: "d" for "th" in certain words, "fo'" for "for," and "yo'" for "your." With most of the writers, as with Dunbar, the dialect probably came more from literature than from folk speech.

Thematically, most of the dialect literature other writers produced at this time built on and was compatible with Dunbar's own, displaying the same effort to synthesize elements of gentility with those of black distinctiveness in the creation of an image of black folk life. It did this chiefly by presenting folk Negroes as a simple people who had the sort of love of pleasure Dunbar had discussed in his *Saturday Evening Post* essay on Negro society.

The simplicity was evoked in several ways. One was by presenting folk Negroes as the homely repositors of a simple wisdom and an uncomplicated approach to the problems of the world. This was especially apparent in the substantial body of what might be called "advice" poetry, in which the voice of the folk was used to offer encouragement and solace in the face of adversity. W. Felix Waters, in a poem published in the Methodist *Southwestern Christian Advocate*, gave fairly typical advice of this sort:

> Oh, sometimes yo' heart is werry.
>   Keep a-prayin' anyhow,
> An' de way seems mighty drerry,
>   But to Fate jes' make a bow;
> When we's true like Paul an' Titus,
> Dah is many fo'kes will slight us,
> An dah's some who's gwinter fight us—
> Nothin' in de worl' kin hite us;
>   Keep a-prayin' anyhow.[5]

By evoking a simple but strong faith, Waters tried to bring together the piety that had long characterized black poetry with the emerging form provided by dialect work.

The same may be said of the substantial body of dialect writing that focused on human emotions. As was true for Dunbar, most such writing dealt with emotions that were familiar and easily understood. James Edwin Campbell, in some ways the earthiest of dialect poets, evoked the love of mother for child in his "Negro Lullaby":

> Mammy's baby, go ter sleep,
>   Hush-er-by, hush-er-by, my honey;
> Cross de hyarf de cricket creep,
>   Hush-er-by, hush-er-by my honey.
> Hoot owl callin' f'um de ol' sycamo'
>   'Way down yon'er in de holler;
> While de whip-po'-will an' de li'l screech owl
>   Dey des try dey bes' to foller.[6]

The affection of mother for child, associated with the beauties of nature, calls to mind the Victorian ideals of life that earlier black writers had celebrated in a more genteel fashion, here presented in a way that stresses the natural, simple virtue of the folk. The evocation of a rural simplicity was closely tied to the genteel, conservative "antimodernism" found in Dunbar's work as well.

But if there was much in the larger black dialect tradition that did little more than echo Dunbar, stylistically and thematically, there were

---

5. W. Felix Waters, "Thoughts of My Childhood," *Southwestern Christian Advocate*, XXXIV (April 6, 1899), 5.

6. James Edwin Campbell, *Echoes from the Cabin and Elsewhere* (Chicago, 1895), 33.

also elements in this larger tradition that moved away from genteel ideals, more pointedly and more self-consciously than Dunbar had ever done. One sees a good example of this in a poem by Junius Mordecai Allen, entitled "Eureka." Narrated in dialect by a man who has read of a medicine intended "ter make er cullud man git white," and for only a dollar, the poem makes a mockery of commonplace understandings of race. According to the narrator:

> It straightens out yer hair,
> En yer gits pale en paler
> 'Tell yer skin is lily fair;
> Fum a darkey, yer er Injun,
> Den er Chinaman, en den
> Yer stan's up Mr. White Man
> Wid de other white men.

The results would be spectacular; the speaker foresees joining a white church and wearing "white-folks clo'es" and even plans for a career in politics.[7]

To be sure, much of the satire in Allen's poem is aimed at white society, focusing on the arbitrary character of white racial ideas. The point had been made many times, but Allen used the apparent simplicity of his dialect-speaking narrator to make fun of the ways of white people. Not only did the poem raise the black man by "grades"—a slap at social Darwinist ideas of cultural evolution—but like some modern Dance of the Dead, it brought white pretensions low by refusing to take seriously white claims to racial superiority. The narrator's apparent simplicity serves, in part, to subvert white oppression.

At the same time, however, there is a less-than-veiled burlesque of blacks who, like the genteel authors of earlier times, sought to place their hopes for racial salvation in aspirations to gentility. Despite its humor, the poem is among the most thoroughly pessimistic about the prospects of assimilation of any I have seen. Like Dunbar, Allen revealed a sense of the intractability of racism; the need to turn to magical potions is a sign of desperation. But most telling of all is Allen's consistent use of a strict classification scheme—a white church, "white-folks" clothes, white politics. Although there was certainly a foundation for such a scheme in black folk culture,[8] and Allen may have been attempt-

7. Junius Mordecai Allen, *Rhymes, Tales and Rhymed Tales* (Topeka, 1906), 61–62.

8. On separatist elements in Afro-American folk ideas, see Sterling Stuckey, *Slave Culture: Nationalist Theory and the Foundations of Black America* (New York, 1987), especially Chapter 1.

ing to evoke that culture in his poem, it was a perspective quite different from that of other writers, who resisted the categorization of the American mainstream as, somehow, white. Thus, in this poem, assimilation *has* become a matter of duplicating white ways, not of expressing one's own fully American character. Allen's narrator makes an implicit claim that, in a segregated society, such an assimilation is not a promising undertaking.

"Eureka" is only one poem, of course; but it provides in microcosm—and in a somewhat radical form—an approach to thinking about black life in America that may be extended to dialect writing generally, especially given the place that that writing came to occupy in black literature. Although Allen's poem went farther than most black writing in its rejection of and pessimism about the possibilities of assimilation, it revealed the extent to which the popularity of dialect literature, taken as a whole, signaled a new look at assimilationist ideals and aspirations by middle-class black writers. That they should have produced dialect literature at all could have been the result of many motives, including commercial ones. That they should have liked it, however, indicates a growing disenchantment with gentility as a way of life and a strategy for racial progress. It was not a radical move; theirs was not a thorough disenchantment. The close ties between dialect literature and elements of gentility indicate the limits on their departure from older norms. But culturally the vogue for dialect writing turns Dunbar's psychology upside down, pointing to a growing ambivalence on the part of middle-class black people about the attractions—and possibilities—of entering mainstream America.

Indeed, in the minds of at least some writers, dialect work represented more than an edging away from an assimilationist, genteel faith. Picking up on elements visible in Victoria Earle Matthews' "Aunt Lindy," some writers sought to make dialect writing represent an approach to the obverse of assimilationism—that is, the recognition of a genuine black distinctiveness that could give substance to a black racial identity.

Dunbar himself sensed this connection between dialect writing and racial identity, with great discomfort. Allen implied it, with desperate humor. For others, however, this aspect of dialect writing was strong and wholly positive. In a turn-of-the-century discussion of black literature at Hampton Institute, the prominent southern educator Lucy Laney urged black writers to draw on the traditions and dialects of the folk Negroes of the South, much as Scottish writers had done for the folk of Scotland. When she concluded her remarks by saying, "Too many of us are Anglo-Saxon Africans," she made clear the connection between dialect and interest in a distinctive black identity.[9]

This appreciation for black distinctiveness was, as a limited departure from older norms, one of the first significant ways in which black writers sought to adapt and redefine what remained a middle-class outlook on the world. As such, it was part and parcel of the historical processes that made assimilationist hopes more and more difficult to maintain.

As the black middle class found itself increasingly excluded from the American mainstream and increasingly dependent on the black community, its members had to find meaning in black life and, hence, in being black. Tying dialect to distinctiveness was an expression of that need. The fact that middle-class writers and readers enjoyed dialect literature is a measure of their ability to make positive an identity that was easily seen, and that earlier generations had seen, as largely negative. Had they been unable to do this, dialect writing would never have attained the popularity it did. But black writers were able to make dialect writing a more positive form. They did so by creating their own approaches to it, approaches that defused its negative connotations and served the ambiguous needs forced on black people by the changing conditions of the 1890s.

The crux of what black writers did with dialect was summarized in an essay by the educator-scholar Anna Julia Cooper in her 1892 book *A Voice from the South*. Discussing the need for a literature that would capture what was distinctive in the black American experience, Cooper wrote: "There is an old proverb, 'The devil is always painted *black*—by white painters.' And what is needed, perhaps, to reverse the picture of the lordly man slaying the lion, is for the lion to turn painter."[10] Although Cooper herself was no great fan of dialect, as critic Mary Helen Washington has stressed, Cooper's comment aptly summarized what other writers did with the form. Whatever the sources of black dialect

9. This comment appears as part of William S. Scarborough, "The Negro as Portrayer and Portrayed," *Southern Workman*, XXVIII (1899), 362. On this, see August Meier, *Negro Thought in America, 1880–1915: Racial Ideologies in the Age of Booker T. Washington* (Ann Arbor, 1963), 266. Interesting evidence of the connection between dialect writing and identity appears in the publication of dialect work, by an American writer, in the pioneering pan-African publication, *African Times and Orient Review,* published in London. See Charles D. Clem, "Fetch Dat Slippah Heah," *African Times and Orient Review*, I (1912), 92.

10. [Anna Julia Cooper], *A Voice from the South by a Black Woman of the South* (1892; rpr. New York, 1969), 225.

writing, the most crucial aspect of this literature was that, in the hands of black writers, it became a black literature. When black writers wrote in dialect, they took the form out of the hands of whites and made it their own. In doing so, they radically shifted the context of dialect writing and changed its entire thrust. The negative connotations of dialect literature were undermined, because it was harder to view it as a weapon of racism in the hands of black writers. Indeed, one can even see a touch of irony here, as a literary device used to deny creativity and intelligence in blacks was now used creatively by black people themselves. Some of the pleasure this writing gave to black readers may have come from an appreciation of that irony. Irony itself was not, after all, unknown in black literature.

Still, black writers also found ways to use dialect that fulfilled Anna Cooper's injunction for a black literature. For one thing, they formulated dialect works in ways that departed from plantation-tradition excesses, reclaiming its subjects as human beings rather than simple caricatures.

The effort to rescue folk Negroes from caricature appears in both the satirical poems and the sentimental verses of the dialect poets. One sees it, for example, in the extent to which other dialect writers matched Dunbar in turning to folk materials for their works, giving an accurate foundation to their literary presentations of folk life. The folk perspective conveyed in Allen's "Eureka" has already been noted. But many poets turned to specific elements in folklore and folk culture. For instance, several used hoodoo as a basis for their works. Charles Roundtree Shoeman wrote a long poem, "Lucindy and de Hoo Doo," based on what he described as an actual superstition—namely, that "if a live frog be placed in a perforated box, and taken to an ant-hill, that when the ants have eaten the frog to a pile of bones, a hooked bone and a scale will be found among them. It is thought by hooking the hook into a woman's dress, it will cause her to love the person doing so, even against her will. But should the frog croak while dying, it is believed that it will make the conjuror deaf." Frog bones were recognized as lucky in southern black folk belief, and it is likely that the belief Shoeman based his poem on existed among rural southerners. The poem itself is a narrative of an effort to use such a trick on "Lucindy." Unfortunately, the conjuring lover is killed by a train, and Lucindy is set free from his spell.[11]

11. Charles Henry Shoeman, *A Dream and Other Poems* (2d ed.; Ann Arbor, 1899–1900), 164–71; see Newbell Niles Puckett, *The Magic and Folk Reliefs of the Southern Negro* (1926; rpr. New York, 1969), 315.

Other dialect writers drew on folktales. In a story entitled "Why the Black Man Is Called a Coon," Eugene Berry wrote of a slave named Billy, who is offered his freedom if he can tell what is underneath a box. Billy has no idea and says: "Well, Massy, you have got the old coon at last. I cain't tell ye what's under de box." Berry concludes: "So since that time the negro has been called a coon. The box contained an opossum." Berry's story is a rather poor retelling of a traditional folktale that plays on calling blacks "coons," a tale generally known as "Coon in a Box." In the folktale, the stumped slave mutters, "Master, you got this old coon at last," and wins his reward. The box conceals a raccoon.[12]

A source of a rather different sort was one of the more popular black religious creations of the period, John Jasper's famous sermon, "De Sun Do Move." Jasper was a notable Baptist preacher in Richmond, Virginia, minister of the largest black Baptist church. This sermon, which he estimated having preached at least 275 times, inevitably drew a large audience—including whites—and captured the kind of folk simplicity so popular in dialect literature. Jasper, who had been a slave preacher, used a commonsense religion to deny the scientific view that the earth revolved around the sun. Rather, he declared, it was the sun that moved. He proved it by referring to the story of Joshua, who was to avenge himself against his enemies in battle before the sun went down. "Joshua asked God to stop the sun. What do you suppose that God was going to tell Joshua to tell the sun to stop when it was not moving. God had some sense if Joshua did not." Besides, Jasper concluded, "Could the sun go down if it was not moving?"[13]

Because it encapsulated a key perspective in dialect literature, the sermon was an attractive source for black writers who used the form. Powell W. Gibson used its main theme in a 1904 poem to evoke the simplicity of folk thought:

> Jes tell me how de Sun gwine rise
> Ef de Sun doan move.
> 'Splain me dat you folks what's wise:
> I know de Sun do move.[14]

---

12. Eugene Berry, *Fact and Fun: A Book of Thrilling Stories, Etc.* (N.p., [1907]), 16–17; Arthur Huff Fauset, "Negro Folktales from the South (Alabama, Mississippi, Louisiana)," *Journal of American Folklore*, XL (1927), 264–65.

13. Account in Richmond *Planet*, December 21, 1895.

14. Powell Willard Gibson, *Grave and Comic Rhymes* (Alexandria, Va., 1904).

James Weldon Johnson, in collaboration with his brother, John Rosamond, used the same theme for one of their dialect songs, "De Bo'd of Education":

> Dey tell us dat de earth aint flat
> And dat de sun dont move.
> Now dat's an easy thing to say,
> But mighty hard to prove.
> For Joshway told de sun to stop,
> And it dont need no provin',
> Dat he would not ha' spoke to de sun that away
> If the sun had not been movin'.[15]

If much in dialect writing seems patronizing, much also had strong foundations in black culture and traditions. In building on such foundations, black writers made a visible effort to create a dialect literature that was different from much of the white plantation tradition and that was tied to real aspects of black life.

They also advanced beyond white writing in turning dialect writing in the direction of protest. This was particularly the case in the works of Elliott Blaine Henderson. Not well known, Henderson was typical of black poets in that most of his work was self-published, done up for him by job printers in his native Columbus, Ohio. Nevertheless, Henderson had a long career as a poet. He published five volumes of poetry between 1904 and 1915, mostly dialect works, with such titles as *Darkey Ditties*, *Darky Meditations*, and *Uneddikayted Fo'ks*.

Much of Henderson's poetry was derivative stylistically and thematically (his "Good Bye, Honey—Good Bye" was a virtual paraphrase of Dunbar's famous "Negro Love Song"); but he introduced protest subtly and often deceptively. The protest is especially deceptive given Henderson's frequent use of such words as *coon*, *darkey*, and *niggah*, which were prominent in minstrelsy but found in the writing of few other black poets. His "Seems Dey's No Place" is typical:

> Well er coon kin go to kollege
> Git his head chucked full o' knowledge,
> Till he knows ez much ez Solomon de wise.
> He kin study an' summize,
> Count de stars up in de skies,

15. [John Rosamond Johnson], "De Bo'd of Education," words by James Weldon Johnson, music by John Rosamond Johnson (New York, 1906).

> Seems dey's no place
> Fo' de eddeekayted coon.

The rest of the poem deals with the problem posed in the last two lines of the stanza. Indeed, the poem becomes almost a dialect summary of Solomon Brown's "He Is a Negro Still," decrying a society that cannot appreciate the abilities of educated black men and women. Another poem, "What We Gwine to Do?," is an equally plaintive protest against injustice. Noting that "dis kentry's gittin' wussah / Fo' de po' and he'pless coon," Henderson wrote:

> Dey lynch him on de lef'
>   An' dey lynch him on de right,
> Dey cum an' git er niggah
>   In de day an' in de night.
>
> Whut we gwine to do?
>   Hain't dey no whah in de lan'?
> Hain't dey fo' de niggah
>   Not er kin' an' he'pin' han'?[16]

The open despair expressed in these poems sets Henderson apart from most other dialect poets—Allen, in "Eureka", for example, had masked desperation with humor—but the poems also show dialect poetry as something very different from plantation-tradition white writing. To be sure, Henderson, like others, wrote poems dominated by humor and affection; but he also understood despair and incorporated it into his writing.

Protest was, of course, not part of the white plantation tradition, and this in itself represented a way in which at least some black writers rescued the dialect-speaking folk from white caricature. These writers knew that the folk were neither blind nor fools. In adding an element of protest, they presented a much fuller picture of their subjects as human beings.

At the same time, however, black writers also neutralized the negative connotations of dialect literature by presenting it in such a way as to make clear how different they were from folk Negroes. This may have been a literature celebrating black distinctiveness, but it was not a signal of a radical departure from assimilationist ideals. As noted earlier, few went as far as Allen did in "Eureka," treating those ideals and the American mainstream as exclusively "white." Thus writers still made some

16. Elliott Blaine Henderson, *Plantation Echoes: A Collection of Original Negro Dialect Poems* (Columbus, Ohio, 1904), 10–11, 14–16.

effort to keep their distance from their subjects. One way they did this was by not devoting themselves exclusively to dialect work. Dialect poems, for example, usually appeared in volumes that contained other kinds of poems on a range of subjects, sentimental and racial. Poets who published mainly in magazines usually engaged in both dialect and standard English writing. More striking, dialect poems, in particular, usually appeared hand-in-hand with verse that dealt with black heroism or that bitterly excoriated American prejudice.

Thus, for example, Katherine Davis Tillman—an activist with the National Association of Colored Women as well as a writer—produced a volume containing a poem entitled "Sen' Me Back to de Souf," which portrayed an old man's homesickness for his home in the rural South. The poem was filled with memories of southern scenes and descriptions of the simple pleasures of rural life. The same volume also included "Clotelle—A Tale of Florida," a narrative poem describing the attempted seduction of a slave girl by her master and concluding with her subsequent suicide. The book contained, as well, a poem entitled "Our Cause," in which black Americans were encouraged to "fight hard, fight e'er for every right / That's granted by our Charter's might!"[17] Charles Shoeman, author of "Lucindy an' de Hoo Doo," also included neoabolitionist and antilynching poems in his collection.[18]

Examples could be multiplied, but the point is clear. Black poets between about 1895 and 1906 saw no reason to view dialect writing as excluding other kinds of sentiments, among them those founded in racial protest. Something similar could be said about the publication of dialect work in black magazines, since no publication was devoted exclusively to such writing.

The mixture was important because it indicates the extent to which black writers were using notions of black distinctiveness in order to adapt to changing conditions, not in order to create a radical alternative to their older ideals and aspirations. Even as black poets evoked the lives of rural folk through dialect, they also manifested in their other work their awareness of and ability to live up to Victorian middle-class ideals. Thus they organized their work in a way that proved they could preserve their heritage and appreciate the distinctiveness it revealed but that also showed they could transcend that heritage and make their way in the cultural mainstream.

17. Katherine D. Tillman, *Recitations* (Philadelphia, n.d.), 8, 10–13.
18. Shoeman, *A Dream*, 31–40, 41.

The mixture is important also in helping to emphasize the complexity of the position these writers occupied toward the subjects of their dialect work. That they could accurately portray much of folk life, including folk perspectives, indicates that they were far from unfamiliar with the main features of black folk culture—whether, like Dunbar, they consciously sought it out or, as was certainly the case for some, because it was a familiarity born of experience. As we saw in the case of Allen, the portrayal could be quite subtle. Henry Louis Gates, Jr., has called attention to the importance of "signifying" in Afro-American expressive forms,[19] and it is possible to see examples of signifying—of saying one thing to mean something very different—in dialect poetry. Three examples are Allen's "Eureka," in its subtle ridicule of white—and elite black—society; Henderson's protest in the framework of "darkey ditties"; and Dunbar's earlier "Antebellum Sermon." This is not to say that the purposes of these poets were somehow tied to folk purposes and defined by folk-derived aims. It is to say that when these writers worked with folk forms, they could adopt a folk rhetoric, a rhetoric that they understood well. But as their efforts at distance make clear, they were not about to undermine their continuing assimilationist aims.

From this point of view, it may be possible to see in dialect literature an example of what has often been called a third-generation phenomenon in American ethnic groups, though modified for black Americans by the experience of slavery. For writers of the early post-Reconstruction period, life in the rural South was closely bound up with the plantation and slavery—and with memories too close and painful to be easily incorporated into a popular, light literary form. Writers of the 1890s were further removed from at least some of the realities of plantation life and were thus able to deal with that life less painfully. Structurally and thematically, they still had to tame those memories; but dialect writing, given its characteristics, probably succeeded in part because it provided a satisfactory way of linking a past that black writers had come to need with the present.

A few of the scattered remarks by black commentators on the form help support this view of dialect literature. George A. Neale, in an essay on black literature, emphasized the extent to which dialect writing looked to the past when he wrote that "the plantation life was distinctively an American method of existence" and that dialect writing was a

19. Henry Louis Gates, Jr., "The Blackness of Blackness: A Critique of the Sign and the Signifying Monkey," in Gates (ed.), *Black Literature and Literary Theory* (New York, 1984), 285–321.

method for its literary preservation. He added: "The people who made the plantation, who made the South different from the North, are still among us. But they are fast assimilating the conglomerate civilization of the country. Another half century will see the negro character entirely eliminated."[20] An introduction by John H. Smythe to a popular book of dialect poetry took a similar view:

> The crudities of speech portrayed in these poems, in some—will provoke laughter, in some contempt, and not infrequently offend the sensitivities of some; and yet they serve to remind us of the misfortunes of our ancestry, and the cruelties of an alien people. But the progress made and being made by us in learning—convinces us that this patois is not natural to the American blacks, but simply marks the transition of African illiteracy to an alien tongue. A hundred years hence when illiteracy among Negroes of America shall be less pronounced than it is among the masses of whites—now, this patois will prove interesting and amusing to our posterity—whose command of English and European languages will not be inferior to that of the American scholarly class of to-day.[21]

Smythe, a Richmond political leader and former diplomat, could approve of dialect poetry because the people it portrayed were different from the emerging Negroes of the turn of the century. Part of the pleasure came from the quaintness of the form. But black writers could feel confident that the work would appear "quaint" only if it were effectively tamed, thematically and structurally.

This stance toward the black distinctiveness evoked by dialect work set black writers apart from others working in a similar vein at the turn of the century. Black writers were not the only ones to explore questions of identity in America during this period. Just as problems of race and racism were having an effect on black Americans, other changes in American society and in the American economy were raising questions of identity for different groups of Americans. Regionalist and local color writers have already been noted in this regard; in addition, there were important literary movements involving immigrants, women, and those who sought to capture the lives of farmers and workers. To a surprising extent, as Werner Sollors and other scholars have argued, writers from all these groups raised similar issues, focusing on the ambivalences of being both American and "other" and on the need to bring together

20. George A. Neale, "A New Negro Poet," *Howard's American Magazine*, VIII (1901), 335.

21. John H. Smythe, "Introduction" to Daniel Webster Davis, *Idle Moments: Containing Emancipation and Other Poems* (Baltimore, 1895), 6.

those two attributes. The ideal, in the work of ethnic writers especially, was that of a fusion, in which the elements of an "Old World" otherness would be combined with those of American life, as one constructs an identity by holding onto the traditions of the past while embracing the virtues of the larger American society.[22]

It might be possible to see in this light the early approach to identity advanced by dialect writing, as black writers laid claim to a heritage that was rich and distinctive. But the presentation of that poetry and the stated attitudes toward it make such a reading hard to sustain. If there was anything these writers would not let go of, it was gentility; the virtue of the tradition that dialect represented lay in the apparent fact that it was on the way out. There was no effort, at this point, to create a fusion of cultures. The effort was, instead, to confront the past and to find a way to celebrate it while proclaiming one's own emancipation from it. As David Fine has noted of turn-of-the-century Jewish immigrant writers, there was in their works a strong emphasis on "reconciliation," on the return of the overly Americanized individual to a place in the ethnic world.[23] Such an emphasis was lacking in the works of the early black dialect writers. Transcendence, not reconciliation, was the focus of their works. Whatever the strength of emerging concerns about identity, those concerns still confronted aspirations formed in strongly assimilationist terms.

In addition, and from this point of view, it is possible to understand an important rhetorical role that dialect writing was assigned by at least some turn-of-the-century writers. Black writing was always conceived of as a weapon against prejudice, and dialect work was no exception. When an admirer of Dunbar wrote, "The Afro-American people would justify their freedom and presence as a part of this nation if they did no more than call attention to Dunbar when their defamers begin a derogation of them, and base calumniators roll their sour tongues," this point was clearly made.[24] But as Dunbar's admirer implied, the rhetorical purposes of black writing meant that this work, like that within the genteel tradition, was still addressed to an implicit white audience as well as to a black one. After all, a body of literary evidence against

22. Werner Sollors, *Beyond Ethnicity: Consent and Descent in American Culture* (New York, 1986), 71.

23. David M. Fine, *The City, the Immigrant and American Fiction, 1880–1920* (Metuchen, N.J., 1977), 106.

24. "Paul Laurence Dunbar," *Colored American Magazine*, X (1906), 162.

prejudice would have been meaningless in that regard if it were not addressed to those whose minds needed changing.

Dialect writing had the potential to draw whites in to a rendering of black life that accorded more fully with the assimilationist aspirations most of these writers continued to portray in their works. It could do this by evoking relatively familiar black folk-types and, from there, moving the white readers to a deeper understanding of a black people previously unfamiliar to most Americans—a people whose lives embodied Victorian ideals and principles. It could use stereotypes of difference to bring home the more desired message of similarity.

It is hard to say for certain that this was a conscious strategy on the part of every writer. Dunbar used an argument along these lines in trying to justify his own dialect work to himself and others. It was written in part, he said, to gain a hearing. Other writers may have had similar notions, even if they did not share Dunbar's misgivings about dialect work itself. In any case, such a strategy was implicit, at least, in the structure of virtually every work embodying the dialect tradition.

It was also a strategy that allowed black writers to move directly from dialect to a form of protest that was clearly directed toward a white audience. One can see this strategy, for example, in the inclusion of dialect and protest works in the same setting. One can also see it in a few individual works from this period. It was especially notable in a long poem by Franklin Henry Bryant, "In Days Gon' By," published in his 1903 book *Black Smiles*. The poem was set after slavery and took the form of an old man's reminiscences of plantation days, of youth, of friends, and even of his old master. On the surface, the poem actually appears well within the plantation tradition, so great is the fondness it expresses for bygone days. Even "ole massa" comes in for a tribute. Having spoken of his "lub" for ole massa, "dough he use to put me froo," the narrator describes the white man's kindnesses—his refusal to whip a woman, his refusal to put the dogs on a runaway. Still, the narrator recognizes that slavery was filled with evil. At one point he recalls the story of "Sindy May," who sought to escape "wid her pooty little baby." The narrator had himself tried to help Sindy May, but she was caught. The hounds killed her baby, and the beautiful Sindy herself was fatally injured. Although the narrator remarks that "ole missus" was heartbroken by Sindy May's suffering, the evil of slavery was plain.[25] This

25. Franklin Henry Bryant, *Black Smiles: or, the Sunny Side of Sable Life* (Nashville, 1903), 27–37.

poem appeared to be close to the plantation tradition in showing the devotion of slave to master, but the closeness was deceptive. The devotion was certainly something more than the blind loyalty writers such as Thomas Nelson Page and Joel Chandler Harris liked to celebrate. Bryant's narrator had no illusions about slavery's cruelty. And the graphic account of the deaths of Sindy May and her baby powerfully overshadows the professions of love and loyalty that take up much of the poem.

In this, Bryant, like other dialect writers, also replicated folk tradition. During the 1930s, in an effort to preserve a past about to be lost, a concerted effort was made to interview surviving former slaves about their experiences under the institution. Reading those narratives, one is often struck by the way in which protest was veiled as former slaves described their lives. Professing not to have suffered so much themselves, individuals peppered their accounts with tales of cruelty and atrocities on other plantations. Displacing aggression, they could still deliver harsh indictments of slavery through the recounted sufferings of others. In a world in which direct confrontation of the larger society could be dangerous—as it was in 1903 and as it remained in the 1930s—displacing aggression was necessary. But so was finding a way of making people listen to the story of racism's cruelty, in slavery or in freedom. Moving from comfortable stereotypes, for a white audience, to subtle protest was a way of doing this; and dialect literature provided a form that was especially suited to the task.

The strategy of couching protest in a language that white readers would find comfortable does much to explain the literary career of one of the most controversial dialect poets of this period, Daniel Webster Davis. Davis has long been vilified by literary historians. Sterling Brown has referred to him as a black Thomas Nelson Page, and Jean Wagner has written that he had little on his mind beyond flattering white people. Davis was not so harshly treated in his own time. His work was widely published in black periodicals around the turn of the century. Indeed, he was even invited to contribute to the anti-Washington *Voice of the Negro*, which he did. And when the racial activist John E. Bruce planned his "Anthology of Negro Poetry," he included only two dialect pieces, both by Davis.[26]

26. Sterling A. Brown, *Negro Poetry and Drama* (1937; rpr. New York, 1978), 37; Jean Wagner, *Black Poets of the United States from Paul Laurence Dunbar to Langston Hughes*, trans. Kenneth Douglas (Urbana, 1973), 141; J. W. E. Bowen to Rev. D. Webster

Still, Davis was an ardent follower of the policies of Booker T. Washington. Davis' "Stickin' to de Hoe," for instance, was nothing more than a presentation of Washington's ideas in dialect form:

> Larnin' is a blessed thing
> An' good cloze berry fin',
> But I likes to see de cullud gal
> Dat's been larnt how to 'ine'.[27]

Local color entered into Davis' works—he published the usual tributes to food and partying—but he was, more than anyone else, the poet of accommodation.

Davis was a leading figure in the black community of Richmond, Virginia, where he was born a slave in 1862. He attended public schools in that city, graduating from high school at age sixteen. By eighteen, he had become a teacher; and he continued to teach until his death, in 1913. He was also a minister, having been elected pastor of the Second Baptist Church in 1896. This post, too, he held until his death.[28] During his career in Richmond, Davis was extremely active in city politics and civic life; he was also in great demand throughout the country as a public speaker on racial matters.

Davis, like Dunbar, believed there were special properties in the "Negro character." In his portrayal of that character, Davis even veered toward the older tradition of romantic racialism, declaring at one point, for example, that the Negro "stands as a monument to faithfulness to humble duty, one of the highest marks of the Christ-life."[29] In general, however, Davis' views cohered with those of writers such as Matthews and Dunbar, as he tempered ideas of distinctiveness with ideas of gentility. Not surprisingly, Davis' dialect poetry reflected his ideas of black distinctiveness and thus cohered with the main themes developed by other black dialect writers.

What set Davis apart was that he was the most prominent of the dialect writers to put his literary work to clearly political uses. Capitaliz-

---

Davis, May 10, 1904, in Daniel Webster Davis Papers, Virginia Historical Society, Richmond; John Edward Bruce, "Anthology of Negro Poetry—A Collection of Poems by Negro Poets," n.d., ms. in Arthur A. Schomburg Papers, Schomburg Center for Research in Black Culture, New York Public Library.

27. Davis, *Idle Moments*, 57.

28. Lottie Harrison, "Daniel Webster Davis," *Negro History Bulletin*, XVIII (1954), 57.

29. Daniel Webster Davis, "The Sunday School and Church as a Solution of the Negro Problem," in Alice Dunbar Nelson (ed.), *Masterpieces of Negro Eloquence* (New York, 1914), 296.

ing on black writers' literary strategy of moving from familiar stereotypes to the presentation of a less familiar, assimilated black America,
Davis used his dialect writing rhetorically in a way that helps reveal the
characteristics of the form.

As a prominent black leader, Davis often spoke before audiences that
were largely—or entirely—white. He made his poetry an integral part
of his speeches. His popular lecture "Paying the Fiddler," for instance,
took off from a party poem, "Ole Virginny Reel," moving to the proverb
that if people wanted to dance, they had to pay the fiddler. From there,
Davis could frame an indictment of racism, asserting that white America
ultimately would pay for its history of injustice to blacks. "For every
unjust act, for every lynching, for every burning, for every unfair convic-
tion, for every crime against truth and right," Davis declared, "America
must pay the Fiddler," as an oppressed people continued to claim social
justice. "Jim Crow's Search for the Promised Land" included recitations
of his poems "Sense 'Kinley's 'Nogurashun" and "De Linin' ub de
Hymns"—the former a rejection of party loyalty, the latter a typical
tribute to black folk religion. The speech itself, however, urged the
recognition of black progress since antebellum times and, in a break
with strong Washingtonianism, stressed the fundamental importance of
protecting black Americans' right to vote.[30]

As these examples show, there are some grounds for reevaluating our
ideas about Davis' positions on racial questions. He was hardly a man
willing to sell out his own race in order to please the white folks,
accommodationist though he may have been. It is more accurate to see
him as a man carefully attuned to his white audience, one who believed
his message of racial justice would fall on indifferent or hostile ears
unless he could make his audience comfortable with him, unless he
could put himself and the audience, as much as possible, on friendly
terms. His dialect poetry, evoking familiar stereotypes, could have done
this. Booker T. Washington often did something similar in his addresses
to white audiences, using homely stories and remarks to preface his
message of racial uplift.

The need to create a friendly rapport with a white audience was
made especially important by the character of the increasingly virulent
racism of the period. The ugly side of white ideas of black dependence,
the side that asserted black savagery, was reaching its apogee when

30. Daniel Webster Davis, "Paying the Fiddler," typed speech, in Davis Papers; Daniel
Webster Davis, *'Weh Down Souf, and Other Poems* (Cleveland, 1897), 22–24, 54–56;
Davis, "Jim Crow's Search for the Promised Land," ms. lecture, in Davis Papers.

Davis was making his career as a speaker. Davis could use his dialect poetry to counter that image and as a way to soften the frequently strong words favoring racial justice that he directed to his audiences. Open demands were dangerous for Davis to make and would, in any case, have got him nowhere. Or so he apparently believed. But threats framed by the voice of the noncontroversial plantation Negro were less risky; the voice itself served as a nonthreatening exordium to a message challenging the substance of race relations in the South and the rest of the nation.

This may explain, in large part, Davis' great popularity with white audiences. And there is no doubt of his popularity. In one account of a speech of his in Toronto, the reporter—himself white—described applause so strong that Davis' words were "drowned," this after the audience had been visibly moved throughout the presentation.[31] Davis, more than any other black writer, used his poetry to exploit the strategic possibilities of dialect forms.

Were there costs in Davis' technique? Such critics as Sterling Brown and Jean Wagner think so, since Davis' strategy involved, from their point of view, a willingness to be what white people wanted him to be, whatever his dedication to racial justice. Making his message palatable would also have undercut its force. It is not hard to see Davis as playing the very part Dunbar tried so hard to avoid. But what about dialect writing considered, more generally, as a major phenomenon in black writing and reading at the turn of the century? The popularity of dialect writing represented an issue that certainly caused little apparent trouble for Davis and other members of the black literary community at the time. But it was a major issue in the work of James D. Corrothers, paradoxically one of the period's most accomplished dialect writers.

Corrothers brought his own approach to dialect writing. On the one hand, he shared much of the psychological ambivalence about dialect writing that plagued Dunbar. On the other, and unlike Dunbar, he was especially aware of the place of dialect work in black literary life at the turn of the century; and his ambivalence on that score was equally strong and especially significant. More than anyone, Corrothers raised grave doubts about the sociological significance of dialect as a literary form—doubts of a different order from the kinds of concerns Dunbar

31. Charles Gallaudet Trumbull, "International Doings at Toronto," *Sunday School Times*, XLVII (1905), 373, copy in Davis Papers.

had felt, doubts that raised fundamental questions about the black literary community of Corrothers' time.

Like Dunbar, Corrothers was born in the North (in 1869) and was
raised in a white environment. Indeed, his grandfather, who raised him,
was a white man who had been married to a black woman. As a young
man, Corrothers tried to learn prizefighting. He also worked as a journalist before coming into contact with the noted temperance lecturer
Frances E. Willard, who helped him to attend Northwestern University.
His later career was varied. He continued in journalism after his studies
at Northwestern, and he also entered the ministry. He was ordained in
the A. M. E. Church and later became a Baptist and, finally, a Presbyterian—"convinced," he said, "that my race needed religious training
along the higher lines." Like other poets, Corrothers created a great deal
of sentimental verse and poetry on racial themes. Indeed, one of his first
published works was "The Psalm of the Race," a long poem that repeated
many of the major racial ideas of the period. But, like Dunbar, Davis, and
others, he was best known for his work in dialect. His dialect poetry
appeared in such major white journals as *Century*. He is best remembered for a single work that combined dialect poetry with narrative and
gave it an urban setting, his 1902 book *The Black Cat Club*.[32]

The Black Cat Club is an unusual work. Stylistically and thematically,
it marks Corrothers as a real innovator within the dialect tradition.
Although Corrothers wrote a great deal of dialect poetry that did not
differ from the mainstream of the black dialect tradition, *The Black Cat
Club*, with its urban setting, was removed from both the ties to gentility
and the usual modes of black distinctiveness found in that tradition. It
was as thematically distinct from other black dialect writing as Dunbar's
The Sport of the Gods was from the mainstream of black sentimental
fiction. *The Black Cat Club* also took an approach to dialect that was
founded less on literary precedents than is apparent in other dialect
work. Corrothers made extensive use of slang that appears much closer
to folk speech than to dialect-tradition writing, and he produced a
dialect that went well beyond the simple misspellings of literary dialect.
The language of the book and its tone have a flavor of realism that makes
The Black Cat Club a striking piece of work for its time.

32. John Livingston Wright, "Three Negro Poets," *Colored American Magazine*, II
(1901), 411–12; James D. Corrothers, *In Spite of Handicap: An Autobiography* (1916;
rpr. Freeport, N.Y., 1971), quotation on p. 237; Corrothers, "The Psalm of a Race,"
Howard's American Magazine, IV (1900), 358–59; Corrothers, *The Black Cat Club:
Negro Humor and Folklore* (New York, 1902).

Corrothers represented the book as "a series of character studies of Negro life as it may be observed in the great cities of the North"; and, like Dunbar and others, he wrote that there were distinctive traits of character to be seen in black Americans. "The Negro is *himself* everywhere," Corrothers wrote, "educated or uneducated." The chief characteristic Corrothers stressed was humor, an ability to have fun with life. He wrote that such a presentation was entirely true to life and claimed that his sources were themselves from life, including the "many quaint Negro expressions, droll sayings, and peculiar bywords, used by Negroes universally." In addition, he claimed to have drawn on "old Negro folk-lore tales" learned from older relatives and others. "Believing them to be worthy of preservation," he declared, "I have endeavored to retell them faithfully through the medium of the 'Black Cat Club,' a setting which, I hope, will give the reader a clearer insight into certain phases of Negro life and character."[33]

Corrothers' treatment of black life in *The Black Cat Club* received generally high marks from his contemporaries. Braithwaite, a conservative, wrote an early review of the book. He claimed to admire it very much, describing it as "praiseworthy in its method." The equally conservative Charles Alexander, an editor and an ardent Washingtonian, vouched for its accuracy and wrote that readers would agree that Corrothers' "pictures are accurate if they will take the pains to make a careful inspection of the kind of lives herein exhibited." He added, "The humorous side of Negro life furnishes an abundance of material for smiles and laughter." Corrothers, however, revealing his own ambivalence about the project, said some years later that he had written dialect only because he had been encouraged to do so by a white Chicago editor and, pleased with his skill at it, had decided to try a sustained production. In the intervening years, he said, he had "grown to consider the book a very poor one, and regret exceedingly that it was published."[34]

The Black Cat Club consists of fourteen chapters, really vignettes, organized around the activities of the club, a Chicago "literary society" established by a group of black men of less-than-elite pretensions. Most are barely literate, and all are given to drawing a razor in the heat of

33. Corrothers, *Black Cat Club*, 7–8.
34. William Stanley Braithwaite, Review of James D. Corrothers' *The Black Cat Club*, *Colored American Magazine*, V (1902), 151; Charles Alexander, Review of James D. Corrothers' *The Black Cat Club*, *Alexander's Magazine*, III (1907), 259; Corrothers, *In Spite of Handicap*, 139.

argument; the level of their discussions is hardly elevated. Much of the book uses the vehicle provided by this club to satirize various black groups and points of view current among blacks during the period, including the important place given to dialect writing in black literature. The central figure in the book is Sandy Jenkins, founder, president, and poet laureate of the Black Cat Club. Sandy is a typical dude, "dressed to kill" but clearly lower class. His dialect is heavy, his ideas are primitive, and he carries with him a black cat, among other charms, with which to hoodoo his enemies. As a poet, he creates a wealth of dialect verse on such subjects as fighting, hoodoo, and possums. The book follows Sandy and his companions through the club's activities, in their dealings with representatives of the black middle class and the black church, and in Sandy's romance with the ethereal, genteel Miss Sybill Underwood, of Terre Haute. At the end of the novel, Sandy and Sybill marry, and he becomes the industrious owner of a catering business. But the "plot," such as it is, is always minor, subordinated to the humor of individual episodes.

Several of Corrothers' vignettes make obvious reference to black folk traditions. One chapter, "Ghosts, Witches, and Hoodoos," offers a range of hoodoo tales that have close connections to traditional Afro-American beliefs. Another chapter, "Tales of Slavery Days," includes a version of "Master's Gone to Philly-Me-York" and a few other, similar tales. Other vignettes are closer to burlesque. In one, a debate among club members quickly degenerates into a shouting match and then into a brawl, complete with razors. In "Near to Nature's Heart," the club members present a number of grandiloquent orations demonstrating their ignorance of both geography and English. "Good Eatin's" fits well into dialect tradition, as members compare favorite foods and "recipes."[35]

But the book's real force comes from its satire. Corrothers at one point depicted a black church interested in saving the souls of Sandy and his band and a minister who urges them to convert—while reminding them that "we haven't much money to carry on our good work." He also introduced a "society woman," a sewing lady, who speaks the voice of uplift by urging the men to reform and treating them as a group that belongs to the "past generation." Later, when this same "modern" woman fears that she has been hoodooed, she quickly changes in character and becomes a real friend to Sandy and his friends.[36]

35. Corrothers, *Black Cat Club*, 95, 129ff.
36. *Ibid.,* 48, 50, 102.

Corrothers' satire was especially sharp in an oration delivered before the society, "De Eddicated Cullud Man." Much of the oration is simply a dialect statement of Washington's philosophy. At one point, Sandy describes "de thriftless eddicated cullud man whut de colleges am scatterin' promiscuous' th'u' ouh lan', as some lan'-po fahmah tu'ns his cattle out to pick a libbin' foh deyse'fs, whahevah dey kin fine it," and condemns the college graduate who "stan's 'roun' on de con'ah, wid a cigah in his mouf—happy as a big sunflower!—makin' mashes on de yellah gals, an' braggin' 'bout de *"vancement uv his people!"* " Washington's hostility to liberal education, as opposed to technical training, for most blacks was well known; and Sandy merely puts that opposition into his own words. Book-learning, he goes on to say, has done nothing to make such a man as he describes useful; indeed, it has only filled his head with useless knowledge to the point that the graduate "cain't talk nothin' but Greek an' Latin, an' cuss you in Trinogometry."[37] Washington himself did not put the view much differently, although he did state it more grammatically.

Soon, however, a point different from Sandy's begins to emerge from the episode. Sandy offers a tribute to Washington, declaring, "Dat man's doin' a heap mo' good in de Souf den all de graddiates whut's a-slanderin' uv 'im an' writin' resolutions." He continues, tellingly, "Look at de genamuns uv dis club! We ain't got much book l'arnin', but we has lit'a'ly cahved ouh way to fame an' fortune." The allusion to carving is appropriate; and if Washington's opponents seemed ineffectual, Washington's program was hardly recommended by the achievements of the members of the Black Cat Club. In another passage, Corrothers reduced Washington's program to an absurdity as Sandy pictures, in apparent seriousness, the affluent victim of a lynch mob saving himself by threatening to have his heirs foreclose on his lynchers should they complete their act.[38]

In this passage, Corrothers revealed his own sense of the ambiguity of celebrating folk life. The passage stresses both the failure of accommodationism and the inability of folk Negroes to overcome—even to understand—the realities of racial oppression. If Corrothers intended the book to reveal something of "the Negro himself," he was not entirely pleased with what it revealed.

More significantly, certain passages in the book serve as a reflexive

37. *Ibid.,* 55–57.
38. *Ibid.,* 58, 59–60.

commentary by the author on dialect work as such. This commentary comes in the form of the book's treatment of Sandy, its main character. Not only is Sandy a budding dialect poet, but his fame is spreading beyond the boundaries of the club. Tracing Sandy's career, Corrothers sharply satirized the vogue for dialect writing by black writers. He did this first by delineating Sandy's relationship with Sybill. In her first admiring letter to Sandy, she compares him to "Longfellow, Shakespere [*sic*], and James Whitcomb Riley combined,"[39] a rather unlikely collection of poets and one that says as much about Sybill's own lack of knowledge as it does about Sandy's ability. Later, when Sandy visits Sybill in Terre Haute, he is lionized by the locals in the "Lotus Literary and Social Club," to whom he gives a reading of his poems. Treated as a "great colored leader and poet," Sandy is royally received. The Terre Haute visit is a telling account of the ease with which a dialect writer, upon receiving the slightest recognition, can become a celebrity among black readers. It satirically undermines any effort to take the rest of Corrothers' book too seriously.

It might be too much to see *The Black Cat Club* as a thinly veiled attack on Dunbar's reputation among black readers—a reputation that rested as much on Dunbar's race as on his accomplishments, Corrothers' book would imply. But an element of such an attack is present. Corrothers himself was conscious of the problems raised by dialect writing. In his autobiography, he wrote that before he started doing such work, "I had always detested Negro dialect as smacking too much of '*niggerism*' which all intelligent coloured people detest," although he professed an admiration for Dunbar.[40] He may have remained ambivalent enough about dialect writing to use his book as a vehicle in which to comment on what he saw as an uncritical reception of popular dialect writing by the black audience and to convey a sense that dialect writing could never really escape those negative connotations that the weight of literary tradition had given to it.

Certainly, the book's ending rests on this theme. Sandy and his comrades are invited to perform in a church, and they do so in a most respectable manner—but the respectability is uneasily maintained. At one point, two members of the group threaten to come to their usual blows. Sandy, whose masterpiece is a poem about fighting with razors, is praised with the kind of words often spoken of Dunbar: "No race can

39. *Ibid,* 49.
40. Corrothers, *In Spite of Handicap*, 137.

afford to ignore its poets. No race amounts to anything unless it has produced its poets. Did you hear that? But—but—the Negro race has produced Sandy Jenkins! Now, then, let us feel proud."[41] There is nothing in the book to prepare one for such praise, unless it is offered tongue-in-cheek. Sandy, in fact, proves his attachment to his usual principles when, offered the opportunity for a college education by a wealthy white man, he compromises by taking an educated wife and accepting financial backing for a start in business. The reference to Dunbar is thinly veiled here—he too had turned down white offers to send him to college and had married into the black elite—as it is in the remarks introducing Sandy to the church. Corrothers' conclusion subtly presented his own disenchantment with, and alienation from, much that was contemporary in black literature, especially the vogue for dialect work.

The main satirical episodes of *The Black Cat Club* indicate that Corrothers' disenchantment may have been a result of the fact that dialect writing came along at an awkward time in black American history. It was a period when external threats to the community were at their highest, as Jim Crow became southern law, along with disfranchisement and lynching, and as social Darwinist intellectuals proclaimed the inferiority of nonwhites. It was also a period when internal dissensions among blacks were particularly vociferous, as leading black men and women had to choose sides in the debate over Washington's successful accommodationist policies. Corrothers' book indicated that the very enterprise of dialect writing meant accepting a position in such events, and a side in such debates, that was problematic. It implicitly asked, was that "distinctive identity" of folk culture really one to be celebrated, or was it closer to the world of Sandy Jenkins and his club? Could dialect work really be done without a tacit acceptance of white stereotypes, and, thus, was embracing those stereotypes not, ultimately, an accommodation with racism? In short, Corrothers conveyed a doubt that dialect work could ever be made the basis for a positive racial identity, and, decrying its popularity, presented it as, ultimately, an acceptance of a racist society. Thus, Corrothers implied, while dialect writing might have seemed, in the early stages, a relatively convenient way to go after a broad audience—and Dunbar's success had proved that this was possible—thoughtful blacks could never have pursued dialect writing without a host of related, significant issues having been

41. Corrothers, *Black Cat Club*, 243–44.

raised. Corrothers went straight to the heart of those issues in his satirical *Black Cat Club*.

If Dunbar felt great psychological ambivalence about writing dialect literature—an ambivalence Corrothers shared—Corrothers' work reveals an awareness of problems in the willingness of his black contemporaries to accept dialect forms as popular entertainment and even literary achievement. If his work displays a measure of ambivalence about gentility, it barely hides an undercurrent of bitterness about the pressures to create a distinctive black identity and about the way many middle-class black people seemed to be going about it. Corrothers' humor overlaid a peculiarly tragic sense of American racial life, a sense in which neither the aspirations of the past nor the answers of Corrothers' present seemed very satisfying. It is no wonder that Corrothers came to regret the book. Nor is it surprising that, toward the close of his career, he escaped from such a tragic vision by choosing the assimilationist aspirations that *The Black Cat Club* also found problematic. His last poems, published in *Century*, were, with one exception, in standard English and filled with the language of genteel protest.

At the same time, *The Black Cat Club* is a book that in its very anger confirms the significance and meaning of dialect literature for many black American writers. By Corrothers' time, that literature had come to play an integral part in black literary life and was treated with fondness by readers and writers alike. Corrothers was one of the few writers to look at the role of dialect writing with anything like a critical point of view, moving beyond Dunbar's personal and psychological ambivalence to a more sociological appraisal—an appraisal that underscored the ambiguity of this early effort by black writers to come to terms with a changing racial environment.

The identity concerns that underlaid dialect literature also found subtle expression in more traditional literary works produced by black writers at the turn of the century. There was, to be sure, a kind of cultural lag between articulated racial ideals and the emerging structure of feelings that one sees in Dunbar's poetry—or in the general run of dialect writing, for that matter. That such a lag should have existed, given the painfulness of directly confronting an increasingly difficult situation, is not surprising. There remained a strong lure exerted by the American mainstream, and the strength of the lure was embodied in a continuing tradition of genteel, cultured writing.

The strength of genteel forms is shown in both the work and the popularity of William Stanley Braithwaite, one of the most prominent writers of this period. Braithwaite was a major figure in black literary circles at the turn of the century. He was active in the development of *Colored American Magazine* and *Voice of the Negro*, and he published a great deal of work in these and other black publications. Although he lacked a college education, his literary accomplishments and ambitions were enormous. In 1906 he published his own anthology of Elizabethan verse; later he published a volume on the Georgian period in English literature. In addition, Braithwaite received some recognition as the editor of an annual anthology of American magazine verse, an effort he began in 1913. It was not, incidentally, until 1915 that this anthology series included a work by a black poet—James Weldon Johnson's "The White Witch."[42]

Braithwaite had a West Indian background. His father, originally from Guiana, had earned a degree from Oxford and a medical degree from King's College, London, and had settled in Boston in 1874. The father died suddenly, however, in 1886; and a similar education was unavailable to young William. Instead, he apprenticed himself to the printing office of Ginn & Co. and began writing verse as well. Later in life he was variously a bookstore manager, writer, and critic.[43]

Braithwaite's literary standards were high, and there is no doubt that he saw himself as more deeply involved with the Western tradition than with black literature. Indeed, critic Sterling Brown has asserted that much of Braithwaite's effort was aimed toward a denial of his race. Even some of Braithwaite's contemporaries made the same charge. Silas X. Floyd, a writer who was also closely involved with *Colored American*, felt called upon to compare Braithwaite's works with those of Dunbar, much to the disadvantage of Braithwaite; he declared, "William Stanley Braithwaite is hailed by the unthinking, the unknowing, or the untrained, as the leading poet of the colored race (it would be an insult to Mr. Braithwaite to call him a 'Negro,' from all I hear) in this country." Such words seem too strong. Not only did Braithwaite deeply involve himself with black journals, but he also offered encouragement to young black writers even as he drew on those who were already established. James Weldon Johnson was one of many who turned to Braithwaite for critical readings of his work. And in 1902, disappointed in the

42. James Weldon Johnson, "The White Witch," in William Stanley Braithwaite (ed.), *Anthology of Magazine Verse for 1915, and Year Book of American Poetry* (New York, 1915), 160–62.
43. William Pickens, "Braithwaite," *Voice of the Negro*, IV (1907), 119–21.

quality of existing black periodicals—despite his own involvement with them—Braithwaite sought to involve Charles Chesnutt in a plan to create "a magazine for the Negro in America," one that would "create a backbone for a Negro school of writers in the country" and that would meet the distinctive needs of black Americans.[44]

Little of Braithwaite's work was devoted to racial issues, a fact that set him apart from other black authors and poets. He did write a few magazine pieces on racial topics. A 1902 short story, "The Quality of Color," dealt with interracial romance and the tragic force of white American taboos. A 1904 story, "The Returning Road of Dreams," satirized the controversy between Booker T. Washington and W. E. B. Du Bois—here they were "Dr. Hushington" and "Dr. DePois"—with Braithwaite emphatically taking the side of the latter. He also wrote a poem in tribute to the abolitionist William Lloyd Garrison, published in 1906 in *Alexander's Magazine*. But these were, certainly, exceptional works on his part. His earliest volume of his own poetry contained only one poem that even remotely addressed racial concerns, a tribute to the abolitionist-poet John Greenleaf Whittier.[45] Braithwaite was above all a poet of nature and love—enamored of the works of Keats and Dante Gabriel Rossetti—who sought to create a genteel literature that was, in most ways, devoid of racial identity. Both his work and his prominence indicate the extent to which such a literary sensibility continued to appeal to and express the aspirations of a significant part of the black literary world.

But the turn of the century also saw at least a groping toward new poetic images within the framework of conventional forms. These images related to the growing interest in black distinctiveness. Although it did not happen often, at least a few writers began to celebrate, for example, a distinctive black femininity. This femininity was little different from that of the sentimental tradition, but it was couched in a language that emphasized that a genteel black woman need not appear

44. See, *e.g.,* Brown, *Negro Poetry and Drama,* 50; James Weldon Johnson, "Scrap Album," n.d., in Scrapbooks (of his interests and activities) and William Stanley Braithwaite to James Weldon Johnson, July 29, 1914, both in James Weldon Johnson Collection, Collection of American Literature, Beinecke Rare Book and Manuscript Library, Yale University; William Stanley Braithwaite to Charles W. Chesnutt, November 29, 1902, in Charles W. Chesnutt Papers, Fisk University Library Special Collections.

45. William Stanley Braithwaite, "The Quality of Color," *Colored American Magazine,* V (1902), 67–75; Braithwaite, "The Returning Road of Dreams," *Colored American Magazine,* VII (1904), 367–68, 509–15; Braithwaite, "The Liberator: An Ode on the Centenary of William Lloyd Garrison," *Alexander's Magazine,* I (January, 1906), 5–7; Braithwaite, *The House of Falling Leaves* (1908; rpr. Miami, 1969), 104–107.

nearly white. Aaron Belford Thompson, a printer, wrote "To Helen," a poem that deliberately stressed his love's black appearance:

> Oh Helen! thou art passing fair,
>> With locks of sable hue;
> So glossy is thy curly hair,
>> Surpass thy beauty few.

He continued:

> I look upon thy dark brown face,
>> Thy laughing eyes I see;
> Could I with gifted power but trace,
>> Thy love in store for me!

In another work, "Our Girls," Thompson celebrated "our Ethiope maids! / Her crisp curly locks, in beauty arrayed." It was a start, an attempt to separate the ideals of gentility from a context that depended on a closeness to "white" physical characteristics.[46]

The effort was made more ambitiously in Kenneth M. Young's otherwise unremarkable novel of the eternal triangle, *Selene*, published by the author in South Carolina in 1896. The novel was pure romance and devoid of any overt elements of protest or identity; but it was set apart for its day, if only by Young's description of his heroine, Selene, from the point of view of the male protagonist: "For he declared the most beautiful girl upon whom he ever looked was not a blonde of golden tresses, hazel eyes, aquiline nose and marble-white hands; nor was she a brunette cast in Anglo-Saxon mold; but, twin sister of Venus, a direct descendant of the African race, of form superb."[47] Selene's beauty was wholly unrelated to any physical similarity she might have to a white ideal, although her virtues were those of the typical genteel heroine.

What both Thompson and Young were attempting to do was to broaden what gentility could mean, not simply by saying that blacks could be genteel, as earlier writers had done, but by saying that the main cultural categories of gentility were themselves too narrow. As Young implied, dark skin could be as pure as alabaster and dark beauty as striking as that fitting the "Anglo-Saxon mold."

Anna Julia Cooper tried to do something similar by broadening religious categories in her manuscript poem "Aunt Charlotte." Cooper, who had long expressed an interest in creating a distinctive black litera-

46. Aaron Belford Thompson, *Echoes of Spring* (Rossmoyne, Ohio, 1901), 3; Thompson, *Morning Songs* (Rossmoyne, Ohio, 1899), 8.
47. Kenneth M. Young, *Selene* (Spartanburg, S.C., 1896), 6.

ture with roots in folk tradition, drew on the spiritual "Swing Low, Sweet Chariot" to create an image of an old woman looking back on a difficult life and forward to her heavenly reward:

> Swing low, sweet Chariot, swing lower—
> Way down for the humblest and poorest;
> From the pearly white gate where thou soarest
> To the hole of the pit where I cower.
> In bondage my mother conceived me,
> In bondage my first breath I uttered,
> Eight babies in bondage I've suckled,
> And prayed the prayer bond-women muttered.[48]

Quite unlike much of the dialect writing of this period, Cooper's poem drew on folk tradition not to express ambivalence about gentility but to broaden it, to show how it could encompass the lives and sufferings of the folk. It did so by translating folk forms into a conservative poetic language.

Efforts to broaden the base of gentility remained extremely tentative, helping to stress, yet again, the continuing attraction of genteel ideals as well as the conservative characteristics of black writers. Only a few writers moved much beyond Thompson, or Young, or Cooper— except for those who clearly signaled their departure from gentility by the use of dialect. Dunbar was a striking example of one who did. Others approached his radicalism, though to a more limited extent.

One of these writers was David Bryant Fulton, a journalist who became active in burgeoning black consciousness movements later in the twentieth century. At about the time Dunbar was beginning his career, in 1892, Fulton published his *Recollections of a Sleeping Car Porter* under the pseudonym Jack Thorne. These recollections were essentially vignettes taken from the life of a man who worked as a pullman car porter—a job Fulton had held for a time; they recorded encounters with various kinds of fellow porters and with passengers, as well as events in different settings through which the porter passed. Fulton described scenery, local customs, and colorful characters; and although he included one narrative in which he protested white prejudice, he devoted most of the book to such local color sketches.[49] The sketches

48. Anna Julia Cooper, "Aunt Charlotte," c. 1902, typescript poem, in Anna J. Cooper Papers, Manuscript Division, The Moorland-Spingarn Research Center, Howard University.

49. Jack Thorne [David Bryant Fulton], *Recollections of a Sleeping Car Porter* (Jersey City, N.J., 1892).

were unusual in the extent to which Fulton ignored genteel conventions in favor of a fairly faithful approach to black—and white—life, an approach without the overt detachment from folk society found structurally and thematically in the dialect tradition. It was as if Fulton were saying that conventional evidence of faith in the American mainstream need not be a crucial part of black literary life, a rather unusual statement to make in 1892.

Alice Dunbar's departure from older literary norms was somewhat different from that of Fulton. The wife of Paul Laurence Dunbar, she lived in his shadow—or in the shadow of his memory—throughout her career. Her writings were not voluminous; she wrote a number of magazine articles and some verse, along with two books of short stories. One, *Violets*, was published in 1895, before she met Dunbar. The other, *The Goodness of St. Rocque*, was issued in 1899 by her husband's publisher, Dodd, Mead. After her marriage to Dunbar ended, so, too, for all practical purposes, did her literary career. Her most notable publication after 1906 was a 1914 edited volume, *Masterpieces of Negro Eloquence*, which contained major addresses of leading black orators.[50]

As the leading student of her work, Gloria Hull, has stressed, much of Alice Dunbar's writing was little removed from the mainstream of the black genteel tradition. *Violets* was particularly sentimental, the title story telling of a young girl who sends her lover violets tied "with a tress of her pretty brown hair." But by Easter the young girl has died; she lies with her "fair, young face pressed against the satin-lined casket." Her lover eventually marries; and some years later, he comes across the violets. He cannot remember who sent them and tosses them in the fire. As they burn, he sighs "a long quivering breath of remembrance." Other material in the book was similar. Although at the time of its publication the book received a good review in an obscure black magazine called *Monthly Review*—whose press, apparently, also published the book— there was little out of the ordinary in it. In 1913, Alice Dunbar wrote to Arthur Schomburg, then beginning to assemble his great collection of black literature, to tell him she was "heartily ashamed" of *Violets*, urging him, "Please don't want 'Violets' in your collection; such sheer slop as that would spoil the whole." A copy of *Violets* nevertheless became part of the Schomburg Collection.[51]

50. Nelson (ed.), *Masterpieces of Negro Eloquence*.
51. Gloria T. Hull, *Color, Sex, and Poetry: Three Women Writers of the Harlem Renaissance* (Bloomington, Ind., 1987), 40; Alice Ruth Moore, *Violets and Other Tales* (N.p., 1895), 17; Charles S. Morris, Review of Alice Ruth Moore's *Violets and Other Tales*, in

Alice Dunbar liked *The Goodness of St. Rocque* a good deal better, and her reputation could comfortably rest on this collection. Her husband, in an interview, once said that his wife wrote "much better prose" than he did;[52] and if these stories do not quite prove him correct, they more significantly reveal a writer who was as willing as he was to take black literature in new directions and who contributed to weakening genteel conventions. Set in southern Louisiana—including Mrs. Dunbar's native New Orleans—the stories in *The Goodness of St. Rocque*, though sentimental, often achieve the kind of realism for which Paul Dunbar strove in *The Sport of the Gods*; they also show an imaginativeness in plot and characterization that set them apart from the work of Alice Dunbar's contemporaries.

Hull has linked the stories collected in *The Goodness of St. Rocque* with the works of such other turn-of-the-century writers as Kate Chopin and Sarah Orne Jewett. Such a link is appropriate, because, like them, Alice Dunbar achieves a measure of realism in her fiction through the evocation of local color. But no less significantly, given the context of black literary tradition, Alice Dunbar got away from the kinds of characterizations that dominated sentimental writing by focusing mainly on lower-class characters or on folk customs. Thus, for example, the title story deals with a romance involving the ultraelite colored creoles of New Orleans, but the plot ultimately hangs on an effort by the beautiful young heroine to win her love through voodoo. "M'sieu Fortier's Violin" is the poignant tale of a violinist who must sell his beloved instrument in order to stay alive. "Sister Josepha" tells of a young nun—an orphan raised in a convent—who must face a crisis of the spirit when she confronts the temptations of life in the profane world. Alice Dunbar drew on a wide range of plot situations, exploring their emotional character. And if some of the stories were as excessively maudlin as the worst magazine fiction—"Titee," for example, the story of a young boy who sacrifices for an old man—she often created characters and surprise endings that moved significantly beyond the mainstream of turn-of-the-century black fiction.[53]

Monthly Review, III (1895), 157–58; Alice M. Dunbar to Arthur A. Schomburg, July 23, 1913, in Schomburg Papers.

52. "Won Success in Rapid Strides," interview with Paul Laurence Dunbar in Salt Lake City *Tribune*, March 2, 1902, clipping, in Paul Laurence Dunbar Papers, Ohio Historical Society (microfilm ed.).

53. Hull, *Color, Sex, and Poetry*, 50; Alice Dunbar, *The Goodness of St. Rocque and Other Stories* (1899; rpr. College Park, Md., 1969).

Perhaps the most unusual departure from gentility was a work written by John S. Durham, a scion of a wealthy Philadelphia family. Durham was the author of one of the more distinctive works published during this period—"Diane: Priestess of Haiti," a 1902 novella of romance and intrigue set in the palace of the president of Haiti, which appeared initially in *Lippincott's Magazine*. Durham himself had an unusual background. Educated as an engineer, he found that discrimination made a career in that field virtually impossible for him; so he earned a law degree at the University of Pennsylvania. He soon became extremely active in politics, making a deep impression on Booker T. Washington. During the 1890s, he served as American consul to Santo Domingo and Haiti. As a writer, he did some newspaper work for the *Philadelphia Evening Bulletin* and produced nonfiction on Haiti and on the economic condition of black Americans. While he was writing "Diane," in the late 1890s, he was employed as an agent for American sugar interests in Haiti. His interest in Haiti was strong; indeed, he initially intended to make "Diane" "a complete study" of Haitian life presented in the form of "a native love story." It would be difficult to claim that Durham achieved such an ambitious goal, but the novella was unusual and important in other, no less significant ways.[54]

The plot of "Diane" revolves around the frustration of a scheme by German businessmen and Haitian conspirators to overthrow the Haitian president and to bring the island's government under the control of a German syndicate. The scheme is foiled by the combined efforts of the German ambassador and the president himself, both of whom are straightforward, honorable gentlemen. They are assisted by Alcide, a young Haitian soldier and servant to the German ambassador, who at various points is accused of treachery but who emerges as the hero of the piece. Within the story of international intrigue is a love story involving Alcide and the title character, Diane. Diane is the daughter of a voodoo priest who hopes she will follow him in the profession. He opposes her engagement to Alcide; and as a result, his own voodoo practices become woven into the plot, as he seeks to influence Diane's life. All works out in the end, as the plotters are defeated and the lovers are united.

Aside from its international intrigue, unique in black literature from this period, the novella stands out in other ways as well. One of these

54. See William Toll, *The Resurgence of Race: Black Social Theory from Reconstruction to the Pan-African Conferences* (Philadelphia, 1979), 34–35; John S. Durham to Charles W. Chesnutt, September 14, 1909, in Chesnutt Papers.

ways is its Haitian setting, which allows white and black characters to appear as equals—on the side of evil as well as good. Relationships between the president and the German ambassador, for example, are marked by precisely the kind of behavior one would expect of men in their positions. The racial variable plays no part in their dealings with each other. The same may be said on the other side, as white and black villains are equally sinister. Even the relationship between the ambassador and Alcide is very different from what one might expect of a white employer and his black servant. It is as if Durham was showing, however subtly, what a world of white and black people could and should be like.

But the most remarkable thing about the novella, and what takes it outside the genteel tradition, is the portrayal of Diane. In many ways, she resembles the typical genteel heroine; she is well mannered, soft-spoken, and beautiful. And her appearance is close to white; she has "features almost Grecian in their outline" and "soft and tractable" hair. But Durham supplemented this stereotyped characterization with an eroticism that had never been used by a black writer before.

One sees this eroticism in Durham's description of a ritual in which Diane is initiated into her place as a priestess. After a series of preliminaries, she appears before the company: "She was in spotless white. . . . Her neck was decorated with a long string of minute silver beads, falling down on her sturdy chest, generously exposed. On her wrists jingled bangles of silver coins; and the silver, in all the glint of newness, and the plain skirt, bleached to dazzling whiteness and set against the fine satin-like texture of her skin, put her as one apart from the other women. . . . Her gown was fitted close over her body, and the modulation of her hips and the movement of her thighs attracted furtive glances from the men as all bowed their reverence and passed on." A similar eroticism marks Durham's description of Diane's dancing before a group of the conspirators. She is forced to serve as the mistress of the ringleader, a fate she accepts with resignation. In one episode, the two of them are listening to a local band. Hearing the music, Diane "leaped . . . as if she could restrain herself no longer. The drummers caught her feeling, and their music graded itself down to a softly modulated rhythm. . . . She abandoned herself to the feeling, and just back of the centre lamp in the dark shadow began the body-dance of the country revels."[55] Here, too, was a passage unlike any found in other black works of the day, an important reaching toward a sense of black distinctiveness that departed dras-

55. John S. Durham, *Diane: Priestess of Haiti* (Philadelphia, 1902), 388, 407, 458.

tically from white-approved models, including those of plantation life. No other work of the time had anything like the sensuousness found in Durham's "Diane."

It is difficult to know how much Durham himself thought of the innovative aspects of "Diane." It is, however, clear that Durham had some ambivalence toward the gentility that defined virtue in much of the literature contemporary with his own. He expressed this ambivalence most clearly in an essay on Haitian society that appeared in *Voice of the Negro* in 1904, in which he asserted that "the Haytian has not had those contacts with Teutonic civilization which unman the Negro while they refine him."[56] Durham seems to have found in exoticism a way of expressing the quality that had resisted "unmanning" and that could serve as a basis for a black identity, an alternative to the middle-class attributes cultivated by other writers. Durham's Diane had her similarities to the genteel creatures of the past, but in important ways she displayed a freedom from genteel restraints unprecedented in black writing. The creation of her character was a major departure from the cultural attachments of the past and an important statement of how deep an ambivalence about past strategies and aspirations could begin to go by the early years of the twentieth century.

56. John S. Durham, "The Hidden Wealth of Hayti," *Voice of the Negro*, I (1904), 144.

IV

The Literature of the Color Line and the Meaning of Race, 1896–1908

In looking at the vogue for dialect poetry or at such an edging away from gentility as the embryonic exoticism found in John S. Durham's "Diane," one sees the emergence of a real tension in black American literature. This tension was the product of trying to hold to a culture that prized the main features of middle-class American life while living in a society in which the possibilities of entering the American middle-class mainstream appeared increasingly remote. Dialect and exoticism represented an effort to alleviate that tension by creating a notion of black distinctiveness that was not too dangerously close to white stereotypes—although Dunbar and Corrothers, in particular, had strong doubts that such an effort could be successful—while still serving as an adequate focus for a stronger emphasis on racial identity. Some writers, however, saw the tension as deeper and more pervasive than anything that dialect writers and those who, at this stage, celebrated blackness sought to address. For these writers, the tensions in black American life could not be easily resolved; and their works reflect their sense of the real difficulties involved in coming to terms with being black in America during the darkest years of the nadir.

Such writers as George Marion McClellan, Pauline Hopkins, Sutton E. Griggs, and Charles W. Chesnutt felt the changing character of American racial life especially keenly. They portrayed their feelings vividly in a series of works written on the traditional theme of racial mixture, using it to confront directly the various meanings of the color line and of racial identity. They were not alone. So well did this motif capture the feelings of many writers that, however important it had been in the past, they were especially drawn to it in the late 1890s and during the early years of the twentieth century. An unprecedented number of works of fiction, in particular, either used interracial romance, or sex, as a key plot device or featured mixed-race protagonists whose very ancestry served as the basis for plot development.

This was true of white writers as well as black in the changing racial climate of the late nineteenth and early twentieth centuries. Werner Sollors, in his recent extended account of ethnicity and literature, has shown how, historically, a wide range of writers confronting immigrant as well as "racial" experiences in America have turned to stories of intermarriage and racial mixture in an effort to come to terms with being an "ethnic" in American society. Based on his account, the years around the turn of the century seem to have been especially productive of such works.[1] Literary historian William L. Andrews, in a more focused study, has also noted a concentration of such novels in the late nineteenth century. Looking specifically at novels dealing with racial mixtures involving Afro-American characters, he has shown how white as well as black novelists of that time deliberately cast off older approaches to racial mixture—the theme of the "tragic mulatto," for example—in order to deal with the specific problems of assimilation and segregation in nineteenth century life. The Negrophobe Thomas Dixon, for example, sought to use a fear of racial mixture in such fictional arguments for black subordination as *The Leopard's Spots* and *The Clansman*. George Washington Cable and Albion Tourgée, white writers more sympathetic to black aspirations, used the motif of racial mixture and related issues of assimilation and racial identity in order to build the case for black rights, if not racial equality.[2]

The works of black writers fit well into this general context of writing on racial and ethnic mixtures, but with a concern of the writers' own for questions of identity and of their place in American society. Whereas many European ethnic writers simply took the motif of intermarriage as a powerful symbol of their own "Americanization," and whereas such writers as Dixon, on the one hand, and Cable and Tourgée, on the other, looked hard at the social implications of racial mixture, for many black writers the motif of racial mixture provided a vivid metaphor for the difficulty of reconciling the demands of being black and American at the same time.

Much of the literature of racial mixture responded to the issues of the turn of the century as Harper's *Iola Leroy* had, by stressing the need to

1. Werner Sollors, *Beyond Ethnicity: Consent and Descent in American Culture* (New York, 1986), 66ff., 149–56.
2. William L. Andrews, "Miscegenation in the Late Nineteenth-Century American Novel," *Southern Humanities Review*, XVII (1979), 13–24.

choose an identity with the race out of feelings of a familylike loyalty as well as out of political necessity. Or it stressed, as had Victoria Earle Matthews' "Eugenie's Mistake," the possibility and desirability of finding happiness within black society. For example, Ruth Todd, in her story "The Octoroon's Revenge," told of the love of Lillian, a daughter of one of Virginia's most distinguished white families, for her father's black coachman. The two elope, causing great consternation until it is learned that Lillian, raised a Virginia aristocrat, is really the child of her father and his octoroon slave—having been switched for her father's white child at infancy. Mary Louise Burgess-Ware, in a 1903 story, wrote of the love between two cultured young people, a love broken up when it is revealed that the girl has black ancestry. Upon learning the news, she decides to devote her life to the service of her people. However, it is soon learned that her former lover also has black ancestry, and the romance is fulfilled. The ties with Matthews' story, in particular, are obvious and emphasize the way in which the motif of racial mixture could give added weight to racial identity—but without really threatening middle-class ideals.[3]

These ties were fully exploited in one of the more romantic novels of the period, J. McHenry Jones's *Hearts of Gold*, published in 1896. The novel focuses on events in the lives of Regenia Underwood, physically "white" in appearance but actually the racially mixed ward of an abolitionist family; Lotus Stone, a cultured Afro-American physician; and Clement St. John, a black newspaper editor. The novel is filled with evidence of the gentility of the black elite and with some of the most overwritten dialogue produced by any writer of this period. But at its core are the dilemmas and difficulties in the life of Regenia. For one thing, she is greatly desired by one Dr. Frank Leighton, a white ne'er-do-well who is indifferent to her virtue and willing to commit any deceit to have her. Regenia herself, though she has had few contacts with black people, having been raised in Canada, recognizes her duty to her race and goes South for a career teaching black children. Lotus, who has a proper, genteel affection for Regenia, is also devoting his life to providing medical care for the people of the rural South. As the story progresses, Lotus finds himself unjustly accused of a crime and, barely escaping a lynch mob, sentenced to a southern labor camp. Clement, acting the part of a white man, helps Lotus escape—in a scene reminis-

3. Ruth D. Todd, "The Octoroon's Revenge," *Colored American Magazine*, IV (1902), 291–95; Mrs. M. Louise Burgess-Ware, "Bernice, the Octoroon," *Colored American Magazine*, VI (1903), 607–16, 652–57.

cent of abolitionist accounts of escapes from slavery. Eventually, Lotus receives clemency from the governor; and all ends well when he and Regenia marry.[4] There is little original in the novel, except, perhaps, for an extended indictment of the southern prison system through the account of Lotus' stay in the labor camp. But in portraying the dedication of Regenia, Lotus, and Clement to black people despite other possibilities—all could pass—and any attendant problems, Jones stayed clearly within the tradition defined by Harper's novel.

Holding to a black identity was thus treated as having great importance during this period. Along these lines, most writers decried the existence of the color line that divided black people from one another as well as from the larger society. In her 1903 story "The Folly of Mildred," Ruth Todd used a common phrase in condemning her title character for choosing a light-skinned man solely on the ground of color, claiming that "character, not color," should be the key attribute in dealing with other people.[5] Stories of light-skinned protagonists who chose to identify with their race were important ways of getting at an issue that was practical as well as symbolic in the black community.

There was, however, a problem with the continuing use of the motif of racial mixture as it had been developed by Harper and Matthews. Above all, it made for an approach to questions of racial identity that could not bear much examination. So long as writers stayed strictly within the confines of plot and characterization defined by Harper or Matthews, or even by their abolitionist and neoabolitionist forebears, these problems did not emerge. But when writers of this period moved outside those confines, when they struck out in independent literary directions, they revealed historical and moral issues that pointed to real tensions in regard to questions of identity—tensions made strong by the conflict between the push toward identity and the pull exerted by the American mainstream.

To some extent, the tensions were similar to those that characterized dialect writing. Specifically, while there was a value put on racial identity, there was also a real ambivalence about creating an identity that seemed to compromise one's claim to be, above all, an American. But the issues raised by the motif of racial mixture took that ambivalence to a depth that was not wholly apparent in other aspects of turn-of-the-century black writing.

4. J. McHenry Jones, *Hearts of Gold* (1896; rpr. College Park, Md., 1969).
5. Ruth D. Todd, "The Folly of Mildred: A Race Story with a Moral," *Colored American Magazine*, VI (1903), 364–70.

The problems this motif could reveal appeared, for example, in the work of George Marion McClellan, a writer who was born in Tennessee and educated at Fisk University and at the Hartford Theological Seminary. McClellan was a teacher in Louisville, Kentucky, when he did most of his work. In many ways, he was extraordinarily traditional; but he published a major collection of fiction in 1906 that was far from ordinary in its use of the traditional motif of racial mixture. The collection, entitled *Old Greenbottom Inn*, used the setting around the fictional inn, which had been converted into an industrial school for Negroes, as a focus for stories dealing with a number of elements of racial life and race relations. The title story, in particular, showed the difficulties that could arise out of an unusual treatment of racial mixture as a literary motif.

"Old Greenbottom Inn" begins with a description of its Tennessee setting and of the Negro industrial school, then moves back to antebellum times to trace a story of racial mixture and interracial romance with tragic consequences. The owner of the old inn, McBride, is quarreling with his wife over a decision to sell one of their slaves, a young quadroon, while retaining her infant daughter on the plantation. The quadroon's daughter is, of course, McBride's as well; and Mrs. McBride wants to sell the child, Daphne, along with the quadroon mother. "She's a nigger brat," Mrs. McBride declares, "and she'll bring disgrace and ruin along her track as her mother has done."[6] McBride stands firm against selling the girl, but the young mother is sold. Subsequently, McBride dies in the Civil War. Ten years later, Daphne remains in the area but is now a prize student in the Industrial School, where she continues to love her childhood sweetheart, John Henry. John Henry had himself been a slave on the McBride plantation and had comforted Daphne when her mother was sold away. He is now also a prize student.

During this time, Mrs. McBride's own daughter, Eunice, and her daughter's fiancé, Joseph Cramer, return to the homestead from Louisville, where both are beginning their careers as artists. Overhearing Daphne singing opera, Joseph is enthralled and begins a campaign to win her love, despite her race. Daphne's own sentiments are clear. When young Joseph offers her his hand and puts on his best manners, she quickly rebuffs him, asking if he can "insult your hostess by offering me, a Negro girl, your hand and calling me Miss Daphne?"[7] Still, she is attracted to the sensitive, artistic young man; and the relationship

6. George Marion McClellan, *Old Greenbottom Inn and Other Stories* (1906; rpr. New York, 1975), 14.
7. *Ibid.,* 48.

blossoms until, ultimately, Daphne becomes pregnant. John Henry, in a fit of jealousy, confronts Joseph. The two fight; and, in the struggle, Joseph Cramer is killed. John Henry flees but is captured by a mob and lynched.

At its conclusion, the story contrasts the images of the two young victims. Joseph lies in state, clean and beautiful in death. John Henry's body is mutilated, swinging in the breeze and jeered by the victorious mob. His mother mourns: "She had lifted her face to pray to her God, but he was gone from his throne. He was swaying to the breeze with hemp and death in the gray dawn over the bridge of Moore's creek." The story then shifts to Easter morning, when Daphne's child is born. The young mother lies next to the baby and, looking at the child, begins to cry. Old Aunt Jemima, caring for them, rushes to the bedside. "'I believe dat po' thing in dar is gwine 'stracted.' And such she could but believe for she could not understand what she saw when the mother's cry brought her to the bed to see her clutching the little child's hands with such wild words about it. The little babe had sucked its finger till the blood was drawn to the finger tip, making it blood red, and then held it up as if for the mother to see. In that hour of weakness and confused senses, by some law of memory, the young mother was little Daphne again." And as little Daphne, she remembers the words of her former mistress and repeats them: "She's a nigger brat with poison in her blood."[8]

The significance of Daphne's words, with their cutting irony, is brought home by the brief denouement to the story. Mrs. McBride and her daughter, the daughter who had such promise, are brought low, joining "that class designated by the Negroes of the South as 'pore white trash.'" They are forced to sell the inn, which becomes the center for the colored normal school that Daphne and John Henry had earlier attended. The school itself comes under black leadership and grows rapidly. Indeed, the story even implies that the "energetic young Negro" who takes over the school is Daphne's child. But the irony is clear, as the "once famous Inn, which in times past entertained Negro traders, passed for an inheritance to the Negroes, where there is now new life and new hope in the new order of things, while Greenbottom Inn, as it was, is only a memory."[9]

McClellan's story is one of the most complicated works from this period. Its ending is almost Washingtonian in holding out the develop-

8. *Ibid.*, 82, 85–86.
9. *Ibid.*, 86–87.

ment of separate black institutions as a key to racial progress. The school that takes over the inn even sounds a little like Tuskegee Institute—a source of pride that black people could take in black leadership. At the same time, the story is, in a sense, the negative side to at least one part of Harper's *Iola Leroy*. Daphne's original refusal of Joseph's love is much like Iola Leroy's rejection of her young white doctor. Iola goes on to a productive life because she sticks by that refusal. Daphne suffers great tragedy because she does not. In this, McClellan's story fits well, if from a different point of view, into the period's tradition of fiction based on racial mixture.

But what makes McClellan's story complicated is its departure from the kind of story Harper told, and in ways that make it impossible to read the story as a simple parable of identity. At the heart of the story's distinctiveness is the fact that, although Daphne is in many ways a typical sentimental heroine, her relationship with Joseph and her pregnancy bespeak a view of love—interracial or otherwise—that was far from common in turn-of-the-century sentimental writing, black or white; and this view certainly sets the work apart from Harper's, which had a strong sense of sexual propriety. In McClellan's story, passion is an important characteristic of love; and the author did not openly condemn either Daphne or Joseph for succumbing to it in their love for each other. He even went so far as to describe Daphne's pregnancy as the "almost inevitable result" of a relationship as strong as theirs.[10]

In addition, McClellan's story stresses that Daphne's affair with Joseph is not sordid, despite its ungenteel outcome—at least, not as it is developed. Joseph is neither a seducer nor a scoundrel; he is no Frank Leighton, for example. He is, instead, a free-spirited figure whose love for Daphne, despite racial norms, is real and strong; and Daphne has ample cause to return that love. At one point in the story, Joseph even saves her life when she is endangered by a raging bull. As a result of his love for Daphne, moreover, Joseph comes to understand the evil of prejudice. McClellan was thus not using racial mixture as a literary convention to expose simple white perfidy in contrast to black virtue. The possibility of true love across racial lines is something he treated as natural and normal. The tragedy occurs because the larger society does not treat it that way and thus forces the feelings of the two young lovers into illicit channels.

In his portrayal of interracial love, McClellan made Daphne a charac-

10. *Ibid.,* 64.

ter not too different from the classic tragic mulatto developed in ante-bellum fiction. But the significance of such a character in McClellan's story has less to do with Daphne's ancestry in tragic mulatto fiction than it does with the relationship of her character and her situation to the framework provided by McClellan's overt message of racial solidarity. McClellan may have intended to teach the importance of racial identity in this story; but in developing the characters of Joseph and Daphne, he also produced an indictment of racism that questioned much of what other writers had produced on behalf of such an identity.

Above all, McClellan exposed the meaninglessness of the issue of "choosing" to be black in a racist society. It is not simply that the choice itself is meaningless. For anyone fair enough to pass, the choice could be real and meaningful enough. (It was, to take a literary example, for Harper's Iola Leroy.) The tragedy of McClellan's story, and the aspect of the issue he emphasized, was that one should have to choose at all—that Daphne, for instance, should not be able to fulfill her relationship with Joseph. For McClellan, the matter of choice was an artifact of an irredeemably racist society, not a positive act. And it was not that McClellan was simply looking back to earlier ideals and aspirations. In stressing solidarity, he was a writer of his own time, as he was in raising the very issue of choice. It was, rather, that in creating the characters Daphne and Joseph—characters more realistic than an Iola Leroy—and in taking a less genteel view of relations between men and women, McClellan exposed a layer of feeling that intensely complicated the issues of identity and solidarity, that made those issues seem less clear-cut than they appeared in the works of more idealistic, more ideological writers.

In the way that McClellan told his story, then, he undercut any simple message of racial solidarity that one might want to take from the text by presenting racial feeling as the product of cruel, artificial social norms rather than as a matter representing some kind of transcendent racial reality. Indeed, the reality may lie more in Daphne's final delirium and in a world where God has "gone from his throne" than in the apparent success of the industrial school. This is because the hopeful future represented by separate institutions is founded, McClellan's story says, on an unnatural submission to inhuman norms. The conclusion is, thus, far from optimistic, as at least one reviewer of the period recognized. This reviewer, writing in *Alexander's Magazine*, suggested that, at some places, a reader could "discover the note of optimism, of pride in the achievements of the Negro," but that the "tendency" of McClellan's work seemed to be "a lingering on the iniquities, the shame, the horror and the cruelties to which the race was helplessly exposed in the dark days before the war"—and, he might have added, after the war too.[11] The review was to the point. In a real sense, the "optimism" of separate institutions was born, McClellan's story said, from horror and cruelty; and it was based on "achievements" made necessary by prejudice. Again, if McClellan intended to write a story affirming racial solidarity, he actually produced one that, like Dunbar's work, called into question the emotional basis of such solidarity. And more than Dunbar, McClellan also revealed strong doubts about the moral basis of that solidarity—on either side of the line.

McClellan was not the only writer to move away from an easy treatment of the literary motif of racial mixture and to reveal meanings in it that most other writers were unable or unwilling to touch upon. Such an exploration of the significance of racial mixture was a dominant characteristic of the works of three of the most prolific black writers of the late nineteenth and early twentieth centuries: Pauline Hopkins, Sutton E. Griggs, and Charles W. Chesnutt. The work of each casts new light on the tough questions of identity and assimilation, questions that few other writers explored so deeply or significantly. Their work forms an appropriate focus for any discussion of the literature of the color line at the turn of the century.

Pauline Hopkins was among the most ambitious black writers in early twentieth century America. She was, primarily, a novelist who can be placed in the familiar category of sentimental protest writers. Nevertheless, working within the confines of essentially romantic plot lines, Hopkins developed stories and characterizations that gave added dimension to black literature as it was developing in her day.

At the time Hopkins was doing her most important work, she was literary editor of the *Colored American Magazine*, from 1900 to 1904. During this period, she produced four novels—two of them serialized in *Colored American* (one under the pen name Sarah A. Allen)—and a number of articles and short stories. She also published, in 1905, a little book entitled *A Primer of Facts Pertaining to the Early Greatness of the African Race and the Possibility of Restoration by Its Descendants*, a question-and-answer book on the ancient Egyptian background of Afri-

---

11. Review of George Marion McClellan's *Old Greenbottom Inn and Other Stories*, in *Alexander's Magazine*, VI (1908), 88.

can and American blacks.[12] Fired from *Colored American* when it was taken over by Booker T. Washington, she began to do some writing for *Voice of the Negro*. After about 1905, her writing career came to an abrupt, unexplained end. She died in a fire in 1930.

Hopkins was born in Portland, Maine, in 1859, and did not take up fiction until she was forty years old. Her earliest success as a writer, however, came in 1874, when she won a temperance essay contest in Boston. This contest was sponsored by the famous black abolitionist-author William Wells Brown; and Hopkins won it with an essay filled with the main themes of genteel morality. From the late 1870s and through the 1890s, she devoted much of her time to her "Hopkins' Colored Troubadour Quartette," a concert group that performed spirituals along with some classical selections and that included other members of her family. In 1882 the Boston *Daily Globe* described Hopkins as "Boston's favorite colored soprano."[13]

Hopkins also did some writing as part of her activities with her theatrical company, creating dramatic sketches for the troupe to perform. One surviving sketch, "Peculiar Sam," gives a sense of the kind of sketches she created. It is a rather typical story of a group of slaves escaping from their plantation to Canada. Virtually all of the characters speak a heavy dialect—although the hero, Sam, loses his when he attains his freedom—and the play is filled with plantation-style humor as well as black heroism. The sketch, which was first performed in 1879, helps show not only the survival of older, abolitionist-derived forms in black writing but also something of the theatrical antecedents for a black-written dialect literature of the sort that, in little more than a decade, would make Dunbar so popular with white and black audiences alike.[14]

12. Pauline Hopkins, *A Primer of Facts Pertaining to the Early Greatness of the African Race and the Possibility of Restoration by Its Descendants—with Epilogue* (Cambridge, Mass., 1905).

13. Pauline Hopkins, "The Evils of Intemperance and Their Remedy," ms. essay, c. 1874, in Pauline Hopkins Papers, Fisk University Library Special Collections. Sample programs are in Pauline Hopkins' scrapbook in Hopkins Papers. The quotation from the Boston *Daily Globe* is also in Hopkins' scrapbook.

14. Pauline Hopkins, "Peculiar Sam; or, The Underground Railroad: A Musical Drama in Four Acts," 1879, typescript, in Hopkins Papers. See Robert C. Toll, *Blacking Up: The Minstrel Show in Nineteenth-Century America* (New York, 1974). For a fuller account of Hopkins' life, see Ann Allen Shockley, "Pauline Elizabeth Hopkins: A Biographical Excursion into Obscurity," *Phylon*, XXXIII (1972), 22–26. See also Abby Arthur Johnson and Ronald M. Johnson, "Away from Accommodation: Radical Editors and Protest Journalism," *Journal of Negro History*, LXII (1977), 325–38.

As Hopkins moved out of the theatrical world and into literary life, she helped mold the ambiguous literary consciousness of early twentieth century black American writers. As literary editor of *Colored American*, she pushed that leading secular magazine toward publishing an eclectic range of literature, including dialect writing, sentimental stories, and protest. Although Hopkins' role on the magazine cannot be precisely documented, some estimate may be drawn from the relative paucity of literary material in *Colored American* following her firing.[15]

Hopkins' encouragement of a wide range of work by black writers is important, because it helps provide a perspective on the rather narrow focus of her own writing. Although she did do some experimental writing on unusual subjects, such as spiritualism, and even did one work about a Washington street urchin, the bulk of her fiction was overwhelmingly dominated by protest, framed by stories about interracial love and racial mixture. The few critics who have written about Hopkins' work have tended to treat it as offering little more than a variation on the theme of the tragic mulatto. Such a reading is not without foundation, since Hopkins did draw heavily on that theme in several of her works. Still, she tended to treat the familiar subject of racial mixture in unfamiliar ways.[16]

Hopkins' use of racial mixture as her key focus emphasizes some of the ambiguities in black literature during this period. Some of her writing looks back to the tradition established by *Iola Leroy*, stressing the importance of racial identity. Her 1902 short story "A Test of Manhood," published under the pen name Sarah Allen, is the tale of a young man, successfully passing, whose plans are disrupted when his mother appears and he is unable to reject his race if it means disavowing his love for her. But far more revealing of Hopkins' usual focus is her rather long story published that same year, "Talma Gordon," a tale of murder and false accusations centering around the proposition that "amalgamation" must occur when two races exist in close proximity to each other—a

15. For an assessment of Hopkins' significance to the magazine, see Abby Arthur Johnson and Ronald Maberry Johnson, *Propaganda and Aesthetics: The Literary Politics of Afro-American Magazines in the Twentieth Century* (Amherst, 1979), 4–9.

16. Pauline E. Hopkins, "The Mystery Within Us," *Colored American Magazine*, I (1900), 14–18; Hopkins, "General Washington: A Christmas Story," *Colored American Magazine*, II (1900), 95–104. On Hopkins' use of the tragic mulatto theme, see Claudia Tate, "Pauline Hopkins: Our Literary Foremother," in Marjorie Pryce and Hortense J. Spillers (eds.), *Conjuring: Black Women, Fiction, and Literary Tradition* (Bloomington, Ind., 1985), 56; Mary V. Dearborn, *Pocahontas's Daughters: Gender and Ethnicity in American Culture* (New York, 1986), 142–44.

proposition dramatized by the interracial marriage of the story's protagonists. Identity is thus subordinated to profoundly assimilationist
goals, which are symbolized by the belief that all racial barriers, even
those prohibiting interracial love and marriage, will fall in a truly integrated society. This is the point of view that dominates Hopkins' work.[17]

The depth of Hopkins' assimilationism and its relation to literary
trends are shown most fully in her novel-length works. The earliest, and
the one published in book form, is *Contending Forces*, which appeared
in 1900. Hopkins set forth her purposes as a writer in a four-page
introduction, where she described herself as motivated "in an humble
way to raise the stigma of degradation from my race." Fiction, she
believed, was a peculiarly good way to do this; she wrote, "It is the
simple, homely tale, unassumingly told, which cements the bond of
brotherhood among all classes and all complexions." And she asserted,
beyond this, a special role for the black writer. Fiction could capture the
manners and morals of any community, and black writers had the responsibility to tell the truth about their people. "No one will do this for
us," Hopkins claimed. "We must ourselves faithfully portray the inmost
thoughts and feelings of the Negro with all the fire and romance which
lie dormant in our history, and, as yet, unrecognized by writers of the
Anglo-Saxon race."[18] But as her story makes clear, her call for a black
literature was one that took very seriously her own assimilationist
ideals.

Contending Forces begins on a large, wealthy North Carolina plantation. Supporting the usual critical account of Hopkins' work, it draws on
the traditional theme of the tragic mulatto. The plantation is owned by
Charles Montfort, a Bermuda planter who came to the United States
with the abolition of slavery in the English colonies; he lives there with
his beautiful wife, Grace. All would be well except that Mr. Montfort is
believed to be considering freeing his slaves. Worse, there is also a
rumor that Mrs. Montfort has Negro blood in her veins. As a result, two
dialect-speaking poor whites, notably one named Pollock, resolve to
wreak havoc on the family. They murder Charles and force Grace and
her two children, Jesse and Charles, into slavery. Grace kills herself. Her
son Charles is fortunate enough to be purchased and taken away by a

17. Pauline E. Hopkins [Sarah A. Allen], "The Test of Manhood: A Christmas Story,"
Colored American Magazine, VI (1902), 113–19; Hopkins, "Talma Gordon," *Colored
American Magazine,* VI (1902), 271–90.
18. Pauline E. Hopkins, *Contending Forces: A Romance Illustrative of Negro Life
North and South* (1900; rpr. New York, 1971), 13–14.

mineralogist, thus missing the horrors of southern slavery. Jesse is forced into bondage but, at the first opportunity, escapes to Boston.

Hopkins then shifts the scene to the late nineteenth century and to the rooming house of a responsible black Boston family consisting of Dora Smith and her two children, William Jesse Montfort Smith and Dora Grace Montfort Smith. Needless to say, the given names are significant. Will and Dora's father, Henry, died when they were children; and now the brother and sister are responsible for keeping the family going. Will has left school in order to support the family; he and Dora have the kind of devotion to family so prized by Victorian Americans.

The story revolves around the love affair between Dora and John Langley, a young mulatto who becomes the story's villain; and the one between Will and Sappho Clark, a beautiful and sophisticated quadroon lodger at the Smith's house. These affairs are complicated by the fact that John is also attracted to Sappho, who consistently rebuffs his advances. John, it seems, has an inherited tendency for wrongdoing. Indeed, his middle name is Pollock, signifying his descent from one of those poor whites who had been responsible for Mrs. Montfort's final agonies—though he is unaware of this aspect of his ancestry. At an antilynching meeting, he learns that Sappho was once a virtuous girl who had been forced into prostitution by a white uncle. This quickly becomes his trump card in his effort to win her.

John wastes little time in making his knowledge of her background known to Sappho, threatening to reveal all if she will not marry him. She refuses but, in her shame, feels she cannot marry Will either; broken, she flees to New Orleans. There, after a short stay in a convent to regain her health, she takes a job as a governess in the home of a wealthy colored widower. Dora and John also end their engagement, in her revulsion at what he has done. The story, however, ends happily. First, one Charles Montfort-Withington, an Englishman, appears. He has heard Will making a public speech and, impressed, desires to know more about the race. Needless to say, the family connection is discovered. Dora and Will are Jesse's descendants and heirs to a Montfort fortune. Dora marries a black educator of some renown, and takes her place at his side. Will, now wealthy, receives the education he deserves, attending Heidelberg University, and then returns to find Sappho, whom he locates and marries. John dies while chasing after gold in the Klondike.

Contending Forces offers, in many ways, a fairly conservative treatment of racial mixture. Not only is the fate of Mrs. Montfort much like that of the traditional tragic mulatto, but, as Howard did in his traditional work *Bond and Free*, Hopkins took pains to show how the enslaved Mrs. Montfort is more cultured than those who reduce her to bondage. At one point, she is described as, in appearance, the perfect southern belle. Hopkins also used racial mixture as a key source for irony. This is shown most clearly in the case of Sappho, a virtuous girl reduced to prostitution through white cupidity—and by a member of her own family. In addition, Dora's destiny shows the same kind of devotion to race that Harper portrayed in her racially mixed heroine Iola Leroy.

What stands out in the book, however, is that the catalyst for its happy ending does not come from any choices Hopkins' protagonists make. It comes, rather, from the choice by an Englishman, a successful white man, to acknowledge his kinship with the black Smith family. The appearance of Montfort-Withington in the lives of the Smiths creates a powerful structural contrast with the appearance of whites in the earlier Mrs. Montfort's life—the life of the tragic mulatto. The fate of Will and Dora is directly opposite to that of their ancestor, because their biological kinship with the white world—the mainstream—is openly acknowledged. Thus, unlike Harper, who turned the tragic mulatto motif upside down, but something like Boucicault in his London version of *The Octoroon,* Hopkins filled in the blank implicit in the tragic mulatto story, showing what the alternative must be to the sad fate of the victim of mixed blood.

By doing so, Hopkins added a particularly bold statement to the traditional assimilationist argument. She showed what that argument, taken seriously, must entail. Hers was not simply a reiteration of the desire to enter American life. Rather, she was taking the assimilationist argument to its logical conclusion, giving voice to a deep feeling that happiness is tied not simply to the absence of exclusion but to the open, ready inclusion of blacks in the larger society. By using racial mixture and kinship as she did in *Contending Forces*, she stressed how thoroughgoing the assumptions behind an assimilationist argument had to be.

Indeed, in one brief passage of the novel, Hopkins showed just how thoroughgoing her own assimilationism could be. In this passage, looking back over the Montfort family history, Hopkins argued that many black Americans, like Will and Dora, had profited from "the infusion of white blood, which became pretty generally distributed in the inferior black race during slavery." This "infusion," she said, "must be productive of some valuable specimens." If not meant sarcastically, the comment seems, on the surface, shocking, in line with a then-current tendency on the part of whites to explain the brilliance of, say, a Frederick Douglass or a Booker T. Washington by referring to their white ancestry. But this is not at all what Hopkins was about. John Langley too, after all, was the product of an "infusion of white blood" into black; and this had as much to do with his villainy as it did with Will and Dora's virtue, because he was the descendant of "crackers," combining "the worst features of a dominant race with an enslaved race." Far from arguing that white blood was necessary for racial improvement, Hopkins was, again, stressing the artificiality of racial barriers as such. Taking a hereditarian position, to be sure, she asserted that it was the ancestral inheritance of the individual that mattered, not simply an inheritance based on race. This is what made Will and Dora more like, say, their actual kinsman Montfort-Withington, though he was white, than like their racial "kinsman" John Langley. Hopkins' theory of "bloods" was a frank symbolization of what a bourgeois, individualistic assimilationism must entail.[19]

Contending Forces, published two years before "Talma Gordon," was not as radical as that short story, which moved beyond distant kinship to the much more controversial subject of interracial marriage. But Hopkins' next two novels, serialized in *Colored American*, did broach that subject and, roughly contemporary with "Talma Gordon," matched that story in their treatments of it. The first of these novels is "Hagar's Daughter," which appeared under the pen name Sarah Allen in 1901 and 1902. The novel begins with a version of the tragic mulatto story, as Hagar, the beautiful young wife of a southern planter named Ellis Enson, is discovered to have black ancestry. In her grief and despair, she jumps with her child from a high bridge crossing the Potomac, apparently to her death. The scene is virtually identical to a similar episode at the conclusion of William Wells Brown's *Clotel*. But Hopkins departed from the usual treatment of the tragic mulatto. Commonly, in such stories, the heroine's tragedy is a result of the sexual hypocrisy of the white man. In Hopkins' story, the element of sexual hypocrisy does not appear. Hagar decides upon suicide because Ellis has apparently died while trying to arrange for their removal to Europe, where they can continue to live openly as husband and wife, away from the prejudices of white America. Like McClellan's "Old Greenbottom Inn," Hopkins' "Hagar's

19. *Ibid.,* 86–87, 89, 90–91.

Daughter" held out the possibility of a real interracial love that triumphed over prejudice.[20]

But Hopkins also went a step further than McClellan in her treatment of interracial love. As the word *apparently* in the synopsis indicates, neither Hagar nor Ellis actually dies in the early going of the novel. After spinning a complex tale of Washington intrigue, set twenty years beyond the apparent deaths of husband and wife, Hopkins reunited them through a series of coincidences. Again, Ellis, knowing full well Hagar's background, wants her to be his wife, creating a marriage that makes race irrelevant. The only tragic sidelight is that a young white man in love with Hagar's daughter spurns the girl because of her ancestry. In the end, he sees the error of his ways; but he cannot do anything about it. She has died, the victim of a fever. Here, of course, is the tragic mulatto, but presented in a way—balanced by her parents' happiness—that displays the alternative to, rather than the inevitability of, the young girl's tragic end, an alternative that even her misguided young man has come to see.

"Hagar's Daughter" was a frank espousal of the possibility and rightness of interracial romance. It was like "Talma Gordon" in this regard, portraying a perspective consistent with but still more fully assimilationist than that of *Contending Forces*. Hopkins recognized that if racial barriers were to be represented as truly possible to overcome, then even the barrier to intermarriage had to be seen as artificial. Critic Claudia Tate has pointed out that marriage as a source of identity and stability was important in all of Hopkins' novels.[21] In "Hagar's Daughter," Hopkins used interracial marriage to encapsulate a vision of the irrelevance of racial identity in a decent world.

Hopkins similarly used interracial marriage in her third novel, "Winona," which appeared in *Colored American* in 1902.[22] Like *Contending Forces*, it features a young man and woman of mixed heritage; but the setting of this novel is the antebellum American frontier rather

20. Pauline Hopkins [Sarah A. Allen], "Hagar's Daughter," *Colored American Magazine*, II (1901), 337–52, 431–45; III (1901), 24–34, 117–28, 185–95, 262–72, 343–53, 425–35; IV (1901), 23–33, 113–24, IV (1902), 188–200, 281–91; William L. Andrews has noted that William Dean Howells used a similar device in dealing with an interracial romance; see Andrews, "Miscegenation," 18–19.

21. Tate, "Pauline Hopkins," 65.

22. Pauline E. Hopkins, "Winona: A Tale of Negro Life in the South and Southwest," *Colored American Magazine*, V (1902), 29–41, 97–110, 177–87, 257–68, 348–58, 422–31.

than turn-of-the-century Boston, and Hopkins spiced the novel with tales of frontier violence and adventure. The story features Winona and her brother, Judah, children of a white man who has become an Indian chief and his quadroon wife. Soon after the story opens, the old chief dies and the young people are befriended by an Englishman named Maxwell. Maxwell is in America searching for the heirs of Lord George Carlingford. One of these heirs he knows to be living in Missouri, but the other is now lost, and it is Maxwell's task to find him. Impressed by Winona's refinement and Judah's manliness, Maxwell decides to take them back to England to be educated. Before he can do this, however, the two young people are captured by slave catchers and cast into bondage.

The rest of the novel focuses on their efforts to escape from slavery. By coincidence, having been taken South, Winona and Judah become the slaves of Carlingford's known descendant. When Maxwell, in the performance of his own duties, discovers this, he spirits them from the plantation; and all three meet with John Brown, then conducting his war for a free Kansas. They stay on to fight until, finally, Brown makes it possible for them to get to Canada. Upon arrival, it is discovered that the old chief was the lost son of Lord George, making Winona and Judah rightful heirs to the Carlingford fortune. In England, Maxwell and Winona marry, with Lord George's blessing. Judah, appreciating the greater freedom of England, also settles there and becomes a soldier for the queen.

"Winona," because of its setting and its elements of adventure, reads almost like an antislavery novel. But, like "Hagar's Daughter," it makes much of the possibility of real, interracial love. Both Winona's father and Maxwell are like Ellis Enson in dealing humanely and properly with the women they love, despite the presence of Negro blood. Here, too, Hopkins showed the positive alternative to the protest against exclusion—the real acceptance of blacks as members of the American family. Her use of interracial marriage, and her evocation of romantic feelings underlying such marriage, allowed her to mobilize an assimilationist possibility that most writers confronted only implicitly.

Indeed, it is impossible to ignore the element of courage in the conclusions to both "Winona" and "Hagar's Daughter." Whites had long made a bugaboo of "social equality" for blacks and, especially, of the possibility of intermarriage; in fact, one angry white reader of *Colored American* complained bitterly to the magazine about Hopkins' treatment of the subject. Few blacks had responded by asserting that intermarriage was good (although, to be sure, instances of intermarriage involving prominent blacks were well known). Most had referred, instead, to the way in which strictures on intermarriage threatened the chastity of black women or had argued, defensively, that blacks had no more desire for intermarriage than did whites. One may recall Crummell's acerbic remark on the relative fidelity of black men to black women in marriage; and as critic Mary Dearborn has emphasized, there are elements of such concern in Hopkins' work.[23] But in going beyond this familiar position to dramatize the virtue—even the necessity—of intermarriage in a decent society, Hopkins revealed the depth of her assimilationism and the implications of all the genteel assimilationist writing in black literary tradition. She also illuminated the reasons that the ambivalences of turn-of-the-century black writing were so hard to resolve. The emotional underpinnings of a genuinely assimilationist view were both strong and hard to state.

Hopkins herself succumbed to those ambivalences in her final novel, "Of One Blood." In this work, she denied herself the happy, assimilationist conclusions of the other novels and began to think about the countervailing demands for racial identity. Serialized in *Colored American* during 1902 and 1903, the story dramatizes the idea that dominated Hopkins' later *Primer on African Greatness*—that American blacks were the descendants of the creators of ancient Egypt and Ethiopia.[24] Given the thrust of that idea in black thinking, the novel shows important changes in Hopkins' work as a writer. The story focuses on the career of Reuel Briggs, a Harvard medical student who is fascinated with trance states. Although he has black ancestry, Briggs is, to all intents and purposes, a white man; and he is believed to be such by his fellow students. Soon after the story opens, Reuel has a dream in which he sees a beautiful woman. Shortly thereafter, attending a concert by the Fisk Jubilee singers, he actually sees his vision. Her name is Dianthe, and she sings soprano with the group. Sometime later, after a series of strange happenings, Reuel again meets Dianthe; but this time it is at the hospital, and she appears to be dead. Recognizing her "death" as a case of suspended animation, Reuel revives her; and the two ultimately marry. Because of her earlier illness, Dianthe has forgotten her race and as-

23. Dearborn, *Pocahontas's Daughters*, 142.

24. Pauline E. Hopkins, "Of One Blood; or, The Hidden Self," *Colored American Magazine*, VI (1902), 29–40, 102–13, 191–200, 264–72, 339–48, 423–32, 492–501, 580–86, 643–47, 726–31, 802–807.

sumes herself to be white. Reuel and Dianthe, it appears, will enter society as a white physician and his wife.

Unfortunately, Reuel has a friend, Aubrey Livingston, who is aware of Dianthe's background and Reuel's as well. Arranging for Reuel to take a position as staff physician on an African archæological expedition, he seeks to seduce Dianthe and to make her his mistress. To further his scheme, he also plots to have Reuel killed in the African wilderness. Reuel escapes death and, exploring a tomb, accidentally enters a secret chamber. There he is confronted by a marvelous people, descendants of the great tribe that created ancient African civilization. Finding that he has a lily-shaped birthmark, they acknowledge him as a descendant of Cush, the founder of their tribe. Despite his American marriage to Dianthe, he is given the hand of Candace, their queen, to join her in ruling over the Cushite people. Still, he remains troubled about Dianthe. Luckily, the Cushites have preserved many ancient skills; and through them, Reuel is able to learn of Aubrey's plot and Dianthe's torment. He returns to America and tries to rescue Dianthe. And he learns that she, too, has the fabled birthmark. They are brother and sister, separated in slavery. Unfortunately, however, he is too late to rescue her; she is dead, poisoned by Aubrey. Aubrey, too, Reuel learns, has black ancestry. Not only that, he is their brother, also separated from the family during slavery. Still, Aubrey is taken prisoner by Reuel and, according to custom, is forced to commit suicide. Reuel returns to Africa, where, reunited with Queen Candace, he rules over his people, teaching them the ways of the modern world.

"Of One Blood" is a fantastic tale, one that anticipates the romantic adventures of a Saturday afternoon movie serial in its exoticism and fantastic coincidences. But however fantastic the story, Hopkins wove the cruel ironies of interracial romance into her work, using them as the key motivating factors for all her characters—and as measures of her protagonists' nobility and her villains' wickedness. It was the inability to deal with race decently that made for cruelty in Hopkins' literary world, here just as in *Contending Forces*. But Hopkins' last novel differs significantly from the first three. In the earlier works, she created fantastic denouements that envisioned a world far more humane than that of turn-of-the-century America and developed a form for race relations that was, in many ways, far ahead of its time. This novel, despite a somewhat happy ending—for Reuel, at least—offers no such view of a hopeful future. She even gave up her theory of "bloods," with its implicit individualism, in favor of a more racially structured world, as the title indicates.

This revised view of the world and the ancient African setting, taken with the novel's rather ambiguous ending, indicates that, by the end of her literary career, Hopkins was beginning to see problems in the wholehearted assimilationism of her earlier works. In its evocation of ancient Africa, "Of One Blood," along with the later *Primer*, shows a writer moving toward an appreciation of black distinctiveness, even if ancient Africa was the most assimilationist theme in the rhetoric of distinctiveness. The relatively ambiguous ending works the same way. Reuel comes out all right, but he is unable to protect Dianthe—not to mention his brother—from the corruption of a racist society. "Of One Blood" is the obverse of Hopkins' earlier novels, an indication of her awareness that her effort to escape the ambivalences of American society by turning to fantasies of interracial kinship and marriage could not be wholly effective.

Still, Hopkins was an important figure in the development of black writing in the early twentieth century. Certainly, her work helps illuminate the underlying aspiration of assimilationist goals by showing the kinds of relationships that must exist between black and white Americans in a decently ordered society, especially in a society built on genteel virtues. Hopkins was, in her first three novels, willing to say the unsayable, although she couched her words in a romantic sentimentalism that made them more hopeful than threatening.

Sutton E. Griggs is a more confusing writer of this period, in that it is not always possible to get a clear sense of his intent from his works. Even recent criticism is sharply divided on the significance and meaning of Griggs's writing. Robert Bone has found Griggs's work to display, on occasion, a "fanatical Negro nationalism" and to be, at other times, "conciliatory to the point of servility." Hugh Gloster, the most thorough student of Griggs's writing, has seen his work as an inspiration to later "New Negro" ideals of the Harlem Renaissance and to 1960s militance. Arlene Elder has stressed Griggs's focus on the black community, finding Griggs among the first black novelists to write about black concerns for a predominantly black audience, and particularly about the need for economic and political independence. Richard Yarborough, by contrast, has stressed Griggs's own ideological murkiness, finding some ties to militant ideas but stronger connections to the racial conservatism of

Booker T. Washington. There is much to recommend Yarborough's view, because it is indeed difficult to draw any clear ideology—or even any clear pattern of ideology—out of Griggs's work. One reason for this is that, more than most of the writers of this period, Griggs seems to have been especially aware of and unable to come to grips with the ambiguities that were so strong in black ideas and concerns during the late nineteenth and early twentieth centuries. As Elder has said, his novels center clearly on the "tensions and ironies" of black life at the turn of the century.[25]

Sutton Griggs was born in Texas in 1872. His father was a prominent Baptist leader in the state, and he prepared his son for a similar kind of success. Griggs attended Bishop College and Richmond Theological Seminary (now Virginia Union University) and subsequently ministered to churches in Virginia, Tennessee, and Texas. During his later career, he achieved some prominence in the National Baptist Convention, serving on its editorial board for a number of years. He was a civic activist and a popular speaker on racial matters. Charles Alexander, in a review of one of Griggs's novels, said of him: "From the standpoint of commanding eloquence, the superior of Sutton E. Griggs has not yet appeared on the American platform. With this gift of oratory, he has secured a hold upon the hearts of his race that it would be hard to estimate."[26]

It is more difficult to assess Griggs's impact on black literature. Many modern critics agree with Elder that Griggs, more than other black writers, was writing mainly for a black audience; and both William Loren Katz and Hugh Gloster have argued that Griggs probably had more black readers than did either Dunbar or Chesnutt. Griggs himself, however, complained loudly about the lack of support he received from black readers. He once sent a copy of one of his novels to Kelly Miller—a prominent black educator and writer—and received a kind reply calling it "a wonderful work" and predicting "great success." But such a response was unusual. When he later sent the novel to twenty other black leaders, none had any comments for him; and according to Griggs,

25. Robert A. Bone, *The Negro Novel in America* (Rev. ed.; New Haven, 1965), 33; Hugh M. Gloster, "Introduction" to Sutton E. Griggs, *Imperium in Imperio* (1899; rpr. New York, 1969), i; Arlene A. Elder, *The "Hindered Hand": Cultural Implications of the Early African-American Fiction* (Westport, Conn., 1978), 69, 100; Richard Alan Yarborough, "The Depiction of Blacks in the Early Afro-American Novel" (Ph.D. dissertation, Stanford University, 1980), 501.

26. Patricia Diane Watkins, "Sutton E. Griggs: The Evolution of a Propagandist" (M.A. thesis, Howard University, 1970), 1–6; Charles Alexander, "The Hindered Hand," *Alexander's Magazine*, II (August 15, 1906), 32.

sales were very poor. This, he said, was true of his other works as well. Griggs's biographer, Patricia Diane Watkins, has claimed that most of his works probably sold better than Griggs acknowledged. More significantly, however, Griggs never seems to have been part of the larger communities of black writers, either the one that revolved around the black magazines or the one that revolved around such prominent figures as Dunbar, Chesnutt, and Braithwaite. He produced his work in isolation from the main currents of black literature; and while he did rely on at least some of its most prominent conventions, his work showed eccentricities that, perhaps, his isolation produced.[27]

Griggs was the author of five novels, which he published himself between 1899 and 1908. The novels were distinguished from other black works of the period by the great importance Griggs gave to political concerns, as critics such as Bone, Elder, and Katz have noted. But underlying these concerns was Griggs's dependence on themes of racial mixture. The motif of racial mixture played an important role in each of Griggs's novels; and as was true of other writers, his own racial attitudes were strikingly shown by the role he assigned to it. Indeed, his use of that motif helps give some unity to what is otherwise a notably disparate group of books. Above all, it reveals a man whose perspective on race relations had little to do with concerns about either assimilation or identity but who, in staking out his own literary place, was unable to find a fully satisfactory strategy for responding to a deteriorating racial situation. As a result, and however political Griggs's works may have been at one level, the novels undercut politics by presenting a bleak, futile vision of American racial life.

The main lines of Griggs's use of racial mixture and of its meaning for him are most readily apparent in his novel *Overshadowed*, published in 1901. *Overshadowed* tells the story of Erma Wysong, a beautiful orphan whose mother was black and whose father, unknown, was probably white. She lives with her half-brother, John, and is in love with the handsome Astral Herndon. Erma is genteel and beautiful but suffers as a result of all the obstacles to self-improvement posed by poverty. Indeed, she must take a job as a maid to support herself and John, much to the chagrin of Negro society; and Griggs has a fine time ridiculing the

27. Gloster, "Introduction" to Griggs, *Imperium in Imperio,* ii; William Loren Katz, Review of Sutton E. Griggs's *Imperium in Imperio, Journal of Black Studies,* I (1971), 495. See also Wilson J. Moses, "Literary Garveyism: The Novels of Reverend Sutton E. Griggs," *Phylon,* XL (1979), 204–205; Sutton E. Griggs, *The Story of My Struggles* (Memphis, 1914), 191; Watkins, "Sutton E. Griggs," 8–9.

prejudices of what he presents as a not remarkably wealthy black elite.

Erma is also loved by a white man, James Lawson—son of a former governor—who desires to make her his mistress. In his quest, he seeks the help of Dolly Smith, a young mulatto woman of ill repute. Dolly agrees to help, though she hates both the young man and his father; but in the process, it is revealed that the former governor was Erma's father as well and that Dolly is Erma's aunt. In her chagrin, Dolly kills herself; and the young Lawson winds up in prison, framed by Dolly for forgery.

In the meantime, things have not gone well for John. Fired from a job because of racist union policies, John kills the "Master Workman" who is president of the union. He escapes but finally is persuaded to turn himself in. He does and is tried and sentenced to death.

At this point, Griggs gives the novel a fantastic twist. Mrs. Turner, one of the leading black socialites, has decided that many racial problems could be eased if white leaders could learn about the gentility of middle-class black Americans; accordingly, she proposes a number of social hours involving some state legislators and a few young black women of virtue and refinement. The Speaker of the House, Lanier, agrees; and such an arrangement is made. However, at least a few of the legislators are typical white men, who see no virtue in black women, and one of the young ladies is dishonored. Speaker Lanier, extremely angered, devises a scheme whereby the offending legislator will take John Wysong's place on the gallows. The scheme works; and although John is not freed, he is allowed to serve a term in prison—rejecting, as an alternative, emigration to Africa.

By this time, Erma and Astral have decided to get married, despite some opposition from "society." The wedding occurs; and Astral, Jr., is born to the couple. All does not, however, end well. One evening, John returns from prison, a broken man, and dies as Erma answers the door. Erma, overcome, also dies. Astral is disconsolate. Speaker Lanier comes forward to encourage Astral to work toward a better world. Astral, however, cannot be persuaded. Taking his son with him, he buries the bodies of Erma and John at sea and proclaims himself "a citizen of the ocean," ordaining that such a title shall also extend to his progeny "until such time as the shadows which now envelop the darker races in all lands shall have passed away, away and away!" Griggs tried to conclude the novel optimistically, with a prediction that Astral Herndon, Jr., will, in fact, return to bring a new world for the Negro—indeed, that he is ordained by God to do so; but the real message of the novel appears earlier, at the inquest into Erma's death, when Griggs described the close of the inquest by saying, "The last of the official dealings of the Anglo-Saxons with Erma were over." Although blacks might find a few white allies, such as Speaker Lanier, white society itself is simply oppressive. The main characters in this book find relief only in death or escape. Griggs made his own pessimism clear in a brief "proem," where he declared, "*Overshadowed* does not point the way out of the dungeon which it describes, but it clearly indicates the task before the reformer when he comes."[28]

Viewing American society as a "dungeon" and describing Erma's death as a release from being dealt with by "the Anglo-Saxons," Griggs framed his presentation of American race relations in a way that rendered irrelevant any questions of assimilation or identity. For Griggs, the real issue was the active role of racism in black life. The problem was the way in which whites, spurred by racism, interfered with the lives of black people. Whites could not, he suggested, leave black people alone. They had to "deal with" black Americans; they had to make American society like a prison for blacks, a prison characterized by a constant effort to rule the inmates' lives.

The motif of racial mixture serves as a powerful device for getting this point across. In *Overshadowed*, Griggs used racial mixture to show the unremitting, corrupt demands white Americans made on black people. Lawson, seeing Erma, looks upon her only as a potential mistress, causing tragedy all around. An attempt to create goodwill between the races, arranged with the best of intentions, is used by white men to gratify their passions. Griggs's motif also showed the ineffectuality of even those few whites of goodwill, such as Speaker Lanier, in the face of usual white behavior. In other words, racism, for Griggs, involved more than the exclusion of black people from American life—a conception in terms of which notions such as assimilation and even racial solidarity had meaning. Racism involved, rather, an active conflict in which whites were determined to prove that they had the upper hand. The only real sources for satisfaction in such a world lay in revenge—such as that visited on young Lawson or the errant legislator—or escape, either in death or in becoming "a citizen of the ocean." In *Overshadowed*, Griggs made racial mixture a metaphor for the sources of a deep despair.

Such an understanding of racism, and the use of racial mixture to characterize it, was important in Griggs's other novels as well, although

28. Sutton E. Griggs, *Overshadowed* (1901; rpr. New York, 1973), 217, 209, 8.

not always as clearly so as in *Overshadowed*. In *The Hindered Hand* (1905), for example, Griggs appears to have written a novel that conforms, for the most part, to the models favored by other black writers. The book is, in part, a debate between two characters, Ensal Ellwood and Earl Bluefield. Ensal speaks for a conservative approach to racial questions. Earl is more militant, even claiming admiration for the Indians, who opted for death over submission to the white world. Earl remains hopeful throughout the book and, indeed, by the end has devised a plan that he believes will solve the race problem, a Washingtonian plan that apparently has Griggs's approval. But also deeply involved in matters are two young women of mixed race—Tiara, who values her black identity, and Eunice, who seeks to pass. Tiara's fate is a happy one, as, marrying Ensal, she looks forward to a bright future. Eunice's is sadder, however, and takes Griggs far from the common sentiments found in the works of, say, Ruth Todd or J. McHenry Jones. Proved to be of black ancestry, Eunice is assigned by a court to the black race. She promptly goes mad.

It is important to focus on Eunice's fate, because this element of the story undercuts any optimism Earl's plan might be intended to inspire. Griggs did not draw the obvious lesson from Eunice's madness, that passing is a bad thing. He did not follow Harper and others in using her, in contrast to Tiara, as an object lesson on behalf of racial solidarity. Indeed, though Eunice is an unsympathetic character, Griggs presented her madness as an understandable response to her circumstances. This is shown by a concluding passage to the novel. At the book's close, with Ensal and Tiara married and contemplating the future, Griggs remarked that they are prepared to develop a life for themselves in Africa "should the demented Eunice prove a wiser prophet than the hopeful, irrepressible Earl."[29]

This remark places *The Hindered Hand* in precisely the same ideological framework as *Overshadowed*—as a novel concerned about the possibilities of achieving a satisfying life as a black man or woman in a white racist society. Although Griggs did not directly address the issue of dealing with whites in *The Hindered Hand*, it is certainly at the heart of Eunice's problems. Like Erma, Eunice can trace her very existence to a white man's lust. Trying to escape racism by passing, she must confront a white society determined to make her accept her ancestry.

---

29. Sutton E. Griggs, *The Hindered Hand; or, The Reign of the Repressionist* (1905; rpr. Miami, 1969), 298.

Eunice goes mad, at one level, because she knows how much black people must suffer in America and does not have the strength to face it. But, at another level, that of prophecy, Eunice's madness is much like Astral's decision to become "a citizen of the ocean." It is a justifiable effort to do the only thing possible, given unremitting racism—to escape from American life altogether. Even the courageous Ensal and Tiara keep a new life in Africa in their sights.

The point is important, because it reflects on the more overtly ideological elements of the novel, on its presentation of Earl's "plan" for solving America's race problem. It even reflects on Griggs himself, given his other life as an orator and polemicist. Griggs understood that it was one thing to develop strategies for overcoming racism in American life and another to see real, dramatic possibilities for those strategies. Writers such as Harper and Hopkins could see possibilities for confronting racism, because they viewed it as something consisting primarily of barriers to be met and, ultimately, overcome. Because of the active role that Griggs assigned to racism, he saw it as something other than a barrier. Eunice might prove a better prophet than Earl, simply because Griggs had a sense that the issue was, in the final analysis, out of Earl's hands. Earl's plan for solving the race problem might be excellent, but white people might prevent its ever having any effect.

Griggs was, then, of two minds—at least as a novelist. Able to present, as in Earl's plan, a cogent summary of prevailing ideological trends—and *The Hindered Hand* was not the only novel in which he did this, for a lengthy, similar plan took up a great part of his 1902 *Unfettered*—he dramatized a world demanding desperation and escape. It was a world of alienation, even to the point of madness, and of men and women ultimately aware of their inability to control their own destinies, however well conceived their "plans." Griggs also took a fairly conservative Washingtonian position in his oratory and polemical writing. It may not be too much to suggest that his fiction revealed doubts that he was not wholly prepared to confront directly.

This sense of uncertainty powerfully informed Griggs's first and best-known novel, *Imperium in Imperio*, published in 1899. This is the story of the birth and death of a black revolutionary movement, the "Imperium"; it is filled with political discourse and is tragic in its ending. The novel has often been read as an early-day nationalist tract; but as Richard Yarborough has said, Griggs's sentiments were not nearly so clear.[30]

30. Yarborough, "Depiction of Blacks," 487–88.

Griggs often made a good case for racial separation as the novel proceeded, usually on the ground that the United States was irredeemably racist and that black people would find salvation only in violent change or martyrdom. But he also showed great sympathy for more moderate black characters, those who believed that such sentiments were contrary to any cause "for mankind, for humanity, for civilization." As Jane Campbell has stressed, Griggs did not clearly endorse either position. But in light of his other works, there may have been reason for his apparent ambiguity. Rather than taking sides, one may suggest, Griggs was doing the same thing in *Imperium in Imperio* that he would later do in such novels of racial mixture as *Overshadowed* and *The Hindered Hand*. He was stressing the desperate condition of black Americans and the lack of clear strategies for change that had a chance of success.[31]

Interestingly, though *Imperium in Imperio* is not focused on issues of racial mixture, Griggs nevertheless drew on the motif in two episodes to underline his message of desperation. The novel features two main characters, Belton Piedmont and Bernard Belgrave, the latter the illegitimate son of a white political leader. Belgrave confronts racial mixture not only in himself but in his love for Viola Martin, a beautiful, dark-skinned young woman. Looking toward marriage, Viola kills herself rather than take the mulatto Belgrave, out of a belief that racial "intermingling" is slowly destroying the race. As Richard Yarborough has stressed, Belgrave does not necessarily accept the idea. More significantly, however, the experience starts him on the road to a separatist revolution.[32]

One may see why this happens when one reads about Belgrave's experience in light of Piedmont's own confrontation with racial mixture and in light of Griggs's other work. Piedmont, himself dark, falls in love with the light-skinned Antoinette Nermal. They marry and have a child, but the infant is "white" in appearance. Shocked and assuming the worst, Belton decides to devote his life to the race, ultimately assuming leadership of the separatist "Imperium."

The two characters are, as Yarborough says, different from each other;[33] but in one crucial respect, their experiences are the same. Each is brought to a strong realization of racism's force by an experience

31. Griggs, *Imperium in Imperio*, 265; Jane Campbell, *Mythic Black Fiction: The Transformation of History* (Knoxville, 1986), 51.
32. Yarborough, "Depiction of Blacks," 480.
33. *Ibid.*, 480–82.

with the complications of apparent racial mixture (Antoinette's child "darkens" and is identified as Belton's own). Each is led for the first time to see, through an understanding of the implications of racial mixture, the power of a white presence in black American life and the inescapability of that presence in the context of American society. And this, of course, is a familiar story in Griggs's work, dominating both *Overshadowed* and *The Hindered Hand*, as well as *Imperium in Imperio*. Polemicist that he was, Griggs wrote novels that were significant chiefly because they undercut polemic and ideology. They did this because of Griggs's own powerful dramatic awareness of racism as an active force, purposefully interjected into every part of black life. As with Astral's taking to the sea and Eunice's madness, the Imperium's significance lay in its desperate character. Griggs did not have to take sides.

To be sure, Griggs was not always so pessimistic. Two of his novels, the 1902 *Unfettered* and the 1908 *Pointing the Way*, actually strike an optimistic note, and in fairly traditional terms. But when Griggs moved away from traditional plots and characterizations, when he dealt in an original way with the issues raised by the nature of American race relations, he stood out as by far the most troubled novelist of this period, presenting American racism as threatening to both the social fabric and the black psyche. The ambivalences and tensions for black literature at the turn of the century were harsh and profound. Griggs came closer than any other writer to giving them a direct, if problematic, articulation.

If Sutton Griggs dramatized the desperation produced by a racist society, Charles Chesnutt captured the feelings underlying the confrontation with race itself. Acutely aware of the power of racism in American life, he was also faithful to an assimilationist morality of race relations. He knew the tensions inherent in his assimilationist faith, and he was especially skillful at using the motif of racial mixture to explore those tensions.

Chesnutt was a prolific writer. During his career, he published three novels, all on racial themes; two collections of short stories, including one composed of dialect pieces; and a biography of Frederick Douglass. In addition, he published a great deal of short fiction in periodicals ranging from such popular short story publications as *Family Fiction* and *Puck* to such major American magazines as *Atlantic* and *Century*. He had little to do with the black periodicals of the period, although two of his stories appeared in *Southern Workman*, a white-edited journal from the Hampton Institute. Not until W. E. B. Du Bois founded *Crisis* as an organ for the NAACP would Chesnutt deal seriously with black journals, and then only in the twilight of his literary career.

Chesnutt had close contacts with the American literary elite. He corresponded extensively with George Washington Cable, the Louisiana author, and with Walter Hines Page, the North Carolina–born editor of *Atlantic*. He also knew William Dean Howells and, like Dunbar, received great support from him. Moreover, he was well acquainted with the black leaders of his day; he was particularly close to Booker T. Washington—close enough, in fact, to be candid about his strong disagreement with Washington's philosophy while still maintaining their friendship.

Chesnutt was extremely light in complexion. Du Bois once described him as one of "that group of white folk who because of a more or less remote Negro ancestor identified himself voluntarily with the darker group."[34] Indeed, the issue of Chesnutt's race was of some interest, as, during the earliest part of his literary career, the public was largely unaware that he was a "black" writer. Knowledge of his race did not become general until well into the 1890s, when he had already achieved some fame. Moreover, a substantial body of his earliest writing and of his short fiction is essentially "raceless," focusing on other matters.

A writer for the New York *Age*, comparing Chesnutt and Dunbar, noted this quality in Chesnutt's work. "Dunbar thinks and writes as an American black man, for the most part, and there is always present in his work the melancholy note and the tropical profusion which are a part of the African nature, as far as I understand it," the *Age*'s writer commented. But Chesnutt, the writer continued, "thinks and writes more as an American, from the broad standpoint of country rather than of race." Comparing two of the authors' more noted works, the writer concluded, "In 'The Marrow of Tradition,' for instance, it would not be easy to tell that Mr. Chesnutt is an Afro-American by any bias disclosed in his work, while a white man could not have written Dunbar's 'Sport of the Gods' simply because he could not feel and think in the language of that book." Manifesting the usual ambivalence about black distinctiveness, however, the *Age*'s writer predicted for Chesnutt "a higher and more

34. Sylvia Lyons Render, "Introduction" to Charles W. Chesnutt, *The Short Fiction of Charles W. Chesnutt* (Washington, D.C., 1981), 30.

permanent place in prose writing than Dunbar will have in poetic writing."[35]

The *Age*'s commentary points to the ambiguous place Chesnutt occupies in black literary tradition. One measure of this ambiguity is that, although his books were quite favorably reviewed in the black press, he never received the space given to Dunbar, despite the comments in the *Age*. Reviews in the white press were not only positive but showed a general familiarity with his work.[36] In addition, despite his prominence, Chesnutt's influence on black writing is hard to assess. A major writer, he had important publications antedating those of Dunbar. Indeed, his work saw print beginning in the mid-1880s, before Dunbar's career had started. More significantly, by the late 1880s and early 1890s, Chesnutt was an important contributor to the white-dominated form of American dialect writing—the plantation tradition—upon which Dunbar based his early career. But there is no real evidence that Chesnutt exerted any direct influence on younger writers, or on others, at least not in the early part of his career.

At the same time, much of Chesnutt's work did fit squarely into black literary tradition. His dialect and local color fiction helped redeem the image of folk Negroes and was, like that of other writers, clearly based on folk traditions. He also wrote a great deal of protest fiction and drew on themes, characterizations, and plots that were already established in black writing. Indeed, much of his work was dominated by the motif that was especially popular at the turn of the century, the motif of racial mixture. His work was, thus, both part of and removed from the main currents of black American literature during his day.

One can understand the lack of clarity in Chesnutt's relationship to black literary tradition in terms of his own background and experiences. These gave him an uncommon perspective both on the color line and on the purposes and needs of black American writing.

Chesnutt was born in Cleveland in 1858. His parents were free Negroes from North Carolina who decided to try to make a better life for themselves in the North. At the close of the Civil War, the family moved back to North Carolina, to Fayetteville, where Chesnutt's father sought to help his own father begin a grocery business. Young Charles did odd jobs and attended school until, in 1873, he became an assistant to a black educator in Charlotte. From this position, he was able to move

35. New York *Age*, July 20, 1905.
36. Render, "Introduction" to Chesnutt, *Short Fiction,* 50.

George Marion McClellan.

From Daniel Wallace Culp (ed.), *Twentieth-Century Negro Literature* (1902).

Pauline E. Hopkins.

From *Colored American Magazine*, III (May, 1901), 52.

Sutton Griggs.

Frontispiece from *Alexander's Magazine*, II (August 15, 1906).

Charles W. Chesnutt.

Courtesy of Moorland-Spingarn Research Center, Howard University.

Joseph Seamon Cotter.

Frontispiece from *Links of Friendship* (Louisville, 1898).

Angelina Weld Grimké.
Courtesy of Moorland-Spingarn Research Center,
Howard University.

W. E. B. Du Bois.
Courtesy of Moorland-Spingarn Research Center,
Howard University.

Benjamin Brawley.

Courtesy of Moorland-Spingarn Research Center, Howard
University.

Walter Everette Hawkins.

Frontispiece from *Chords and Discords*
(Washington, D.C., 1909).

James Weldon Johnson.
Courtesy of Moorland-Spingarn Research Center, Howard University.

up through the ranks as a teacher until he became principal of a Fayette-ville school. He also became a voracious reader—a lover of the classics and a knowledgeable reader of contemporary literature as well.[37]

Life in North Carolina was not, however, pleasant for an intelligent, well-read young black man. According to his leading biographer, William L. Andrews, Chesnutt felt alienated from the black people he knew in rural North Carolina, and he chafed against the restrictions placed on blacks in white southern society. The situation was aggra-vated after he began to have a family of his own. In his journal, he wrote: "I get more and more tired of the South. I pine for civilization and 'equality.'" He felt a responsibility to work among his people but won-dered if he could not serve the race better "in some more congenial occupation." And he added, "I shudder to think of exposing my children to the social and intellectual proscription to which I have been a vic-tim." By 1883, Chesnutt had his fill of North Carolina; and after a brief stay in New York, he and his family settled in Cleveland.[38]

In Cleveland, Chesnutt worked as a clerk for several years, during which time he also read law. In 1887 he passed the Ohio bar and set up a legal stenography service, which was a great success. According to the Chesnutt scholar Sylvia Lyons Render, Chesnutt was, for a time, the wealthiest Negro in the city. He and his family were also active in some of the major social groups in Cleveland; and by 1910, he was even accepted into the Rowfant Club, an organization of men interested in fine books and printing—an organization that had been, prior to Chesnutt's joining it, exclusively white. Throughout his life, Chesnutt was an active proponent of racial justice, a role acknowledged in 1928, when he was awarded the NAACP's Spingarn medal, that organization's highest honor.[39]

Joel Williamson has described the complexities of Chesnutt's life fully and well. Despite a career as a racial activist, Chesnutt was never committed to a distinctive black identity. His alienation from black

37. William L. Andrews, *The Literary Career of Charles W. Chesnutt* (Baton Rouge, 1980), 2–4.

38. *Ibid.,* 7; Charles W. Chesnutt, Journal and Notebook, January, 1881, p. 37, in Charles W. Chesnutt Papers, Fisk University Library Special Collections.

39. Render, "Introduction" to Chesnutt, *Short Fiction,* 10–11. For Chesnutt's biogra-phy, see, in addition to Andrews' *Literary Career,* Helen M. Chesnutt, *Charles Waddell Chesnutt: Pioneer of the Color Line* (Chapel Hill, N.C., 1952); J. Noel Heermance, *Charles W. Chesnutt: America's First Great Black Novelist* (Hamden, Conn., 1974); Frances Richardson Keller, *An American Crusade: The Life of Charles Waddell Chesnutt* (Provo, Utah, 1978).

North Carolinians was striking. He certainly felt his own superiority to most black people around him. As a teenager, in fact, he actually thought of passing over the color line to live as white. As Williamson has shown, Chesnutt wanted, above all, to be part of the American elite—an elite that happened to be white rather than black.[40] Chesnutt's orientation toward the elite also strongly figured in his approach to dominant black literary themes. Most significantly, Chesnutt could not, like other writers, find refuge for himself in any notions of racial identity that implied at least some withdrawal from the larger society. Devoted to the cause of racial justice, he was, at the same time, a thoroughgoing assimilationist.

Chesnutt's assimilationism was quite radical. Like Pauline Hopkins, Chesnutt believed that the logical conclusion to any hope for complete racial equality lay, ultimately, in the creation of a society in which all racial barriers, including barriers to kinship and marriage, were removed. Indeed, it would be no exaggeration to say that Chesnutt believed that the ultimate solution to the race problem lay in amalgamation, in the gradual disappearance of the physical tokens of race. In a talk entitled "The Future American," given in 1900, he made this point quite clearly, arguing that the process had already begun and that "the formation of a uniform type out of our present racial elements will take place within a measurably near period." In a 1905 address to the Boston Literary and Historical Association, he made a similar point. According to a black reporter, Chesnutt "frankly vilipended the doctrine of 'race pride' and 'race integrity,' which is so uniformly preached to us, and urged amalgamation as the solution of the race problem."[41]

At the heart of Chesnutt's racial ideas was his sense of the arbitrariness of racial distinctions, an arbitrariness that his own identification as "black" helped him appreciate. He objected to a celebration of racial identity, because, for him, race should have no real meaning, in either biological or social terms. This point of view was enhanced for Chesnutt by his recognition of the absurdity of racial distinctions in a society already characterized by racial mixture. He had certainly seen this in his own case, especially since his appearance was so nearly white; and he consistently criticized a system in which, as he bitterly remarked, the "words of the negro song 'All Coons Look Alike to Me'" seemed to be a

40. Joel Williamson, *The Crucible of Race: Black-White Relations in the American South Since Emancipation* (New York, 1984), 62, 65–66.

41. Charles W. Chesnutt, "The Future American," 1900, typescript, in Chesnutt Papers; New York *Age*, July 20, 1905.

guiding principle, in which an "educated man or woman, no matter what his character and ability may be, who has one-sixteenth, or one-thirty-second, or one sixty-fourth part of African blood is counted a negro and is debarred from the privileges of a white man or woman." As early as 1889, Chesnutt produced an essay—which was greatly admired by Cable—entitled "What Is a White Man," in which he vilified southern laws governing racial identity. In 1909, when a well-meaning southern bishop sent him a book defending southern racial policies, Chesnutt responded by both rejecting the bishop's views and expessing his own sense of what the future should hold. He remarked, "If the Creator had intended to prevent the inter-mixture of races, he might in His infinite wisdom have accomplished this purpose by a very simple method, as he has by the physiological laws which prevent the confusion of genera in the lower animals." Like Hopkins, then, Chesnutt did not shy away from the opinion that real human equality meant that all racial barriers between individuals were wrong and that no decent relationship between black and white Americans should be taboo. He knew, at the same time, though, how rigid racial barriers were.[42]

An understanding of Chesnutt's general ideas about race is important, because these views framed the kind of literature he produced and account for the fact that racial mixture represented a major literary motif in his work. For Chesnutt, the key point to be made was that arbitrary racial distinctions served to undermine all that was good and proper in human relations. Somewhat like George Marion McClellan, he used racial mixture as a dramatic device to show how unnatural and tragic such distinctions could be.

The work in which Chesnutt most fully explored the literary motif of racial mixture was his first novel, *The House Behind the Cedars*, published in 1900. The novel was based on the theme of the tragic mulatto; and as Arlene Elder has noted, it departed very little from familiar presentations of that theme.[43] But the ways in which it did so are important and do much to illuminate Chesnutt's ideas. In this novel, Chesnutt dealt not only with the absurdity of race and the problems racial distinctions caused but also with the more explosive issue of

42. In Pauline Carrington Bouve, "An Aboriginal Author: The Work and Personality of Charles W. Chesnutt," Boston *Evening Transcript*, August 23, 1897, clipping, in Archibald H. Grimké Papers, Manuscript Division, The Moorland-Spingarn Research Center, Howard University; Charles W. Chesnutt, Scrapbook II, Miscellaneous Writings, 1900–1909, George Washington Cable to Charles W. Chesnutt, June 12, 1889, Charles W. Chesnutt to William Brown, November 7, 1909, in Chesnutt Papers.

43. Elder, *"Hindered Hand,"* 174.

passing. Both of his main characters move over into white society—at least for a time. Chesnutt did not condemn the effort to pass; nor did he, like Griggs, explore the political implications of such an effort. Instead, Chesnutt used passing in a way that dramatized the confrontation between his assimilationist hopes for American race relations and his belief that racial barriers could not be easily assaulted in a society dominated by prejudice.

The House Behind the Cedars was a long time in the making. It began its life as a rather long story and went through at least five manuscript versions before it was finally accepted for publication. Indeed, Chesnutt's friend George Washington Cable began working it over as early as 1889, and it was first rejected as a story in 1890. Critic Robert P. Sedlak has followed the evolution of the novel and has shown it to be an important document in Chesnutt's growing understanding of his role as a black writer; the story moved from one of a love triangle to one of a social novel and from an attack on internal color prejudice to an indictment of racism as such.[44]

The House Behind the Cedars is the story of Rena Walden, a beautiful, fair-skinned young woman living in North Carolina. One morning, she and her mother are visited by an elegant white man, who reveals that he is, in fact, not white but Rena's brother. He is passing and has become an established lawyer in South Carolina. He urges Rena to join him there and to make her way into white society. With some trepidation, she agrees to do so. There, as the sister of a wealthy lawyer, and under the name Rowena Warwick, she quickly becomes a darling of South Carolina society, falling in love with George Tryon, one of the social leaders. They become engaged. Understandably, the engagement is difficult for Rena, because she knows her background may be discovered. Her thoughts summarize Chesnutt's own sense of the artificial, tragic power of race. "He says he loves me," Rena thinks. "He *does* love me. Would he love me if he knew? . . . I think a man might love me for myself . . . and if he loved me truly, that he would marry me."[45] But Rena cannot really convince herself that this is true. Where race is concerned, she understands, love loses its meaning.

44. George Washington Cable to Charles W. Chesnutt, September 25, 1889, Charles W. Chesnutt to George Washington Cable, June 5, 1890, in Chesnutt Papers; Robert P. Sedlack, "The Evolution of Charles Chesnutt's *The House Behind the Cedars*," *CLA Journal*, XIX (1975), 127, 131.

45. Charles W. Chesnutt, *The House Behind the Cedars* (1900; rpr. Ridgewood, N.J., 1968), 75–76.

And, needless to say, Tryon does discover Rena's secret. He promises not to reveal it but also declares the marriage off. Rena returns to North Carolina, pledged to live as black and to become a teacher. Her mother, Molly, tries to fix her up with a prosperous farmer and former Reconstruction legislator, Jeff Wain, who has little going for him other than a light complexion. At the same time, Rena is deeply loved by Frank Fowler, a dark-skinned and industrious, but poor, neighbor who is wholly unacceptable to Molly. Indeed, Fowler loved Rena before her South Carolina adventure and was even aware of her effort to cross the color line. Rena's teaching job takes her to Wain's home.

William Andrews has noted that Chesnutt intended Tryon to be not a villain but a man entrapped by a wicked system;[46] and, indeed, Tryon cannot escape his love for the beautiful Rena. Accidentally encountering her on a country road, he feels his love rekindled. He has acquired a new fiancée, but the chance meeting forces him to realize the strength of his love for Rena, despite racial taboos. Rena's immediate problem is with Wain. Wain's intentions are anything but honorable; and after one attempted rape, she learns to fear him.

Finally, walking home one night, Rena reaches an intersection of two paths. Coming toward her down one is Tryon; down the other, Wain. Overwrought, she flees into the woods and falls in the underbrush. She is found, but the strain is too great. She is seriously ill and out of her head. The next morning, she again flees into the woods. Finally, she is discovered, insane, by Frank Fowler. She is delirious and proclaiming her hatred of Wain and her love for Tryon. Fowler takes her home; and on her deathbed, she realizes that he "loved me best of them all."[47] Tryon arrives at Rena's door, but he is too late.

The ending is melodramatic, as a number of critics have noted. There is irony in Tryon's belated arrival—he is ready to declare his love when it is too late for his love to have any meaning. One may see in it, too, Chesnutt's effort to show his white readers that racism can hurt whites as much as blacks in the barriers it sets up between individuals. One can even see a criticism of the internal color line in Rena's belated recognition of Frank Fowler's love and devotion.

But it is the relationship with Frank Fowler—a sympathetic character in love with Rena—that helps reveal the real heart of the novel, making it more than a story of a tragic mulatto and making it especially

46. William L. Andrews, "Chesnutt's Patesville: The Presence and Influence of the Past in *The House Behind the Cedars,*" *CLA Journal,* XV (1972), 285.
47. Chesnutt, *House Behind the Cedars,* 293.

revealing of Chesnutt's own ideals and aspirations. Fowler's role in the novel moves one to focus on the question of racial identity and on the kind of alternative to passing that such an identity offers to Rena. On this subject, Chesnutt's novel is extremely clear. In so many ways, the pull of racial identity on Rena constitutes a pull downward, as Chesnutt tells the story. Certainly her career as a rural schoolteacher is a step down from the place she had, at least temporarily, as a belle of South Carolina society. And if Chesnutt objects to Molly Walden's color-conscious rejection of Fowler, this does not lead him to present Fowler as a better candidate than Tryon for Rena's hand. Rena and Tryon do love each other. The tragedy in the story is that racial barriers for which neither is responsible prevent them from ever becoming decently married.

Thus, like George Marion McClellan in "Old Greenbottom Inn," Chesnutt wrote, in *The House Behind the Cedars*, a story about choices and about the effect of racial barriers on choices, making his point as he portrayed the impossible position in which Rena and Tryon find themselves, given southern racial life. Like Daphne and Cramer, they have a love that is not supposed to be fulfilled; and, indeed, it cannot be fulfilled. The only "reasonable" choice for Rena is Frank Fowler; but as even Fowler understands, he is not really in Rena's league, socially and culturally. For her to love him would make even less dramatic sense than would Daphne's love for John Henry—who was at least a college man.

But an even more crucial comparison is with Hopkins, who likewise used, in her own way, the theme of the tragic mulatto. Like Hopkins, Chesnutt understood that assimilation involved more than the absence of exclusion; and in his treatment of Tryon, as opposed to Rena, he portrayed a realization that accepting black people on the basis of a genuine indifference to race, not simply ceasing to exclude blacks from significant areas of social life, was the real obligation of white society. Unlike Hopkins, however, Chesnutt confronted the issue of black identity as well as that of assimilation. He addressed, that is, what it actually meant to be black in the context of assimilationist ideals. And this effort grew directly out of his own experiences and desires.

Chesnutt, with his elitism—and from his own experiences as a rural schoolteacher—keenly felt the limitations racism imposed upon him; and he dramatized his feelings in the kinds of dilemmas he created for Rena. Passing was no solution, as he himself knew, because to pass was to accept, tacitly, the existence of the color line, a line that was inimical to human aspirations. As long as that line existed, no one—and especially no one with black ancestry—could be really free. Nor, however, was racial solidarity an answer, because it too involved the acceptance of conditions that should be morally intolerable. As a result, holding to his assimilationist ideals and maintaining an assessment of American race relations that emphasized the strength and pervasiveness of racism, Chesnutt produced a novel that, because it recognized the overarching reality of being black, was notably pessimistic, untempered by the fantasies of a Hopkins or even the strained optimism of a McClellan. Indeed, he was as pessimistic as Griggs, though on somewhat different grounds. Where Griggs was concerned mainly with the corporate evil of racism, Chesnutt saw tragedy in racism's destruction of the individual soul.

The House Behind the Cedars was not Chesnutt's only work to use the motif of racial mixture to treat racism in this way. A no less powerful example of such a treatment was his short story "The Sheriff's Children." This story first appeared in the New York *Independent* in 1889 and was later reprinted in a volume of short stories entitled *The Wife of His Youth* (1899), a volume that focused on the color line. In this story, Chesnutt brought together the motifs of lynching, racism, and racial mixture in a way that clearly anticipated his first novel. Set in a little North Carolina town, the story begins with the arrest of a mulatto stranger for murder. Not surprisingly, a lynch mob forms shortly after the arrest. The sheriff is warned and goes to protect the prisoner. In his first confrontation with the mob, the sheriff is able to hold his own, at least for a time. But going into the jail, he loses his revolver to the prisoner, who wishes to escape. The prisoner protests his innocence, arguing that he has no chance to leave the town alive. As they talk, the sheriff learns who the prisoner is. He is a son the sheriff himself had fathered by a slave—a slave the sheriff later sold with the child. The prisoner starts to shoot the sheriff but is himself shot by the sheriff's white daughter. As the young man lies wounded, the sheriff thinks of what he might have done to make his son's life better. He pledges himself to secure an acquittal and to make a new life for his son. Going to the jail the following morning, however, he discovers that the wounded man has bled to death during the night. When his son had needed him first, and most, the man who would become sheriff had been unwilling to accept even a semblance of fatherhood. Now that the sheriff has decided to be a father, the son is unable to receive his attentions. The tragic effects of racism are set forth in a way that greatly resembles Chesnutt's exploration of those effects in *The House Behind the Cedars*.

In all the stories in *The Wife of His Youth* Chesnutt set forth a picture of racism as something psychologically as well as socially brutal. In "The Sheriff's Children," he was able to dramatize that psychological cruelty through a tale of parental indifference and fratricide, both of which were rendered doubly cruel because both were determined by a socially induced blindness to family relationships and their meaning—or, in the case of the fratricide, even to their reality. This was the kind of perversion of human relationships that Chesnutt bitterly opposed, the kind of distortion that went most fully against his own sentiments. It made "The Sheriff's Children" a particularly important statement of his views and of his effort to show his readers the brutal reality of a society that needed to change.

To be sure, not all of Chesnutt's fiction on the color line was so clearly pessimistic. In "The Wife of His Youth," for example, Chesnutt actually hewed fairly close to more traditional black literary lines. The story is about Mr. Ryder, the black social lion of a northern city. He is extremely cultured and extremely light skinned. Indeed, he is the dean of the local "Blue Vein Society," so called because anyone acceptable for membership has to be sufficiently light that one can see the "blue veins." Mr. Ryder is without prejudice, or so he claims; but he adds: "We people of mixed blood are ground between the upper and the nether millstone. Our fate lies between absorption by the white race and extinction in the black."[48] Accordingly, he proposes a ball to encourage a feeling of exclusiveness among the Blue Veiners.

Preparations begin for the ball, which is to be as elegant as one might expect. Suddenly, a small, old, and very black woman appears at Ryder's door. She tells her story, but Ryder appears at first not to recognize her. As it turns out, however, he knows her well. During slavery, she was the "wife of his youth." At the ball, and before the assembled multitude, he acknowledges her.

The story makes a comment on the color line within the black community—a line that could produce such a group as a blue vein society. But if, on the surface, the story is a fairly traditional one of racial solidarity—a solidarity vindicated by Ryder's honesty—when read in the light of Chesnutt's other work and in light of his own strong racial ideas, it takes on a very different meaning. Normal human relationships, Chesnutt so often showed, were made unnaturally difficult by the

48. Charles W. Chesnutt, *The Wife of His Youth and Other Stories of the Color Line* (1899; rpr. Ann Arbor, 1968), 7.

power of color prejudice in America. Nearly white people sought exclusivity; relations even among blacks were disrupted by the demands white people had historically been able to make. In the early days, that disruption had been practical, as in the slave owner's separation of married couples. In more recent times, it had become psychological as well as practical, manifested in an internal color line such that light-skinned Negroes would see in their very color a badge of exclusiveness. In either case, it was a distortion. But here was not simply a question of identifying with one's race—of choosing blackness, as Harper and others had urged. The tragedy, to Chesnutt, lay in having to choose at all and in the cruel implications of being forced to make a choice, because to choose meant to accept the false racial consciousness of American society. Ryder's triumph lay in his transcending such views, not as a matter of racial identity but as a matter of acknowledging the humanity of another person and, as Werner Sollors has suggested, the reality of his own past.[49] The problem was that few people were Ryders, from Chesnutt's point of view; and few of his stories ended so happily.

The perspective Chesnutt adopted in his fiction of the color line informed much of his other work as well. His other two novels—*The Marrow of Tradition* (1901), based on the 1898 Wilmington, North Carolina, race riot, and *The Colonel's Dream* (1905), an attack on Washingtonian ideas—were both deeply pessimistic and stressed the power of racism to blind individuals to justice, honor, and human need. The perspective one finds in the color-line works even informed Chesnutt's least controversial writing—the dialect stories of his first book, *The Conjure Woman*, published in 1899 but including three stories that had previously appeared in *Atlantic* and *Overland Monthly*.

The Conjure Woman consists of seven tales, including the opening story, "The Goophered Grapevine." That story begins with the arrival of an upper-class white man and his wife at a North Carolina plantation they have just acquired. The man's name is John, and his narration frames the story. Upon arrival, John and his wife meet an old black man, Julius, who has spent his life there. They are interested in beginning a vineyard and are looking over the existing vines when Julius tells them that the vines are "goophered." This, he says, was done in slavery time. Julius describes the fate of one slave who, unaware of the goopher, ate some of the grapes. When the vines were bare, this slave grew bald; then his hair began to grow back, in little balls, as the grapes appeared, grew,

49. Sollors, *Beyond Ethnicity*, 158.

and ripened. As the vines became dormant, the slave became progressively weaker. Finally, when one of the vines died, so did the slave. Julius advises John not to buy the vineyard and not to disturb the grapes. It later turns out that Julius has, for some years, earned money by selling the grapes from the neglected vines. He does not want any interruption of his business.[50]

This opening story reveals the model that the others follow. In all of them, John provides the narrative framework in which Julius tells a tale of conjuration; and in all, Julius tries to use the tale to preserve a privilege he has come to enjoy. And this is a model that itself indicates that the tales may be read at more than one level. On the surface, in their use of dialect and in the kind of character Julius appears to be—garrulous, incredulous, and a bit crafty—the tales fit well enough into the plantation tradition that white magazines would publish them and white readers would assume, as they did, that Chesnutt was a white writer within that tradition. At another level, however, and as such critics as David Britt and Robert Hemenway have pointed out, these were also stories that undermined the plantation tradition by cloaking a message of protest within its framework. Occasionally, Chesnutt did this by showing the cruelties of slavery in the context of a tale. As Chesnutt's daughter pointed out many years ago, the stories making up the work, though they bore a superficial resemblance to plantation-tradition writing—and especially to Joel Chandler Harris' "Uncle Remus" tales—were also significantly different from it, in that they never glossed over the true character of slavery. Several of the stories described the separation of families, for example, and the harsh physical brutality of the plantation regime. In this, Chesnutt anticipated later dialect work that dealt with protest by such writers as Elliott Blaine Henderson, Franklin Henry Bryant, and even Dunbar.[51]

But even when the protest was not too obvious, as in "The Goophered Grapevine," its message was present. The model Chesnutt followed in his tales is reminiscent of the trickster tradition in Afro-American folklore. Within that tradition, the trickster attempts to use his wits to gain an advantage over a white man and thus to find at least a temporary respite from an oppressive situation. Julius fits into the tradi-

50. Charles W. Chesnutt, *The Conjure Woman* (1899; rpr. Ann Arbor, 1969), 1–35.
51. David D. Britt, "Chesnutt's Conjure Tales: What You See Is What You Get," *CLA Journal*, XV (1972), especially 271, 274, 283; Robert Hemenway, "The Function of Folklore in Charles Chesnutt's *The Conjure Woman*," *Journal of the Folklore Institute*, XIII (1976), 283–309; Helen Chesnutt, *Charles Waddell Chesnutt*, 109.

tion in "The Goophered Grapevine" in his use of trickery to prevent his source of economic independence from being taken over by the white plantation owner. The conjuring itself is an important element, because, as Chesnutt told the tale, it appears to be less an example of black incredulity than an artful dodge. Uncle Julius is no fool, and no object of ridicule. Like traditional trickster tales, Chesnutt's conjure stories are composed around an effort to preserve a measure of independence in the face of a white society, an effort made through the only resources the old man has. In this, Chesnutt not only showed sympathy for Julius but even played the role of the trickster himself, hiding a message of protest in what appears to be merely a bit of plantation-tradition local color. As David Britt has said, Chesnutt hustled the reader as much as Julius hustles the narrator.[52]

But there is another level, too, at which the stories must be read, a level that strongly coheres with the general themes of Chesnutt's other fiction. This level becomes most apparent when one considers, in light of Chesnutt's other work, the central place he gave to the relationship between Julius and the narrator, John. Although other writers—Dunbar in particular—had framed their stories with the words of a sophisticated narrator, only Chesnutt made that narrator an active participant in the drama. And this role of the narrator shifts one's attention away from the content of Julius' stories—a type of content that other writers could use as a basis for identifying a black distinctiveness—to the interaction between white man and black and to the characteristics of both participants.

If one surveys the range of Chesnutt's tales and the quality of Julius' trickery, one soon feels a need to ask, following Britt's remark, who is hustling whom. If, at one level, Julius is usually able to use his trickery to good advantage, Chesnutt also made it clear that John himself is a quick study and is, in most of the stories, well aware of what Julius is up to. As a result, he treats Julius' duplicity with a kind of amused, grumbling tolerance. Julius never poses a real threat to any of John's major aims. John never has cause to feel endangered by Julius' trickery. Perhaps the fact that Julius is essentially unthreatening has to do, in part, with Chesnutt's desire to hold a white audience. But, more significantly, even as Chesnutt used the stories to protest, the stories themselves leave no doubt as to who is really in charge of the plantation. It is not Julius.

From this point of view, it becomes especially important that the

52. Britt, "Chesnutt's Conjure Tales," 283.

plantation owner's voice and the narrator's voice are one, because it helps to indicate the third level at which the stories can be read. The stories are told with an air of amused detachment on the part of the narrator, and the superiority such a tone implies is a superiority the stories themselves bear out. But the tone of the narrator is also the tone Chesnutt adopted when, living in North Carolina, he felt such discomfort in having to deal with the local, rural black folk. The air of superiority one finds in the voice of Chesnutt's narrator, that is to say, is Chesnutt's own; and the stories are framed by his own point of view as well as John's.

Chesnutt saw himself as a cultured and sophisticated man, one who deserved a place in the American elite. In assuming such a narrative voice, he made his claim for that place. If, to some extent, he was like Dunbar in using the device of an outsider-narrator to frame his dialect tales, the tales—and thus the force of the device—were very different from what one finds in Dunbar. They were much more political, much more attached to protest than to psychological ambivalences. This characteristic of the tales means that one should read Chesnutt's narrative voice not as a product of ambiguity about his own identity but, rather, in light of his consistent objection to racial categories. Chesnutt could identify with his narrator because, in terms of background and temperament, he felt himself to be a man like his narrator, regardless of color.

If this is so, of course, then it adds another dimension to the protest one can find in *The Conjure Woman*. In addition to the veiled but explicit protest in Julius' trickery, there is also the implicit protest in all assimilationist writing, Chesnutt's too, as the author set his own skill and sophistication against his readers' stereotypes—the stereotypes that on the surface Julius seems to confirm. By his readers' lights—his white readers, at least—Chesnutt should have been Julius, but he was not. By his authorship of the overall tale, by his ability to assume the narrator's role, and by the very difference from Julius thereby defined, Chesnutt used racial stereotypes in a way that clearly proved them wrong. *The Conjure Woman* thus throws dominant American social categories into confusion, a confusion that reveals their arbitrariness, their lack of fit with reality. Such a message was present in all of Chesnutt's work. His identification with the narrator in *The Conjure Woman* makes it an important element in that work as well.

But, from this point of view, one can also see an underlying current of pessimism in *The Conjure Woman*, as in Chesnutt's other work. It may be instructive, in this regard, to compare *The Conjure Woman*, in its literary characteristics, with Hopkins' *Contending Forces* and "Wi-nona." Each work portrayed a world in which the force of racial barriers was acknowledged but their meaning was denied. Hopkins accomplished this through her fantasies of kinship and marriage, Chesnutt by assuming a particular narrative voice. Both knew how race relations ought to take shape in America—character should mean more than color—and both used literature to see what that would mean. Each could play out the nature of a different world, setting existing wrongs in sharp relief while enjoying the possibilities of a life in which such wrongs were overcome.

But Chesnutt was not Hopkins. She could construct her fantasies in Boston or antebellum America and bring them to realization as her black and white characters acknowledged love and affection for each other. Chesnutt's "play world" was, by contrast, more personal, masked in the assumption of a narrative voice that society would deny him—a denial he acknowledged by making the narrator white—even if he knew himself to be able to assume it. This does not mean that Chesnutt wanted to be white or that he had questions about his own identity. It does mean that he had powerful fears that white America could never recognize human worth across the color line, no matter what the character of the individual. There was much of Chesnutt himself, that is, not only in *The Conjure Woman*'s narrator but in Rena Walden as well.

And this may make *The Conjure Woman* especially prescient as the first major work in Chesnutt's literary career. Critic Jules Chametzky, in a perceptive reading of *The Conjure Woman*, one that stresses the subtle protest embodied in Julius and his tales, has argued that the inability of white audiences to grasp the meaning of those tales drove Chesnutt into more conventional forms of protest fiction. But, perhaps, in literary terms, Chesnutt never really was convinced of his ability to break down the barriers of race, at least not as a black writer whose weapon was his pen. He demanded so much more than all but a few writers, because he understood his assimilationist goals more thoroughly than most. And the progress seemed so slow; indeed, during the prime of Chesnutt's literary career, there were far more backward than forward steps. In assuming his white narrative voice, Chesnutt may well have been giving tacit recognition to a sense that the goals that had motivated black writers since the earliest days were futile, that no degree of literary merit or achievement could overcome the white prejudice that kept blacks outside the American mainstream. As critic Bernard Bell suggests, quoting Chesnutt himself, Chesnutt appears to have learned from the reception of his novels that he could not over-come racism "by the stroke of his pen." Perhaps, even from the begin-ning, Chesnutt sensed this, whatever his ambitions.[53]

As has often been noted, Chesnutt's career, like that of Hopkins, came to something of a premature end. Although Chesnutt did not stop writ-ing completely, as Hopkins seemed to have done, his literary activity after the publication of his last novel, *The Colonel's Dream*, in 1905, was, as his biographer Andrews has described it, "desultory"; and his publications were sporadic. There have been many explanations for this, as Andrews has noted; the most common one was that Chesnutt was discouraged by what he saw as the commercial failure of his later novels.[54] But if, in fact, *The Conjure Woman* really did convey his doubts about the efficacy of black literature, then perhaps the tapering off of Chesnutt's career grew out of failures that were more than com-mercial. Perhaps it grew out of his own awareness that, whatever liter-ary reputation he had created, he had done it during America's racial nadir—a deteriorating racial climate that even his best work had been powerless to affect. Any commercial problems his later work may have had simply confirmed the inefficacy he had always feared.

The writers surveyed in this chapter help remind one of the kinds of issues at stake in turn-of-the-century race relations, from the point of view of at least some black Americans, and help emphasize a side to those issues that is largely emotional and thus easily ignored by histo-rians. Taken with Dunbar's writing, and with the kind of effort other writers expended in developing at least embryonic notions of black distinctiveness, the works of these writers show, above all, how hard it was to create an effective ideological response to the deteriorating race relations of the period. They show the forces pushing toward the cre-ation of a black identity, especially in the absence of viable alternatives. But they also show the extraordinarily fragile emotional base on which any ideology of racial identity had to rest, given that it implied at least a tacit acceptance of an insult. Here was a tension that was hard to resolve, because it was based on powerfully conflicting moods and needs and on ambivalent feelings about the alternatives available to black Americans.

That the ideological possibilities were so slim casts an interesting

53. Jules Chametzky, "Regional Literature and Ethnic Realities," *Antioch Review*, XXXI (1971), 393–94; Bernard W. Bell, *The Afro-American Novel and Its Tradition* (Amherst, 1987), 67.

54. Andrews, *Literary Career*, 261.

light on the major dispute among black thinkers of this period and their partisans—the debate between Booker T. Washington and W. E. B. Du Bois. The differences between Washington and Du Bois grew out of the latter's response to the kinds of ideas Washington had promulgated in his 1895 Atlanta compromise address. Du Bois rejected even the temporary acceptance by blacks of a subordinate position in American society. He urged the continuing demand for total equality and full rights of citizenship and argued, too, for the encouragement of education—and not just vocational education—for blacks. Where Washington asserted the need for cooperation with the "best" white people for racial uplift, Du Bois saw the importance of creating a "talented tenth" of black leaders, cultured and well educated, who could look after the needs of the race. Although Washington had other opponents—notably the Boston editor William Monroe Trotter—after about 1903, opposition coalesced around the brilliant Du Bois, resulting in the foundation of the Niagara Movement and, later, the NAACP as organizations to combat Washington's ideas and influence while agitating for racial justice.

The first point to be made, however, is that Washington's and Du Bois' positions were alike in capturing certain basic cultural concerns of the growing black middle class, at least as those concerns were embodied in much of the literature of the period. Much of this is obvious. Washington, for example, built on the growing sense that black people had to set themselves apart from whites and that achievement had to take place in the context of a distinctive black community. Du Bois, in terms of his goals and ideals, retained an older outlook. Indeed, there are close ties between Du Bois' key political ideas from this time and the main themes of sentimental protest. In particular, one may focus on the ways in which Du Bois stressed both the importance of a liberal education and the rejection of a purely material view of progress. These were major points in his attack on Washington's ideas. For Du Bois, there was a great need to encourage "knowledge and culture." "Patience, Humility, Manners, and Taste, common schools and kindergartens, industrial and technical schools, literature and tolerance,—all these spring from knowledge and culture, the children of the university," Du Bois wrote. "So must men and nations build, not otherwise, not upside down."[55] In its open elitism and its appreciation for the signs of genteel culture, Du

55. W. E. B. Du Bois, *The Souls of Black Folk: Essays and Sketches* (1903; rpr. New York, 1968), 86.

Bois' position had clear affinities with the middle-class underpinnings of genteel traditions of black protest and with assimilationist ideals. It is no accident that both Hopkins and Chesnutt, for example, were opponents of Washingtonianism, finding Du Bois' ideas more congenial.

Not so obvious, however, is the extent to which Washington and Du Bois both created positions that captured much of the ambivalence and tension that characterized black literature as well. Du Bois, urging the creation of a black racial leadership, as opposed to depending on the goodwill of white people, certainly encouraged a turning inward. Moreover, he had a strong awareness of the importance of cultivating a black identity, and he was one of the most important contributors to early, romantic conceptions of black distinctiveness. In Washington's case, the ambivalence was less pointed but no less significant.

The ambiguities underlying Washington's position were most apparent in his extremely popular autobiography, *Up from Slavery*. Although not really in the purview of a study focusing on fiction and poetry, *Up from Slavery* was an important work, a book that had the widest audience of any associated with a black figure prior to World War I. Although, as Washington's biographer Louis Harlan has discussed, the book was put in final form for Washington by a ghost-writer, it was, as Harlan also has shown, based heavily on Washington's own ideas and even on Washington's own words.[56] It was thus an important portrait of an individual and his concerns, and it helps emphasize the pervasiveness of the kinds of issues raised by the works of Chesnutt and Hopkins, McClellan and Griggs.

On the surface, *Up from Slavery* had much in common with another classic American autobiography, that of Benjamin Franklin. It was the story of how a young man, through pluck and determination, was able to rise from the depths of poverty to a rather exalted position in American life. As a scenario, one can see the structure of Washington's life informing his sense of what Tuskegee Institute had done and what the race could do. Indeed, Washington's own success was proof of the possibility of the race's actually attaining its rightful place in American society. But there was an implicit message in the book, too; and it was found in Washington's representation of his own success. To some extent, Washington could measure his success in the achievements of Tuskegee, a black-run institution that brought improvement to the lives of young

56. Louis R. Harlan, *Booker T. Washington: The Making of a Black Leader, 1856–1901* (New York, 1972), 246.

black people. But when Washington most clearly sought to blow his own horn in the book, what he inevitably focused on was his ability to move in white society, to address white people as at least a near equal among them. His Atlanta address was proved a success, for example, by the enthusiastic response to his remarks by leading white southerners. They actually shook his hand, Washington stressed; and this was a striking level of contact between the two races.[57] Much of the book is devoted to detailing Washington's close relations to white people at social and public events.

A crucial point to be made about Washington's *Up from Slavery* is that it was not only a scenario recommending determination and hard work for black success. Nor was it merely a brief in defense of industrial education and political conservatism, although these were all elements in it. It was also a story of a man who had moved very close to achieving the goal for which black leaders had contended for generations. He had come close to acceptance into the American mainstream. And for all his overt talk of keeping the races as distinct as the fingers on one hand in all things social, Washington's life was anything but a life apart from white people, at least as it was represented in his autobiography. If, in reality, Booker T. Washington was often reminded of his race, in his autobiography his was a life of almost unbroken success in moving among the best circles of white society.

In certain essentials, then, *Up from Slavery* helps support the conclusion drawn from the more imaginative works on racial mixture—those that moved beyond standard plots and characterizations and that thus also went beyond formulaic approaches to racial concerns—that old aspirations died hard, if they died at all, among middle-class black Americans. Du Bois built his ideology on those traditional aspirations. Washington's ideology departed from them, but his appeal did not. Historian August Meier has suggested that much of Washington's influence in the black community grew out of his prestige and visibility rather than out of his specific ideas.[58] It was probably the case that his influence was enhanced by the fact that his own life could be portrayed in a way that actually undermined those ideas, keeping the image of the man and his career within a framework that included traditional assimilationist ideals and goals.

What all of this indicates is the extent of the difficulty in formulating a

57. Booker T. Washington, *Up from Slavery* (1901; rpr. New York, 1986), 225.
58. August Meier, *Negro Thought in America, 1880–1915: Racial Ideologies in the Age of Booker T. Washington* (Ann Arbor, 1963), 165.

consistent ideological response to racism in the closing decade of the nineteenth century and the first decade of the twentieth. If it had become clear to many people that older assimilationist strategies had little chance of success, there was also a nagging sense of the negative base on which separationist ideas and strategies rested. And as so much of the literature of this period shows, that nagging sense could be pretty strong. Indeed, it provides an important caveat to the argument historian John Cell and others have made about the rise of segregated institutions in the United States. Cell has argued that there were many black Americans who, in a sense, accepted segregation, because they perceived that the alternative to segregated institutions was not integration but was, instead, the provision of no public institutions to serve black people.[59] At a practical level, Cell is probably correct. There is plenty of evidence to support his argument. But if he is correct, it makes the story he has to tell doubly melancholy, because it is the story of practical men and women choosing a course at odds with all that they felt about themselves and their lives. Rena Walden stands, one might say, as a metaphor for them all.

At the same time, the literature of this period, highlighting as it does emotional and structural underpinnings to the ideologies of Washington and Du Bois, may help account for some of the political complexities of the "age of Washington." One of the striking things about Meier's description of the ideologies and politics of the period is the extent to which support shifted between the two men. Washington's followers often moved into Du Bois' camp. Men who were close to Du Bois' ideas could also work closely with Washington.[60] To some extent, one can explain such shifting alliances in terms of personal factors and power politics. But it may also have been that, ultimately and structurally, the two men were not that far apart and, more significantly, that neither could formulate a wholly satisfying approach to racial issues within the shifting currents of turn-of-the-century American life. The pains and frustrations were too strong and too new. It was possible to feel them but too hard to know what to think about them yet. These were not times for true believers.

59. John W. Cell, *The Highest Stage of White Supremacy: The Origins of Segregation in South Africa and the American South* (Cambridge, England, 1982), 93, 175.

60. See Meier, *Negro Thought*, especially Chap. 12.

V

The Emerging Black Consciousness of the Early Twentieth Century, 1906–1915

By 1906, when Dunbar had died and the literary careers of such writers as Hopkins, Griggs, and Chesnutt had virtually come to a close, the United States had become a determinedly biracial society. In the South, the course toward legalized segregation was fixed, many of the laws on the books. In the North, the segregated character of many aspects of life was assumed, if not given sanction of law. The years after 1906 represent not so much a period of transition as one of culmination so far as American race relations were concerned. It was a period that saw the realization of many white segregationist aims throughout the United States, and this realization powerfully influenced black literature after the era of Dunbar and Chesnutt, Hopkins and Griggs.

To be sure, black writers continued to produce much that fit comfortably within the framework of established forms and conventions. Dialect writing, in particular, continued to be important in black letters after about 1906, although the amount of such work diminished after Dunbar's death. Black writers also maintained a focus on protest and gentility, as they had done in earlier times. Thus, as earlier generations had done, writers of this period continued to write about subjects that evoked strong feeling—death, nature, and love—or about things that allowed them to present proper, middle-class standards, stressing piety and a genteel virtuousness. And for the most part, black writers remained conservative in their use of forms for prose and poetry.

That there should have been such continuity, even in the face of changing conditions, is not surprising. Given the conservatism of most black writing up to this time, one would not expect change to come quickly, unless it was inspired by a spectacular literary impetus, such as Dunbar's success with dialect writing. This continuity also helps to emphasize that long-held ideals and aspirations still had force among middle-class black men and women, serving as an underlying background to any responses to American conditions and events and to any changes that might occur in black literary forms.

Nevertheless, against this background of conservatism, there was a small but noticeable movement toward the reshaping of traditional forms and conventions. This movement might best be described as one toward a more open confrontation with the demands posed by American life and a still stronger willingness to move away from ideals of gentility than appeared at the turn of the century.

One example of a departure from older conventions occurred in a protest novel from this period, Robert Lewis Waring's *As We See It*, published in 1910. Much in the novel conforms with older themes. Waring wrote his novel to portray a middle-class, educated black elite and to pose the Washingtonian possibility of creating an alliance between the best black and white people to overcome the racist excesses of the southern poor whites, the "crackers." According to Waring, the crackers were the source of all southern racial problems, a point Washington had stressed as well.[1] But, significantly, he wrote his novel in a way that would have done little to encourage any alliance between blacks and whites, at least under the circumstances of the early twentieth century, and in a way that departed sharply from traditional means of trying to encourage white support.

Waring's novel is the story of two Abe Overleys, one the descendant of slaveholders, the other of slaves. The two Abes are fast friends (as are their fathers) and leave the South to go to Oberlin College together. Also at Oberlin, however, is the son of Nick Lashum, Overley's overseer during slavery. The former overseer is a crude man, but one who has achieved wealth in the postwar South. He is a prototypical cracker, and his son is no better. Young Lashum does his best to get the black Abe out of Oberlin and shows how evil he can be when, on a false pretext, he causes the lynching of Abe's mother and sister. Abe is not content to bear the injustice; and with the knowledge of his white friends, he leaves Oberlin in order to carry out a program of vengeance against the lynchers, whom he pursues and kills, one by one. With the help of his white friends, all elite southerners, he is enabled to escape and to create a successful life in New York.

Such a literary response to lynching was new. Prior to the time

1. Robert Lewis Waring, *As We See It* (1910; rpr. College Park, Md., 1969), 5–6.

Waring wrote, the usual treatment of lynching was—as works by Stowers and Anderson and by Dunbar showed—to stress the horror of the
crime and the suffering of the victim. A few writers had toyed with
stories of resistance. "A. Gude Deekun" published a story in 1903,
"When the Worm Turned," in which the black hero uses dynamite to
thwart a mob.[2] But no one had ever allowed readers to experience,
vicariously, the revenge many believed a lynch mob deserved. Waring
created a powerful fantasy, a fantasy made necessary by the failure of
more peaceful pleas to make much headway against white southern
racial violence. It was an open acknowledgment of a black desire for
vengeance that earlier generations of black writers—apart, perhaps,
from Griggs—had taken great pains to avoid.

And such an open confrontation with a perfectly understandable
reaction to racism remained uncommon, even at the time Waring
wrote. Most novelists and protest poets remained within the limits of
nonviolent response to American racism. But Waring's novel indicates
that the possibility of expressing raw feeling was no longer entirely
closed to black writers. Here was a new sense of the kinds of concerns
black literature could address, one that gave little place to older desires
for respectability in the always assumed presence of a white audience.

The new orientation even affected dialect poetry written during this
time. Although little formal experimentation took place in dialect writing before World War I—that development would have to await the
Harlem Renaissance—a few poets did move beyond traditional bounds
in dialect writing. Most particularly, they began to move away from the
kind of detached presentation of the folk that dominated dialect poetry
from earlier times. One poet who did this was Emory Elrage Scott,
whose 1913 *Lyrics of the Southland* contained several dialect pieces
that avoided the kind of affectionate amusement or condescending
sympathy found in earlier work. The poem "Fix Me," for example, was
an early effort simply to create a poetic rendition of black folk religion
similar to the spirituals in language and structure:

> Oh, Lawd, give me faith an' grace;
> He'p me run dis rugged race;
> Fix me, Lawd, when I go wrong,
> 'Ca'se you know dis lane is long;
> Fix me, Jesus, fix me right.[3]

2. A. Gude Deekun [pseud.], "When the Worm Turned: A Story from Real Life in the
South," *Colored American Magazine*, VI (1903), 226–36.
3. Emory Elrage Scott, *Lyrics of the Southland* (Chicago, 1913), 18.

Wellington Adams, a Washington, D.C., teacher and musician, published a poem in 1914 that effectively brought together dialect and standard English in order to evoke the feelings of folk piety. Using the lines from a Baptist hymn, but rendering them in dialect, Adams wrote "The Passing of 'Old Aunt Maria,' " allowing a line from the hymn to serve as a counterpoint to his description of an old woman's sinking into death:

> "Ah'm near'er mah hom', near'er mah hom' "—
>   Rang out upon the air,
> As old Aunt Maria raised her voice,
>   With song, to God in prayer.
> Her form bend'd o'er by age's firm hand;
>   Her voice, tho' coarse, was sweet;
> While angels seem'd to hover o'er,
>   As though they came to greet.
>
> "Then ebbah ahve been befoh,"
>   Was whisper'd soft, as death
> Was stealing her away from there;
>   And left them all bereft;
> As, one by one, they gather'd 'round
>   And murmured—"She is gone!"
> Yes, old Aunt Maria's task was done
>   On earth, that Sunday morn.[4]

Adams wrote other dialect poems, most of them humorous; but here he tried to take the tradition in directions that looked more seriously at the lives of black folk and, more significantly, without the detachment that marked dialect writing in Dunbar's time.

This empathetic treatment of folk characters became a hallmark of black writing in the years leading up to World War I, as some black writers showed a willingness to identify with the perspectives of their folk subjects. An especially vivid example of this is Maggie Pogue Johnson's long narrative poem "Aunt Cloe's Trip to See Miss Liza Kyle," the story of a country woman's visit to an old friend living in New York City. Aunt Cloe is intimidated by the prospect, having never left the country, and writes to her friend for advice, so that she will appear to be right in style when she arrives in town. Liza Kyle responds by sending Cloe a picture from a magazine, urging her to imitate it. Needless to say, the effort is a failure; and Cloe arrives in New York looking ridiculous. Liza, chagrined at the sight, refuses to acknowledge Aunt Cloe and runs

4. Wellington Alexander Adams, *Lyrics of an Humble Birth* (Washington, D.C., 1914), 22–23.

away. Cloe pursues her home, only to be denied entrance by Liza's servants.

> I flung my shoes right in der face,
>   "No police in de lan
> Kin git me out ob here,
>   Right here I takes my stan.
>
> "Ef dis am de greetin dat you git,
>   When you come in style,
> I'll war ole clos de nex time
>   To see Ole Liza Kyle." [5]

Certainly, one may laugh momentarily at Aunt Cloe's efforts to be fashionable; but laughter turns to sympathy as Liza Kyle, affluent and urban, refuses to acknowledge the old woman. Aunt Cloe is right to have her sense of decency outraged by her unthinking city friend, and Johnson's poem is directed toward making the reader share Aunt Cloe's feelings.

Indeed, it is not too much to suggest that the poem provides an implicit criticism of the middle-class detachment that earlier dialect writers found ways to express. Aunt Cloe is the sympathetic character, but the Liza Kyle with whom she contrasts is, on the surface at least, the very essence of the kind of assimilated figure earlier writers prized. In this poem, Johnson turned the rhetoric of the dialect tradition upside down, implying a kind of falseness in the assimilated black American. One would not want to go too far with such a conclusion in Johnson's case, since the bulk of her work conformed to the pattern appearing in other dialect literature. But this poem does represent a notable departure from the overall thrust of dialect writing as the tradition had developed.

So the dialect tradition remained alive after Dunbar's death, but not entirely unchanged. At least a few poets began to drop the ambivalence toward folk Negroes that had marked the dialect writing of an earlier era. Evoking folk life and folk characters in ways that even urged an identification with them, these poets showed less concern than previous writers had about continually proving a fitness for the American mainstream by stressing the differences between themselves and their folk subjects.

Dialect literature was not the only realm in which black writers

5. Maggie Pogue Johnson, *Thoughts for Idle Hours* (N.p., 1915), 16–23.

showed less concern than their predecessors for a conservative, main-stream literary image. Other works that appeared during this period similarly displayed a shifting orientation toward literary matters.

One of these works, perhaps the most curious one by a black writer of this period, was Joseph Seamon Cotter's collection *Negro Tales*, published in 1912. The qualifier "perhaps" is used because this work comes from a most unexpected source. Cotter was a conservative follower of Booker T. Washington, a respected educator in his hometown of Louisville, a good friend to the most influential whites in his city, and a prolific writer of poetry that did not depart in the least from the genteel sentimentality that had long dominated black verse. An earlier work of his, a play entitled *Caleb, the Degenerate*, had celebrated Washington's ideas while ridiculing many of the positions taken by Du Bois and others among Washington's critics. *Negro Tales* is, however, an unusual book. It is a collection of brief stories, some of which are clearly modeled on folktales. Others have less clear roots and show a remarkable departure from traditional literary modes.

Among the stories clearly based on folktales are an African story, "The Jackal and the Lion," and an Afro-American animal tale with the descriptive title "How Mr. Rabbit Secures a Pretty Wife and Rich Father-in-Law." Both stories have as their central characters the trickster figure so prominent in African and Afro-American traditions. Another tale, "Kotchin' de Nines," a story about playing the numbers, is introduced by Cotter as "a Negro tale current in Louisville." [6] "Faith in the White Folks" fits in with the large body of black folktales that joke about stereotypes and about the subordinate place of blacks in American society.

Among the writings whose sources are less clear, the one that is closest to other black writing is "Tesney, the Deceived," which self-consciously reflects on traditional literary treatments of racial mixture. Tesney is a mulatto servant working for a white family, a girl well loved by all. She is curious about her parentage, because, although she knew her mother, she has never seen her father. She is, however, convinced that he is a certain rich white man. Whenever she sees the man, she thinks, "He is my father. . . . He will give me something some day." On her twenty-third birthday, she receives a ring and is sure it came from him. Somewhat later, however, cruel Aunt Agnes, who wants to arrange a marriage between her son and Tesney, tells Tesney, "Yo' mother wus er ooman nearly white, an' yo' father wus er nigger man." Later, Tesney's

6. Joseph Seamon Cotter, *Negro Tales* (1912; rpr. Miami, 1969), 62.

white employer confirms what Agnes has said. Tesney has deceived herself.[7]

At this point, the story shifts abruptly to the relationship involving Tesney, Agnes, and Agnes' son, George. Tesney becomes ill after learning her background, and the 350—pound Agnes is her nurse. While Tesney is delirious, Agnes has Tesney and George married; and Tesney bears George's child. George is killed in a brawl, and Tesney buries the child alive. There is a terrible storm, and Tesney digs up the child. But during the night, both Tesney and the baby die. Agnes is left to face ten years of agonized guilt for her part in the tragedy.

"Tesney" is a strange story, filled with a grotesqueness utterly unknown in black writing before or during Cotter's time. One would not want to account for it by treating Cotter as an experimentalist. There is nothing in his other work to make one think he would have the literary self-consciousness to engage in radical experimentation. It may simply be that Cotter was an eccentric, at least when he put pen to paper, although there is no corroborating evidence. It may also be that Cotter was, to some extent, drawing on oral sources for "Tesney." Stylistically, the tale shares much with common practices in oral story-telling. Folklorists such as Linda Degh and Daniel Crowley have made much of the ways in which traditional storytellers improvise, deal in the fantastic, and shift scenes radically and abruptly—all in an effort to keep their audiences entertained.[8]

One may see all of this in Cotter's story. Elements of the fantastic appear in, for example, the kind of exaggeration that makes Agnes a 350-pound woman and the grotesquerie of Tesney's burying her baby alive and later digging it up. The flow of the narrative has an improvised quality that likewise resembles oral tradition. One sees this clearly in an account of Tesney's torment after she has buried the baby. She is caught in a thunderstorm; and after a thunderclap, she arises and puts her hand to her ear:

> "My name?" asked she. "It is Tesney." There were renewed thunder and lightning. "My baby?" asked she. "I sent it up. Is it there?" Again it thundered, again the lightning flashed. "Is it not there?" she asked. "I must come with it? All right! Welcome!" She ran to the grave and uncovered the baby. It kicked feebly and gave a faint cry. "I knew you were still here," she said. "The Voice of

7. *Ibid.,* 37, 41.
8. Linda Degh, *Folktales and Society: Story-telling in a Hungarian Peasant Community*, trans. Emily M. Schossberger (Bloomington, Ind., 1969), 84–85; Daniel J. Crowley, *I Could Talk Old Story Good: Creativity in Bahamian Folklore* (Berkeley, 1966), 40–44.

the Clouds said so." A terrible storm was breaking. "Listen, little rascal: We go together. Listen! The Voice is coming. We go! We go!" These were her last words.[9]

The coming of the storm and the "Voice of the Clouds" enter the story only at this point, an abrupt scene setting much like the abrupt shift when the story moves from Tesney's search for her white father to her problems with Agnes and George.

The same may be said of what is certainly the strangest story in Cotter's collection, a tale entitled "Rodney." This is the story of an illegitimate child whose mother is black and whose father is white. Rodney meets his father only once, and their dialogue takes a curious shape, even as it reveals the white man's racism:

> "You have a fine head of hair," said his father.
> "That's what people say," replied Rodney.
> "Are you proud of it?"
> "Should I not be, sir?"
> "Well, my little man, it's a disgrace to you."
> This was the first and last meeting of Rodney and his father.[10]

Following this meeting, most of the story takes place on a single day in Rodney's home. The family is visited by two snobbish women who are servants of a wealthy white family and who are elegantly dressed in their employer's clothing. These women are extremely cruel to Rodney because of his illegitimate birth. The family is also visited by a "professor," who is trying to get Rodney to go to school. He, too, treats Rodney and Rodney's mother with contempt. Rodney offers the professor a drink, then tells him that the women have spit into the glass. His little sister, Mary, goes further, telling the professor that the women "puked into it."[11] After a debate over the difference between spitting and puking, the professor runs from the house, and the family recognizes the love each member has for the others. A satire on black snobbery, this story, too, relies on the sort of grotesquerie, exaggeration, and improvisation that marks much of oral tradition.

Thus it is quite possible that even "Tesney" and "Rodney" had some background in oral tradition, although one cannot trace them to conventional sources in Afro-American folklore. Cotter was fond of telling stories and even organized story-telling sessions and story-telling con-

9. Cotter, *Negro Tales*, 48.
10. *Ibid.,* 23.
11. *Ibid.,* 34.

tests for black children in Louisville.[12] But, in any case, his collection *Negro Tales* offered a striking departure from older modes, even in the language Cotter chose to write down, and showed a willingness to portray a version of black life that was rather far from the images created by earlier writers, even those in the dialect tradition.

This change in orientation informed other areas of black writing as well. For example, the post-Dunbar era saw the diminishing importance of racial mixture as a theme in black literature. To be sure, fairly conventional works relying on racial mixture continued to be written; but they came to take a proportionally smaller place in the body of black literature. In addition, it was no longer necessary, as it seemed to have been in the past, for heroes and heroines to be of mixed background; and even when they were, their ability to lead Victorian lives, though not forgotten, was secondary in importance to other kinds of concerns. What was most important was the difficulties they faced as black men and women. And this was the mark of other fiction written during the period. The ambiguities of identity began to take secondary importance to writing about the difficulties of living in what was clearly categorized now as a "white" society, or even about the life of the black community itself.

A good example of this shift is Thomas Hamilton B. Walker's 1910 novel *Bebbly*. This was the first novel to focus on the black church, using its peculiar problems and disputes as the basis for a plot. Like most novels of the period, it used a romance to provide the main cues for plot development. John Bebbly, who begins the book as a teenage preacher, is in love with Sadie, a pastor's granddaughter, and must compete for her affection against another minister as well as against the demands posed by life in the ministry. Bebbly is a powerful preacher and an effective administrator; and he is able to make a good career by taking over failing congregations and building them into healthy organizations. But he is, above all, a modern minister; and Walker took every opportunity to print contemporary sermons, putting the words into his protagonist's mouth. In the end, Bebbly's love for Sadie is never to be fulfilled; she dies, and he marries another woman. But his ministerial success is great, as he moves from rural Florida to the pastorate of one of the largest churches in Chicago.[13]

Walker was clearly concerned about the state of black religious life

12. Ann Allen Shockley, "Joseph S. Cotter, Sr.: Biographical Sketch of a Black Louisville Bard," *CLA Journal*, XVIII (1975), 333–35.

13. Thomas Hamilton B. Walker, *Bebbly; or, The Victorious Preacher* (Gainesville, Fla., 1910).

and used his novel to express a point of view toward it that was closely tied to concerns for middle-class morality and uplift—for making the church, above all, socially responsible. In this, he maintained the ambiguous view of folk culture that marked the writers of the preceding generation. Indeed, in certain particulars, *Bebbly* resembles Dunbar's "Old Abe's Conversion." But Walker also used the novel to paint a realistic portrait of the difficulties facing the black ministry in his time. Certainly, his championing of a modern ministry echoed that of many educated black ministers of the period, who felt themselves cast adrift in trying to lead less-educated congregations. The novel also portrayed the simple, practical hardships of a ministerial life in which every minister had to be a community leader. The demands on one's time were exhausting, as many ministers testified, and made difficult the kind of human commitments that life and love also demanded. Here, in other words, was an attempt to deal with elements of black life in a way that addressed black concerns for black readers, not in a way designed to reach a white audience.

From a slightly different point of view, one sees a shifting orientation toward older images of literary respectability as a few black poets began to look more frankly, and imaginatively, at traditional sentimental themes—love, for instance. Although sentimental love poetry continued to have a prominent place in black poetry, some poets began to look at love from a different perspective. The Mississippi lawyer Samuel Beadle wrote what was probably the first poem by a black writer to deal openly with divorce—with the possible exception of Dunbar's "Parted"—a poem entitled "The Love That Would Not Keep." Angelina Weld Grimké published "El Beso" in the Boston *Evening Transcript* in 1909, one of the first poems by a black writer to celebrate passion openly and honestly:

> Twilight—and you,
> Quiet—the stars;
> Snare of the shine of your teeth,
> Your provocative laughter,
> The gloom of your hair;
> Lure of you, eye and lip;
> Yearning, yearning,
> Languor, surrender;
>   Your mouth
> And madness, madness,
> Tremulous, breathless, flaming,

The space of a sigh;
The awaking—remembrance,
Pain, regret—your sobbing;
And again quiet—the stars,
Twilight—and you.

A recent student of Grimké's work, Gloria Hull, has noted that this poem created something of a sensation among the *Transcript*'s readers, including Grimké's friends, when it appeared. It certainly represented a major, if unusual, break from the genteel conservatism that dominated black writing prior to World War I. For one thing, it shows a positive attitude toward sexuality that earlier writers—understandably concerned about white stereotypes of black licentiousness—would have been afraid to confront. Durham had come close in his descriptions of the Haitian priestess Diane, but he had tempered his presentation by making Diane typically genteel in her character. In its freedom with versification, moreover, Grimké's poem also shows an atypically free view of poetry itself, a diminished concern for producing verse that looked like poetry according to the most conservative models. Grimké did not publish a great deal of work of this sort, but this particular poem points to an adventurousness that would have been unthinkable in earlier times, given what black writers believed they had to demonstrate about themselves and, by extension, their race.[14]

Something similar may be said of the poetry of Wilson James Jefferson, whose collection *Verses* was published in 1909. Jefferson was a Georgian who studied for a time at Atlanta University and who worked for the post office. Prior to the publication of his volume of poetry, he had a number of pieces printed in such white newspapers as the New York *Independent*, the Boston *Transcript*, and the Springfield (Mass.) *Republican*. Much of his poetry was similar to that of other black writers of the period—conservative in its versification and dealing with nature, love, and religious belief. But it also differed from other black poetry, especially in its range of subjects and its originality of imagery. Jefferson's "Night Worker's Song" exemplifies this work:

14. Samuel Alfred Beadle, *Lyrics of the Under World* (Jackson, Miss., 1912), 19; Angelina Weld Grimké, miscellaneous poems, clippings, in Archibald H. Grimké Papers, Manuscript Division, The Moorland-Spingarn Research Center, Howard University; Gloria T. Hull, *Color, Sex, and Poetry: Three Women Writers of the Harlem Renaissance* (Bloomington, Ind., 1987), 113–14, 117.

> We seize the tangled skein of things
> 　　When tired hands are folded by,
> And night to our unraveling brings
> 　　The glory of the star-set sky.
> Day with its garish charms departs
> 　　And dark, gem-studded, rims our world;
> And peace all-healing seeks our hearts
> 　　From night's dim star-strewn spaces hurled.

More significantly, Jefferson also experimented some with versification, as is shown in these lines from his poem "The Vine":

> This thing I saw about a common vine
> That sprang from common soil;
> Following the nature of its parent stock
> That earth and air and sun
> Had wakened, coaxed and urged
> To full free life,—
> High in the air its tendrils reached,
> Like a thing of sense.
> But not so seeming good or kind.

Jefferson's collection contained only two poems that dealt at all with racial questions—one a tribute to Abraham Lincoln, the other a tribute to William Lloyd Garrison. And while Jefferson broke little thematic ground with his poetry, he, like Angelina Grimké, showed a willingness to experiment that was unusual among black writers of his time and unprecedented in the poetry of earlier generations.[15]

Here, then, was a new focus beginning to appear in black writing between about 1906 and 1915. Certainly, it characterized the works of only a minority of writers. But it was important, nonetheless, as an effort to find stimuli for creativity from sources other than the assumed expectations of a predominantly white America. To grasp its significance, one need only draw the obvious comparison between the kind of poetic freedom sought by an Albery Whitman and that represented by an Angelina Grimké.

To the extent that they involved a new interest in artistic independence on the part of at least some black writers, the changes in black literature become an important manifestation of changing conditions in American racial life as well, especially of the real triumph of segregation.

15. Wilson James Jefferson, *Verses* (Boston, 1909), 8.

It would not do to say that such changes represent some kind of accommodation to racism or that they represent a giving up of assimilationist goals. The characteristics of the writers were too varied to allow for such a blanket generalization. Still, whether they intended to do so or not, these writers began to produce a literature that implicitly proclaimed the inadequacy of traditional literary goals at a time when related social hopes had been all but destroyed. They represent a moving away from traditional literary assimilationism and toward a more independent approach to creative work. Such a move had to have been made easier by the fact that traditional literary purposes no longer made as much sense in a world that was determinedly racist. It may be the greatest of paradoxes, that with increasing social inhibitions, black writers found avenues for real innovation in literary work, for real opportunities to explore their own feelings and their own background.

In most of the writing from 1906 to 1915, the possibility of a literary independence from white expectations was only subtly expressed, only implicitly acknowledged. Nevertheless, beginning in about the middle of the first decade of the twentieth century, there was at least a move toward a more open acknowledgment of the importance of creating an independent black literature, a move framed by a more pluralist conception of American society and American race relations. The most profound and influential thinker along these lines was W. E. B. Du Bois. Not only was Du Bois deeply involved in the ideological wars of early twentieth century black life, but he was also the most versatile thinker on issues of race in America at that time. His articulation of ideas about literature and his ability to put those ideas into practice, both as an author and as editor of *Crisis*, the most influential black periodical prior to the 1950s, made him a leading spokesman for a distinctive black literature during the early twentieth century. Although much that Du Bois had to say was not framed in fiction or poetry, an understanding of his ideas provides an essential clue for understanding some major developments in black literature after the heyday of Dunbar and Chesnutt.

Du Bois was born in Great Barrington, Massachusetts, in 1868, a member of a family that had long known freedom. He grew up in Great Barrington and was a top student there before going South at the age of seventeen to attend Fisk University. His upbringing was not easy. His father had deserted Du Bois' mother shortly after the infant was born, and he and his mother lived in near poverty until Du Bois left home for college. His position as one of the very few black children in a white environment did not make his situation any easier.[16] In any case, Du Bois graduated from Fisk and, after a brief career as a teacher in the South, entered Harvard as an undergraduate. There, he did well enough to be chosen to deliver the commencement address in 1890. He spent the next two years doing graduate work at Harvard, followed by two years of study in Germany. He then returned to Harvard, where he completed his Ph.D. in history. Both at Harvard and in Germany, Du Bois studied with some of the finest minds of his era. And his years in Boston, in particular, provided him with a thorough initiation into America's black elite, as he got to know many of the city's most sophisticated and accomplished black families.

Du Bois' early career was marked by accomplishment. In 1896 his doctoral dissertation, *The Suppression of the African Slave-Trade*, was published as the first volume of the Harvard Historical Studies. In 1896, too, Du Bois spent a year in Philadelphia, under the somewhat grudging auspices of the University of Pennsylvania, doing the research that culminated in his important book *The Philadelphia Negro*, published in 1899. This massive community study, employing both statistical and ethnographic analyses, was the first large-scale study of black life in America.

After leaving Pennsylvania, Du Bois joined the faculty of Atlanta University, where he headed the sociology program and produced the series Atlanta University Studies, which examined different phases of black American society and culture. During this same time, Du Bois was also publishing widely. By the turn of the century, and even before he became the spokesman for the opposition to Washington, Du Bois had become one of the better-known black intellectuals in the United States.

Du Bois' mark was really made, however, with the 1903 publication of *The Souls of Black Folk*, a book that had an almost instant impact on black readers. James Weldon Johnson, looking back on the book's appearance some years later, compared it to *Uncle Tom's Cabin*. The black critic and poet Benjamin Brawley considered it the most important book a black writer had produced up to that time. Much that appeared in the book was not entirely new. Du Bois had begun to make his views known in the late 1890s, when key parts of the book first appeared as

---

16. Allison Davis, *Leadership, Love, Aggression* (San Diego, 1983), 107–10. Du Bois wrote three autobiographies, and they were not always faithful to the facts of his life. Davis has made fascinating comparisons between those facts and Du Bois' various autobiographical accounts.

magazine articles. He expressed some similar views as early as 1890 in his Harvard commencement address.[17]

But *The Souls of Black Folk* had special import. In part this may have been because it was the first real salvo in his war on Washingtonian ideas. As such, it could not be ignored; and, indeed, it did as much as anything to thrust Du Bois into the forefront of leadership for blacks and whites opposed to Washington. Only two years later, he was able to organize the Niagara Movement to coalesce black opposition to Washington. But *The Souls of Black Folk* was more than an attack on Washington. A collection of closely related essays, along with one short story, it sought to create a clear definition of the black experience in America. Critic Stanley Brodwin has described it as Du Bois' "spiritual autobiography"—an effort to create a "truer self," within the context of American life, through a series of meditations on a more general Afro-American identity.[18] The attack on Washington grew out of Du Bois' profound concern for the meaning of being black in America. In this concern lay the basis, too, for Du Bois' specific contribution to the development of black American literary tradition.

The framework for Du Bois' exploration of issues of black identity and culture is provided by a notion he called "double-consciousness," which he brought up in the first essay. Du Bois understood double-consciousness to operate at two levels. At one level, there is the double-consciousness that comes from the difficulty of being both a Negro and an American, of having two identities forced on oneself by virtue of one's exclusion from the mainstream of American society. One is expected to conform to American values but is prevented from enjoying the fruits of doing so. At the other level is the double-consciousness that comes from the lack of communication between white and black Americans, leading to two separate spheres of existence for black people, particularly for educated black people. Behind "the veil," Du Bois argued, there is a vital and significant Afro-American culture—with roots in Africa and in black American folk life—from which black people may draw sustenance; but it is a folk life that can never be fully appreciated in the context of American society. Thus the "twoness" that every black

17. Arnold Rampersad, *The Art and Imagination of W. E. B. Du Bois* (Cambridge, Mass., 1976), 68; Joel Williamson, *The Crucible of Race: Black-White Relations in the American South Since Emancipation* (New York, 1984), 399–400; W. E. B. Du Bois, *Against Racism: Unpublished Essays, Papers, Addresses, 1887–1961,* ed. Herbert Aptheker (Amherst, 1985), 14–16.

18. Stanley Brodwin, "The Veil Transcended: Form and Meaning in W. E. B. Du Bois's *The Souls of Black Folk," Journal of Black Studies,* II (1972), 306–307.

American feels is not simply the negative product of exclusion but is also the product of a conflict between two cultural heritages, each of which has a place in black American life. The creation of a satisfying identity would involve giving full expression to what was American—and, again, Du Bois saw much to admire in the American mainstream—while not rejecting what was distinctively black in character. As Du Bois wrote of the Negro: "He would not Africanize America, for America has too much to teach the world and Africa. He would not bleach his soul in a flood of white Americanism, for he knows that Negro blood has a message for the world."[19]

To some extent, Du Bois' idea of double-consciousness built on themes and dilemmas that had long underlain black writing. It is not difficult to see a relationship between Du Bois' idea and the more general problem of being both black and American that had been expressed in the tension between assimilationist ideals and values on racial identity and solidarity. One may also place Du Bois' ideas in the context provided by the independence from older norms that such writers as Angelina Grimké and Wilson Jefferson were expressing in literary terms. And making such a connection, one can see the idea of double-consciousness as a symptom of the increasing isolation of black Americans from the rest of society. Finally, in giving substance to black identity and looking back toward folk roots, Du Bois was building on efforts found even in Dunbar's poetry and in the theorizing of Anna Julia Cooper, efforts antedating even the earliest of Du Bois' own essays on the black experience.

But if there were precedents in black literature for Du Bois' ideas, Du Bois brought those precedents together and put them in a form that took them well beyond what anyone had done before, particularly in the pervasive role he gave to the substance of a black identity. Whereas Cooper, for example, could see the folk heritage as providing an important historical basis for a black identity and Dunbar had seen the meaning of a folk-based identity in terms of certain "traits of character" remaining alive in otherwise assimilated people, Du Bois saw blackness as something more profound. For him, it was the ground from which every aspect of the black experience grew. Folk life was the clearest manifestation of that ground, because it had not been overlaid with the forms of the "white" world. But blackness was the independent cultural

---

19. W. E. B. Du Bois, *The Souls of Black Folk: Essays and Sketches* (1903; rpr. New York, 1968), 4.

framework ordering the experience of every black man and woman, an element of "Negro blood." Du Bois thus invested the black identity with an innateness and a depth that was quite different from older approaches to the issue.

Indeed, as critic Robert Stepto has stressed, Du Bois' book was more than a portrayal of that black culture. Stepto has described it as "the first true narrative expression of a distinctly Afro-American cultural immersion ritual."[20] To put it more simply, in keeping with the profound innateness he ascribed to black culture, Du Bois constructed *The Souls of Black Folk* in ways that emphasized his own black identity; and this in itself was a major change.

Stepto has done the closest analysis of the ways in which Du Bois conveyed his own position within the black culture. He has shown, for example, how Du Bois revised his earlier work so that, in *The Souls of Black Folk*, his "racial self-identification" became more pronounced and his positive valuation of black culture became clearer. Thus, to take two of Stepto's examples, an article initially entitled "Strivings of the Negro People" became, as the first essay in the book, "Of Our Spiritual Strivings"; and a line that in its initial appearance read "for he [the Negro] believes—foolishly, perhaps, but fervently—that Negro blood has yet a message for the world" was transformed into "for he knows that Negro blood has yet a message for the world."[21] These kinds of changes were directly related to the substantive presentation of a distinctive black identity in *The Souls of Black Folk*.

Du Bois identified the key mark of black distinctiveness in spirituality. He wrote about this spirituality in several ways. One was to contrast black spirituality with white materialism. In the same essay in which he defined double-consciousness, Du Bois spoke of the potential contribution of blacks to American life, stressing that, "all in all, we black men seem the sole oasis of simple faith and reverence in a dusty desert of dollars and smartness." Toward the close of the book, Du Bois heightened the contrast, speaking of the "three gifts" Africans had brought to America: "a gift of story and song," a physical strength to conquer the wilderness, and, finally, "a gift of the Spirit"—an endurance based on finding peace "in the altars of the God of Right." This idea of black spirituality guided Du Bois' ideas on other subjects. In an essay on the New South, he spoke of the region's corruption by American mate-

20. Robert Stepto, *From Behind the Veil: A Study of Afro-American Narrative* (Urbana, 1979), 66.
21. *Ibid.,* 53–54.

rialism and of his fear that blacks, going along with New South ideas, would themselves be corrupted, would lose the spirituality that gave them a positive distinctiveness.[22]

It was from this perspective that Du Bois attacked the work of Booker T. Washington. When Du Bois developed his attack, he did not simply condemn Washington for open accommodationism. He also attacked him for New South vulgarism, for advocating a merely material solution to what were also spiritual problems. For Du Bois, the cultivation of the spiritual was essential; and it was especially important for black people, given that it was a distinctive virtue of the race.

Like the focus on the folk heritage, the assertion of a black spirituality was not entirely new. Black writers had celebrated black spirituality at least as far back as the earliest days of the post-Reconstruction period. It was an element as well of the "romantic racialism" of antislavery writing. But Du Bois went much further with the idea than had earlier writers. Whereas earlier writers had stressed black spirituality either to make an ironic point or to help emphasize black virtue and even gentility, Du Bois presented as something very different from an American genteel piety. It was a basis for claiming, and Du Bois did, that black people were really different from whites and that this difference was to be seen as a good thing.

Du Bois located the essence of a distinctive black spirituality in the roots of black American culture, roots that clearly lay in Africa. Du Bois was one of the first black American writers to offer an appreciation for the African heritage. Writers before him, if they had talked about Africa at all, had focused their attention entirely on ancient Egypt and Ethiopia, viewing ed Africa of the more recent past as having declined from ancient glory. Du Bois, too, wrote about ancient Egypt and Ethiopia; but he also dealt more positively with the Africa of recent history. In a piece on the black church, he wrote, "The Negro has already been pointed out many times as a religious animal,—a being of that deep emotional nature which turns instinctively toward the supernatural." Du Bois accepted such a description, writing, "Endowed with a rich tropical imagination and a deep, delicate appreciation of Nature, the transplanted African lived in a world animate with gods and devils, elves and witches." And so he remained, Du Bois believed, even at the opening of the twentieth century—that native religiosity having been "deepened and strengthened" by the experiences of slavery and racial oppression.

22. Du Bois, *Souls of Black Folk*, 11–12, 262–63.

In his essay on Negro spirituals in *The Souls of Black Folk*, Du Bois attempted to show concretely how African spirituality was transformed into "Sorrow Songs," the black American folk songs that provided America's sole claim to an original music.[23]

Indeed, as both Robert Stepto and Arnold Rampersad have noted, the spirituals themselves played an important part in Du Bois' book. Each chapter begins with an epigraph taken from a spiritual, and the effect is to root Du Bois' text within the heritage he sought to evoke. The use of the spirituals emphasizes Du Bois' own place within black culture by giving an authoritative character to that culture as a source of inspiration. It is to use the spirituals as, in Rampersad's characterization, a "patristic" literature.[24]

Consistent with this effort to root *The Souls of Black Folk* within black culture was the extent to which the tone of the text exemplified Du Bois' understanding of black distinctiveness. This is especially apparent in the chapters where Du Bois discussed history and the social and economic conditions facing blacks in the South. Du Bois made no attempt to write as the impartial social scientist, although the chapters are filled with data on social and economic life and on the ways in which conditions evolved in the years following emancipation. The reports are presented with deep feeling—not with anger or aggressiveness but with a gentle passion that gives them human vitality and in a way that allows Du Bois' own feelings to come through to the reader. Du Bois intended to inform the reader not merely of the facts but of his own feelings about them. He was well aware of this dimension of his book. In a brief discussion of *The Souls of Black Folk* written shortly after its publication, Du Bois spoke of the "tropical blood" that was in him and that was, he thought, revealed by his words.[25]

Spirituality, then, was, important to Du Bois' ideas about race; and he sought to cultivate it in his own presentation of racial concerns. There may have been many reasons that Du Bois turned to such a strong conception of black identity. Werner Sollors has classed Du Bois' work with that of other theorists of ethnicity from this period who sought to create pluralist, fusionist models for an ethnic-American identity. Showing the similarities between Du Bois' ideas and those of Randolph

---

23. *Ibid.,* 198, 251.
24. Rampersad, *Art and Imagination,* 81; Stepto, *From Behind the Veil,* 64.
25. In Herbert Aptheker (ed.), *Book Reviews by W. E. B. Du Bois* (Millwood, N.Y., 1977), 9.

Bourne, Josiah Royce, and Horace Kallen, Sollors has argued that Du Bois urged "the conserving of Negro provincialism" in order to "make it easier to achieve the cosmopolitan and universalist ideal in America." Such a pluralist conception of American society was current during Du Bois' time; and it may be, as Sollors has suggested, that one of Du Bois' contributions was to add black Americans to the pluralist mix other writers had come to celebrate.[26]

In addition, one may see in Du Bois at least a surface similarity to those ethnic—and particularly immigrant—writers who sought to effect a "reconciliation" between past and present through the evocation of a renewed appreciation of their Old World heritage in the American context. Earlier black writers, as we have seen, sought to transcend such a heritage, even as they evoked it in their works. If Du Bois looked to the same sources for black distinctiveness that earlier writers had found appropriate, his attitude toward those sources was markedly different—but not out of line with the attitudes portrayed by such immigrant writers as Abraham Cahan and Israel Zangwill, who stressed the importance of holding to one's Old World heritage while meeting the demands of what they often termed "Americanization."[27]

But one may also see roots of Du Bois' interest in identity in his personal life and background. Psychologist Allison Davis has traced Du Bois' stress on distinctiveness and racial pride to a very personal alienation from white society, an alienation based on his childhood as a poor black youth in a virtually all-white setting; and Sterling Stuckey has emphasized the powerful impression black folk culture—and especially its spirituals—had on Du Bois from the moment he was first exposed to them. No less significantly, as Joel Williamson has argued, Du Bois' ideas had strong intellectual roots in the Hegelian ideas to which Du Bois was drawn during his graduate studies. Du Bois learned to view history on a Hegelian model as a struggle on the part of every people to achieve a consciousness of itself and its own peculiar genius. In *The Souls of Black Folk*, Du Bois combined such a Hegelian model of history with the kinds of ideas about black distinctiveness that had been around for years. In doing so, he gave the ideas a framework that

26. Werner Sollors, *Beyond Ethnicity: Consent and Descent in American Culture* (New York, 1986), 186–87.

27. See Jules Chametzky, *From the Ghetto: The Fiction of Abraham Cahan* (Amherst, 1977), 64–65; Israel Zangwill, *The Melting Pot: Drama in Four Acts* (New York, 1909).

removed much of the ambivalence with which they had long been invested.[28]

But Du Bois' sense of the importance of achieving such a racial self-appreciation can also be seen in terms of the notion of double-consciousness that framed the essays. In defining double-consciousness, Du Bois wrote that it had grown out of living in the American world, a world that allows the Negro "no true self-consciousness, but only lets him see himself through the revelation of the other world." Du Bois continued, "It is a peculiar sensation, this double-consciousness, this sense of always looking at one's self through the eyes of others, of measuring one's soul by the tape of a world that looks on in amused contempt and pity." Here, too, was a difficulty growing out of the fact that black life remained behind "the veil." Whites had no knowledge of black reality, but—as Du Bois saw, giving a kind of clarity to Sutton Griggs's understanding of American race relations—they had both the power and the inclination to define a black reality in which they sought to force blacks to live. One sees Du Bois' understanding of the problem of self-definition in his highly emotional account of his thoughts on the birth and death of an infant son. At the birth, the father's joy is mingled with misgivings: "Within the Veil was he born, said I; and there within shall he live,—a Negro and a Negro's son." The father and mother both dream that their son will become a prophet, leading the race to freedom; but even their grandest dreams are preconditioned by the fact of living in a white world, a world that demands a prophet and a world in which possibilities are defined by the presence of the veil. The freedom to work for self-fulfillment that lay open to the white child was denied at birth to the black infant, "a Negro and a Negro's son." The problem of defining oneself for oneself was crucial; and here, as in other places in the book, Du Bois showed how this was denied to black people.[29]

The Souls of Black Folk was an attempt to claim the power of defining a black reality from whites by pointing to the sources for a personal self-definition and a black self-definition—through its presentation of a black experience with distinctive properties, a real black distinctiveness, with substance. Robert Stepto has argued that as Du Bois immersed himself and his text in a distinctive black culture, he found sources for his own authentication and for the authentication of black

---

28. Davis, *Leadership, Love, Aggression,* 110; Sterling Stuckey, *Slave Culture: Nationalist Theory and the Foundations of Black America* (New York, 1987), 258; Williamson, *Crucible of Race,* 403.
29. Du Bois, *Souls of Black Folk,* 3, 209.

life from somewhere other than white America—and that he was the first black writer to do so.[30] Stepto's argument is important, because it helps emphasize that Du Bois was also the first writer to see clearly how important issues of self-definition were, to see them at the bottom of the kinds of dilemmas black writers had been facing for a long time as they tried to juggle issues of racial solidarity, racial identity, and assimilationist goals. Dunbar may have sensed the importance of self-definition; Du Bois brought it to the fore.

This concern with self-definition is important to note, because, despite the superficial similarities between Du Bois and such theorists as Bourne and Kallen—or between him and his contemporaries among immigrant writers—it was a concern that set him apart. If those other writers, for example, shared in Du Bois' pluralism and in his effort to reconcile past and present, none so clearly confronted the problem of self-definition as such. This was probably because none, despite the demands of "Americanizers" from both within and outside their communities, had to address the powerful, ongoing interference of outsiders in their lives; none had to confront the relentless racism Du Bois, not unlike Sutton Griggs, described in his accounts of race relations. This racism made the very act of self-definition a matter of paramount importance: Du Bois recognized that before one could ask how the self should be defined—a question raised by a range of writers during this period—the first task, for blacks, was to demand the right to define oneself at all.

This awareness of the problems of self-definition gave Du Bois a unique perspective on the familiar issues of assimilation and identity, one differing from the hopeful models others had created. Concerned about identity, Du Bois was no more prepared than such contemporaries as Chesnutt and Hopkins to forego a demand for a place in the American mainstream; and his search for a distinctive black identity remained within the parameters of integrationist ideals. He saw a black American identity as something growing out of a synthesis rather than a rejection of middle-class norms—a combining of the gifts of blacks and whites rather than a choosing of one set of gifts over the other. But he also recognized how difficult this synthesis would be. He described the "American" and "African" selves as "warring" within the individual, and his book usually takes a tone that is more melancholy than hopeful. Its impact on black readers may have had to do more with the way in which

30. Stepto, *From Behind the Veil*, 63–64.

it set forth old dilemmas than with any solutions it offered. The reaction of Jessie Fauset—later to become Du Bois' associate and a major writer herself—is to the point. A student at Cornell when *The Souls of Black Folk* first appeared, she wrote to Du Bois that, when she read the book, she felt that his writing it had been a "personal favor," so well did it capture the difficulties facing the "modern, educated colored man or woman." She continued: "It hurt you to write that book, didn't it? The man of fine sensibilities has to suffer exquisitely, just simply because his feeling is so fine." Focusing on the pain she perceived in the book, Fauset provided a perspective that emphasized the role of long-standing tensions in Du Bois' formulation of double-consciousness.[31]

Still, in stressing the gifts of black folk, Du Bois did reframe the discussion of familiar tensions. Above all, because he could see, with no apparent ambivalence, a substantive basis for a black identity, he was able to place the increasingly sharp dilemmas involving assimilationist desires and segregationist realities under a new umbrella of self-determination, or self-definition. This moved the understanding of those dilemmas to a deeper level, one that went below the issues of exclusion or acceptance and toward an awareness that the aspirations of black Americans involved choices about themselves that had long been in the hands of white Americans. Du Bois proposed, in response, an inward turning and a re-evaluation by black people, on their own terms, of what their place in society should be. The momentum for such a proposal had been developing for some time. One may see it, in literary terms, in the dialect tradition and its background and in the growing creative independence of black writers during Du Bois' time. But Du Bois was the writer who put the proposal in a straightforward way, giving it a foundation in a vision of black American life rooted in the alternative provided by a conception of black culture.

It was from the perspective provided by this reframing of the understanding of the black American experience that Du Bois saw the need for new approaches to literature as well. For Du Bois, the importance of self-determination and the substantive character of a black identity made unusual demands on the black writer. He summarized these demands in *The Souls of Black Folk*, in the context of his discussion of double-consciousness:

31. Du Bois, *Souls of Black Folk,* 3; Jessie Fauset to W. E. B. Du Bois, December 26, 1903, in W. E. B. Du Bois Papers, University of Massachusetts Library, Amherst (microfilm ed.).

The would-be black *savant* was confronted by the paradox that the knowledge his people needed was a twice-told tale to his white neighbors, while the knowledge which would teach the white world was Greek to his own flesh and blood. The innate love of harmony and beauty that set the ruder souls of his people a-dancing and a-singing raised but confusion and doubt in the soul of the black artist. For the beauty revealed to him was the soul-beauty of a race which his larger audience despised, and he could not articulate the message of another people.[32]

Here, in a few words, Du Bois outlined the limitations of much that had earlier been created by black writers, while implying a way to get beyond those limitations. In line with his idea of double-consciousness, and in keeping with the way many black writers were coming to categorize mainstream society and its literature as "white," Du Bois was asserting that much of the literature of the past was built on "white" models and was thus imitative—a "twice-told tale"—which exacerbated rather than resolved the problems of double-consciousness. The duty of the black artist was to tell the story of his own people by creating a literature infused with the spirit of the black folk experience.

With this view of literature, Du Bois provided the first statement of what more recent critics have termed a "black aesthetic"—a sense that, to use Houston Baker's concise definition, there can be "a distinctive code for the creation and evaluation of black art," a code infused, as most theorists have presented it, by the life of the Afro-American folk. Du Bois did not, of course, go as far as many later theorists—into what Baker has called "a kind of impressionistic chauvinism" that makes black literature available only to black readers. Indeed, Du Bois' purposes were exactly in the other direction—to make the black experience available to all readers, to "teach the white world" the knowledge black people had to give. But his pointing toward the uniqueness of the black experience and his urging of writers to capture that uniqueness was an important early statement of what Sterling Stuckey has termed "an autonomous aesthetic" growing out of black folk life and culture.[33]

Du Bois maintained this point of view throughout the years leading up to 1915. In a 1913 essay, he continued to stress the artistic character of the Negro. "The usual way of putting this is to speak disdainfully of his sensuous nature," Du Bois declared. "This means that the only race

32. Du Bois, *Souls of Black Folk,* 5.
33. Houston A. Baker, Jr., *Blues, Ideology, and Afro-American Literature: A Vernacular Theory* (Chicago, 1984), 74, 81; Stuckey, *Slave Culture,* 265.

which has held at bay the life destroying forces of the tropics, has gained therefrom in some slight compensation a sense of beauty, particularly for sound and color, which characterizes the race." That this distinctive gift could be turned to an art that would have worldwide acceptance, Du Bois saw proved in the creations of ancient Egypt, with its Pharoahs of "Negro blood."[34] Again, he did not see the task of turning sensuousness to art as an easy one. The search for distinctiveness could even lead to embarrassing excesses, as he knew. But the search would underlie Du Bois' own literary career.

As a force in black literature, Du Bois was probably more important as an essayist and editor than as a poet or an author of fiction. His role as editor was especially important as, with the founding of the NAACP, he had control of that organization's magazine, *Crisis*. Du Bois had long sought to produce a magazine that would give exposure to the best of black writing. He had sponsored two ill-fated efforts—*Moon* (1905–1906) and *Horizon* (1907–1910)—before taking over the very successful *Crisis*. In all three, he tried to encourage the creation of literature that moved beyond old standards for black writing.[35] But his own contributions to black literature, if sparse—a few scattered poems and a novel during this period—were far from negligible and give major insight into his understanding of black literature and black life.

Du Bois' poetry is an especially important locus for understanding his sense of black distinctiveness. In a poem dated 1899, "The Song of the Smoke," Du Bois celebrated blackness as such, declaring: "I am the smoke king, / I am black"; and in a note of independence, he proclaimed, "I am carving God in night, / I am painting hell in white." Although the poem did not deal with Du Bois' more substantive view of black distinctiveness, it did, as Stuckey has observed, transform blackness into a positive characteristic, engaging in a kind of inversion of categories that could powerfully enhance a positive conception of blackness as a unique source of identity.[36]

The substance of Du Bois' sense of black distinctiveness underlies, more clearly, his poem "The Burden of Black Women," which appeared in *Horizon* in 1907. The opening stanza contains the glimmerings of an exoticism that Du Bois' conceptions of African distinctiveness also

34. W. E. B. Du Bois, "The Negro in Literature and Art," *Annals of the American Academy of Political and Social Science*, XLIX (1913), 233.

35. Rampersad, *Art and Imagination*, 185–86.

36. W. E. B. Du Bois, "The Song of Smoke," *Crisis*, VII (1914), 132; Stuckey, *Slave Culture*, 276.

hinted at; and throughout the poem, Du Bois bitterly excoriated a white world that could neither appreciate the quality of black womanhood nor allow that quality to be revealed.

> Dark daughter of the lotus leaves that
> 　watch the southern sea,
> Wan spirit of a prisoned soul a-panting
> 　to be free;
> The muttered music of thy streams,
> 　the whispers of the deep
> Have kissed each other in thy name
> 　and kissed a world to sleep.

Condemning the white man's lust, the poet asked:

> Who raised the fools to their glory
> But black men of Egypt and Ind?
> Ethiopia's sons of the evening,
> Chaldeans and Yellow Chinese?
> The Hebrew children of Morning
> And mongrels of Rome and Greece?
> Ah, well![37]

Du Bois concluded the poem with the promise of a "Black Christ," who, in virtue, will destroy the corrupt structures whites have built on top of a black foundation. The white world, the poem proclaims, is so deeply sunk in sin that only the black world, with its deep spirituality, can save it.

The theme of black distinctiveness was also raised in another *Horizon* poem, "A Day in Africa." This 1908 poem was surely among the first by a black writer to celebrate African primitivism and exoticism as such, in this case through an evocation of a primitive identification with Nature. And the Africa of this poem was an almost Edenic tropical landscape:

> I rose to sense the incense of the hills,
> 　The royal sun sent crimsoned heralds to the dawn
> She glowed beneath her bridal veil of mist

A primitive closeness to nature was further evoked in a representation of the hunt:

37. W. E. B. Du Bois, "The Burden of Black Women," *Alexander's Magazine*, V (1908), 78–79.

My noon-tide meal did fawn about my feet
   In striped sleekness.
I kissed it ere I killed it,
   And slept away the liquid languor of the noon.[38]

This presumably African feeling for nature, embodied in a love for the prey, stood in sharp, if implicit, contrast to Du Bois' usual treatment of a white society bent only on gain, on using nature for material benefit. And it cohered with the vision of black people, portrayed in *The Souls of Black Folk*, as having a feeling for life that transcended the materialism of the modern world.

A more complex and deeper understanding of black distinctiveness and of the problems of double-consciousness appeared in Du Bois' most ambitious poem, his 1906 "A Litany at Atlanta." This poem was written at the height of the riots of 1906, as Du Bois hurried toward the city, fearing for the physical safety of his own family; it took the form of a litany to raise questions about the place and destiny of black Americans. The poem begins as a confessional. "We are not better than our fellows, Lord," the poet proclaimed, as he accepted punishment for the wrong-doing of his people. "And yet," the poet continued, "whose is the deeper guilt? Who made these devils? Who nursed them in crime and fed them on injustice? Who ravished and debauched their mothers and their grandmothers? Who bought and sold their crime and waxed fat and rich on public iniquity?" The crimes of the whites are far deeper than those of any black man, for they have gone to the soul of both races—the one corrupt, the other pure but frustrated.[39]

Thus the events at Atlanta become a cruel paradox in Du Bois' poem. Black innocence is punished by men who have no concept of virtue— "North is greed and South is blood," the poet said—while even the simplest of black aspirations are greeted with murder, not only in Atlanta but elsewhere in America. And the only white response is hypocrisy: "*Cease from Crime!* The word was mockery, for thus they train a hundred crimes while we do cure one." The poem concludes with the hope that God will send his vengeance, and it beseeches an apparently silent God to hear the prayers of his people. In this paradox is to be found the real tragedy of black double-consciousness—and its importance. At one level, Du Bois expressed the right of blacks to become part

---

38. W. E. B. Du Bois, "A Day in Africa," *Horizon*, III (1908), 5.
39. Rampersad, *Art and Imagination*, 104; poem quoted in W. E. B. Du Bois, *Darkwater: Voices from Within the Veil* (New York, 1921), 25.

of American society, contrasting that right with the frustrating realization that even the most accommodating of black men are to be excluded from society's benefits. At another level, however, is a powerful contrast between an innocent black people, who desire to rely on God and to preserve their spirituality, and a corrupt white world that is devoid of spiritual virtue. At one point, Du Bois' prayers are addressed to a "God of a godless land," emphasizing both the challenge and the significance of maintaining faith in a world in which faith is professed but not lived. To be sure, there are elements of a more traditional black rhetoric of irony in the poem—the sort of irony found in, for example, Victoria Earle Matthews' "Aunt Lindy." But the poem's thoroughgoing sense of the deeper corruption of Western civilization goes well beyond irony to the kind of cultural critique found in *The Souls of Black Folk*. A bitter outcry against injustice, the poem is organized by the sense of black distinctiveness and double-consciousness so important in Du Bois' thought.[40]

But the most complex presentation of the themes that dominated Du Bois' thought appear in his chief work of fiction from this period, his 1911 novel, *The Quest of the Silver Fleece*. This novel is, like other black novels from before World War I, an effort to deal with racial issues in the idiom of the romance. Arnold Rampersad has argued that Du Bois probably learned little from his predecessors among black novelists and seems to have been more nearly inspired by such white writers as George Washington Cable and Frank Norris.[41] This may be so; but in its overall form and in many specifics, Du Bois' novel fell into the main currents of black fiction. At the same time, it was also a novel that served to dramatize Du Bois' ideas about black distinctiveness and his own approach to the tensions he termed double-consciousness.

The Quest of the Silver Fleece is a complicated novel, with several plots going on simultaneously. At the center is a love story involving the two main characters, Blessed Alwyn—known as Bles—and Zora, who enters the book as a darkly primitive daughter of the swamp. At the same time that this relationship is progressing, there is also a story of an effort led by a few white southerners and their northern conspirators to establish a monopoly in the cotton trade. This story of economic and political chicanery deeply involves Bles and Zora, as well, influencing the course of their lives and their relationship. Also weaving in and out

40. *Ibid.,* 26–28.
41. Rampersad, *Art and Imagination,* 116–17.

of the book is an account of the progress and tribulations of the country Negro school, founded by a philanthropic northern white woman. This school has given Bles and Zora the educational foundation for their future lives. And, finally, the novel is a tale of the transformation of Zora from an ignorant primitive to an urbane, sophisticated young woman and a leader of her race. Along the way, Du Bois used the novel as a vehicle for expressing his own views of racial problems, their causes, and strategies for change.

With all these plot lines, it is the character of Zora that holds the book together, serving as the emotional focus of the novel and as the chief medium for conveying Du Bois' concerns. The Zora who enters the novel is unlike any previous heroine in black literature, except, perhaps, John S. Durham's Diane. Above all, she is completely lacking in gentility. Du Bois' first presentation of her is filled with both primitivism and sensuality. She is sighted, out in the swamp, by Bles, who sees her through an opening in the trees: "Amid this mighty halo, as on clouds of flame, a girl was dancing. She was black, and lithe, and tall, and willowy. Her garments twined and flew around the delicate moulding of her dark, young, half-naked limbs. A heavy mass of hair clung motionless to her side forehead. Her arms twirled and flickered, and body and soul seemed quivering and whirring in the poetry of her motion."[42] To Bles, she is a vision; and he is captivated by her.

Bles already has a strong racial consciousness and is attending Miss Smith's school for black youth in the hope of assuming his place as a leader of his people. The very county in which he lives is evidence of the need for such leadership. A "Black Sea," as he calls it, it is corruptly controlled by the white Cresswell family—Cresswell will be involved in the effort to create a cotton cartel—and most blacks are reduced to abject poverty as tenants on white-owned land. Du Bois described tenant farming as nothing other than a species of slavery. For Bles, education and economic independence are the keys to the future of blacks; and he hopes to encourage both.

Zora becomes deeply involved in the effort. Bles persuades Zora to go to school, and together they undertake to transform her swamp into rich cotton land. Zora's school career is not without difficulty. Unsophisticated, she has no idea of decorum or of middle-class morality. Notions of ownership are unclear to her; and, early on, she has to be taught that stealing is not part of the way of life that Bles hopes for her

42. W. E. B. Du Bois, *The Quest of the Silver Fleece* (1911; rpr. New York, 1969), 14–15.

and that the school aims to teach her. She must also face the strong opposition to her education by her mother, old Elspeth, a former slave. Elspeth is an ugly old woman, a reputed witch, who has little respect for Bles's ambitions or what the school stands for.

Indeed, it is Elspeth who, indirectly, causes the first real shock in Zora's life. Accepting the old ways of slavery, Elspeth has made Zora available to Harry Cresswell. Zora has had no sense that there has been evil in this but has accepted it herself as part of her life. One morning, she and Bles, contemplating a picture of the Madonna, begin to discuss purity. Zora wants to know what it is. The Madonna is lily white; and Zora asks, "Bles, what's purity—just whiteness?" Bles responds that it means for a woman to be "just as good as a woman knows how."[43] Zora is satisfied of her own purity, but later the truth comes out. After Zora has been to school, she learns that what she has done with Cresswell has made her impure. Bles, in a fury, leaves her.

By this time, however, Zora has changed, beginning that transformation that will culminate in her taking a place of leadership among her people. She has become special to her teachers, as to Bles, and has progressed rapidly in school. She and Bles have worked hard to make their crop, and have succeeded. She has become industrious as well as educated. Indeed, the crop is beginning to come in when she and Bles break up. Their parting does not destroy her, though it easily could have. Left with the cotton when Bles leaves, Zora succeeds in having it picked and takes it to market. It is of unusually fine quality and fetches a good price. Cresswell, however, tries to take advantage of the situation. Claiming an obscure title to the land, he attempts to force Zora into tenancy by claiming, as well, her indebtedness to him. She resists, realizing that "to work in the fields meant endless toil and a vista that opened upon death."[44]

Zora's salvation comes from a wealthy white woman, Mrs. Vanderpool, who takes her on as a maid. This woman encourages Zora's desire for improvement and opens up vistas to her that even Bles would not have known. Taking Zora to Washington, D.C., she also introduces Zora to the world of American society and politics, even using Zora to deal with blacks in an effort to improve her husband's standing with the national administration. By this time, Zora has become an intelligent and refined young woman; and she proves a capable assistant to Mrs. Vanderpool as well as an apt student of Washington life.

43. *Ibid.,* 98.
44. *Ibid.,* 214.

With Zora's arrival in Washington, *The Quest of the Silver Fleece* becomes very much a political novel. Bles is also in Washington and is heavily involved in the political life of the capital. He is seen as one who can have strong effects on the Negro vote, and his leadership is both sought and resented by the leaders of various political factions. The Cresswells are in Washington, too. Harry is in Congress, using his position to further the aims of his cotton cartel. He has married Mary Taylor, a former teacher at the Negro school, whose northern background is useful to his efforts to involve northern money in his scheme. Du Bois presented white politics in Washington as cynical and corrupt, with no one motivated by anything other than the most venal ambitions. Here, he made clear, is impurity—not in Zora's ignorant and innocent sexual contact with an immoral white man.

Zora herself recognizes the impurity of Washington life as well as the moral complexity of living in the modern world: "I do not belong in this world where Right and Wrong get so mixed. With us yonder there is wrong, but we call it wrong—mostly. Oh, I don't know; even there things are mixed."[45] She has learned more than Bles could ever teach her; she has learned both the difficulty of applying moral categories and the necessity for doing so. She returns to the South, revitalizing the school and successfully taking charge of her own land—humiliating the Cresswells in the process. Bles returns to ask her forgiveness and to ask her to marry him; but she refuses, at first, preferring to devote herself to her work. Despite opposition, including mob violence, Zora succeeds. In the end, Bles, pleading his own unworthiness, is accepted by her as a husband.

According to the critic Robert Bone, Du Bois had, by 1911, become a socialist; thus one purpose of *The Quest of the Silver Fleece* was to emphasize the important connections between economic forces and racial injustice. But Du Bois did not write an economic novel. As the recent critic Bernard Bell has stressed, it was, like other black novels of the period, both romantic and moralistic.[46] Morality, not economics, lay at the center of Zora's transformation. So, too, did Du Bois' own interest in black distinctiveness. There were noble white characters in Du Bois' novel—or at least white characters capable of acting nobly—but the white world of the South and of the nation's capital was distinguished chiefly by its corruption. Du Bois certainly saw the irony of that corrupt

45. *Ibid.*, 328.
46. Robert A. Bone, *The Negro Novel in America* (Rev. ed.; New Haven, 1965), 43; Bernard W. Bell, *The Afro-American Novel and Its Tradition* (Amherst, 1987), 82–83, 85.

world. Treating blacks as moral and intellectual inferiors, white Americans were rapidly creating a social and economic system that was wholly without conscience. The irony was apparent in the character of Bles, a champion of his people who nevertheless gets caught up in that corrupt world. And the irony was especially apparent in Bles's initial rejection of Zora because of her "impurity." So taken in was he by the white man's values that he was incapable of seeing in her a greater purity than that represented by the easily preserved chastity of a New England schoolteacher. The novel was the story of Zora's transformation from primitive to leader. It was also an unfolding of Bles's realization of the beauties of his own people.

If it is possible, in some ways, to place Du Bois' novel within the black literary tradition of romantic protest, it clearly went beyond that tradition in its assertion of black distinctiveness and in its presentation of a kind of intuitive goodness in black people that contrasted sharply with the calculated but corrupt morality of white America. Like other heroines in black literature from this period, Zora has a virtuousness that puts the morality of whites to shame. Unlike those other heroines, however, Zora's moral light comes not from a stronger dedication to middle-class gentility but from an innate quality that could not be destroyed by her contact with a world of material affluence and political influence. Zora is able to maintain this virtue because she remains unawed by whites. She is not taken in by those well-meaning liberals who would force her into the mold of New England respectability, as Bles is. Nor is she corrupted by a desire to emulate white ambition or to pander to white corruption, as is Elspeth and as are the black politicos whose portraits Du Bois drew in his account of Washington life. Zora retains her independence of whites—cooperating with them, to be sure, and certainly learning from them, but never letting them determine her path for her.

Here, then, was a new way of stating some traditional themes; and it was a way that looked in a new direction for black literary tradition. Maintaining the older focus on virtue and morality, Du Bois redefined that focus by looking at moral questions in light of the faith in black distinctiveness that he had given shape in *The Souls of Black Folk*. To be sure, Du Bois' vision was still integrationist. Even here, the Zora who becomes an effective race leader is a Zora who has profited from a liberal education and an exposure to sophisticated white people. She has learned both good manners and good English by the middle of the novel. But Du Bois' integrationist vision was tempered by a perception that black people had a spirituality lacking in white America, a spirituality that ought to be celebrated and preserved. In the sensuous, exotic, but genuinely cultured Zora, Du Bois gave real substance to blackness and genuine dramatic meaning to the synthesis that would produce a black self-definition.

Du Bois was not alone in trying to reframe the tensions facing black Americans, particularly through new articulations and evaluations of black identity in American society. Other writers were also prepared to move, as Du Bois had, beyond more traditional approaches to a black identity. For example, the beginnings of an appreciation for a distinctive black beauty, in works from around the turn of the century, were built upon in the period leading up to World War I by several poets and writers. David Bryant Fulton, under the pseudonym Jack Thorne, wrote a 1912 tribute to black womanhood that expressed a new pride in black beauty, beginning with the oft-cited verse from the *Song of Solomon*, "I am black but comely, O ye daughters of Jerusalem, as the tents of Kedar, as the curtains of Solomon." It was a line, Fulton declared, from "that period in the history of the world when the dominant races were sable races; and the black and swarthy skin was of course a mark of honor; when the women of whose beauties and charms the bards wrote in such extravagant eulogy were colored women, and the warriors and heroes whose praise the women chanted so lustily, as is recorded in both sacred and profane history, were swarthy and black." He concluded his discussion by arguing that the usually accepted translation of the passage from *Solomon* was wrong, that it should read, "I am black and comely." The modification was important, rejecting any apology for physical difference from white standards.[47]

This kind of pride in blackness was especially important in the bibliophilic efforts of one of Fulton's associates from the time, Arthur Schomburg. Schomburg devoted his life and career to researching and recovering the black past. He founded, with John Cromwell and with Fulton, the Negro Society for Historical Research—its letterhead evoking traditional ideas of ancient Africa with a picture of the Sphinx—and began to gather the collection of printed materials by blacks that became the nucleus for the New York Public Library's Schomburg Center for Research in Black Culture. In a 1915 letter to Cromwell, Schomburg reported a conversation he had had with two black Columbia University

47. David Bryant Fulton [Jack Thorne], *A Plea for Social Justice for the Negro Woman*, Negro Society for Historical Research, Occasional Paper No. 2 (Yonkers, N.Y., 1912), 1–2.

students in which he had offered his opinion, familiar from the earliest black histories, that civilization had originated among black Africans and had moved down the Nile to Egypt and thence to Europe. The students strongly disagreed with him, and Schomburg's account of the disagreement is revealing. "The great universities of the North teach us the Caucasian civilization," Schomburg told Cromwell, "and the graduate soon as he leaves its philosophical doors must commence to learn to *think black*."[48] The call to "think black" implied a sense that blacks possess a unique perspective. It was a phrase that would never have been comprehended in the more traditional, and ambivalent, assimilationist-based views of black distinctiveness.

A major statement of this developing position—two volumes worth—was made by William H. Ferris in his 1913 work *The African Abroad*. Ferris, born in New Haven, was a Yale graduate and had attended Harvard Divinity School. He was also involved with Schomburg in the Negro Society for Historical Research and worked as both a minister and a teacher. As historian William Toll has suggested, Ferris was a man of some eccentricity. Du Bois' *Crisis* took note of Ferris' "careless dress, his undecided face, burning eyes and quick endless speech" and noted that more practical blacks tended to cite him as "the awful example of indiscriminate bestowal of higher learning." But *Crisis* also liked his book and found much that was of value in it.[49]

Ferris, who coined the term *Negro-Saxon* to emphasize the dual heritage of American blacks, saw a crucial need to recognize a distinctive Negro character, one that set blacks apart from whites in positive ways. He believed black culture was ultimately part of the mainstream of world cultures; but, like Du Bois, he saw black culture as a valuable antidote to the excesses of white materialism. In a significant passage early in his work, Ferris wrote, "The Negro race will never achieve much if it scatters its energy and attempts to blot out the precious traits of the race," adding, "The Negro possesses those spiritual and emotional qualities which can soften human nature and spiritualize religion and music. Here is his sphere."[50] Like Du Bois, Ferris saw in black spirituality

48. Arthur A. Schomburg to John W. Cromwell, December 23, 1915, in Cromwell Family Papers, The Moorland-Spingarn Research Center, Howard University.

49. William Toll, *The Resurgence of Race: Black Social Theory from Reconstruction to the Pan-African Conferences* (Philadelphia, 1979), 141; "Ferris' Vindication," *Crisis*, VII (1914), 147.

50. William H. Ferris, *The African Abroad; or, His Evolution in Western Civilization: Tracing His Development Under Caucasian Milieu* (2 vols.; 1913; rpr. New York, 1968), I, 34.

the positive gift of black folk that would allow for a genuine self-definition growing out of a synthesis of the African and American identities.

Fulton, Schomburg, and Ferris were not entirely typical of black
thinkers in the first two decades of the twentieth century. The Negro
Society for Historical Research, in which all three were important figures, was itself unique in its strong devotion to black self-consciousness.
Beginning in about 1919, Ferris even became associated with the black
nationalist, emigrationist movement led by Marcus Garvey, taking his
views of black distinctiveness to a point that Du Bois, at the time,
refused to countenance.[51]

But Du Bois' ideas were capable of a less radical formulation and in
these terms had a noticeable impact on black writing. The most influential effort to give his ideas a literary role, outside of Du Bois' work itself,
was Benjamin Brawley's 1915 essay entitled "The Negro Genius," published in the Hampton Institute's white-edited journal, *Southern Workman*. Brawley was a poet, and it was in terms of his ideas about poetry
that his theories of Negro genius developed. He began the essay by
referring to Edgar Allan Poe's lecture "the Poetic Principle," in which
Poe identified three human faculties: intellect, feeling, and the will. Poe
argued, and Brawley agreed, that "the whole realm of esthetics" is contained in the faculty of feeling. According to Brawley, moreover, each of
the "races" of the world seemed to be distinctively characterized by a
special ability in each faculty. The Anglo-Saxon was preeminently gifted
in "the domain of pure intellect"; the Jews showed greatest strength in
areas having to do with the will, especially with morality; and the Negro
race was the race of feeling. Brawley based his position on what he took
to be the fact that all major achievements by black people up to his own
time had been in the arts. He referred to the many gifted black singers,
to the oratory of Douglass, "to the sensuous poetry of Dunbar, to the
picturesque style of Du Bois." Even Washington, he wrote, "proves the
point, the distinguishing qualities of his speeches being anecdote and
brilliant concrete illustration." But this interest in the artistic was not,
he stressed, confined to the educated and the articulate. He spoke of the
love of black people for decoration and color, red being a favorite
because of its brightness. Black churches, he said, were scenes of high
emotionalism and vivid language. The artistic rather than the moralistic
was, he suggested, the center of black religion.[52]

51. See Toll, *Resurgence of Race*, 141.
52. Benjamin Brawley, "The Negro Genius," *Southern Workman*, XLIV (1915),
305–307.

And undergirding all of this was a depth, the product of background and experience, that removed black sensuousness from the merely superficial. This depth was, according to Brawley, "the soul of the race." He wrote, "The wail of the old melodies and the plaintive quality that is ever present in the Negro voice are but the reflection of a background of tragedy." He added: "There is something very elemental about the heart of the race, something that finds its origin in the African forest, in the sighing of the night-wind, and in the falling of the stars. There is something grim and stern about it all too, something that speaks of the lash, of the child torn from its mother's bosom, of the dead body riddled with bullets and swinging all night from a limb by the roadside." Taken together, Brawley found, these attributes and experiences made the Negro the world's greatest romantic, full of feeling and poised to make a major contribution to the world's art.[53]

Brawley was still enough of an assimilationist to see dangers in his position. At one point he took pains to stress that blacks should not be limited to artistic fields and that different individuals had different talents, which each should be enabled to pursue. But his conclusion was still clear, as was his debt to Du Bois. "Every race has its peculiar genius," he argued, and that of the Negro was "in the field of the artistic." Literature, along with sculpture, painting, and oratory, held limitless possibilities: "Already his music is recognized as the most distinctive that the United States has yet produced." In coming to these conclusions, Brawley was merely carrying forward ideas that Du Bois had crystallized—ideas that, in pointing to an innate black spirituality, went back even further than that. But, whatever the germ, the formulation of a full-scale literary theory based on such ideas was original and important.[54]

It would be easy, certainly, to overstate the implications of Brawley's ideas. There was nothing, for example, demanding a sharp break with the major forms of black writing—and, indeed, Brawley's own poems are testimony to that. In terms of both form and content, Brawley was a conservative, sentimental poet, as were most black writers during this period. Though he spoke of a distinctive "Negro genius," Brawley's "black esthetic" was really little more than a claim that blacks could do good, sentimental artistic work and that they were uniquely qualified to do so. But this conservatism on Brawley's part does not lessen his

53. *Ibid.,* 307–308.
54. *Ibid.,* 308. On Brawley, see August Meier, "Some Reflections on the Negro Novel," *CLA Journal,* II (1959), 171–72.

significance. What Brawley showed is the real influence Du Bois' ideas could have on black thinking. Though Brawley was a conservative writer, he nonetheless followed Du Bois' lead—to return to Robert Stepto's analysis of authentication—by placing even black sentimental poetry within a black cultural matrix, giving it a kind of literary independence and a role in self-definition that it had not had before.

One writer who sought to embody Brawley's point of view in his own work was Fenton Johnson. Although Johnson was to make his strongest literary mark as a writer associated with the Harlem Renaissance of the 1920s, he published a great deal prior to the coming of World War I. Not really a radical poet, either stylistically or in terms of his main themes and images, Johnson nevertheless took pains to put his work in a black cultural context; and he subscribed fully to the kinds of ideas Brawley and Du Bois had presented about black culture during this period. In a long introduction to one of his collections of verse, the 1916 *Songs of the Soil*, Johnson spoke of what he saw as the unique character of black people, a character that was "oriental and primitive" and "richly endowed with emotion."[55] All of Johnson's early work displayed a growing effort on his part to embody such ideas in verse.

Johnson published three prewar volumes of poetry; they were mixtures of standard English and dialect poems, much like the works of other poets of his time. Indeed, his first volume, *A Little Dreaming*, published in 1913, broke little new ground, although Johnson did do some experimenting with free verse in a couple of poems. In his second volume, published in 1915, Johnson went somewhat further in an effort to stress black distinctiveness, even as he experimented more with verse forms. One sees something of both these tendencies in his long poem "Ethiopia," an epic of black history beginning in ancient Ethiopia and moving to Johnson's own time. Its final stanza is particularly telling:

> And thus I sing the song of Ethiop
> Though I am dwelling in a stranger's land,
> A lonely minstrel, born to serve and love
> Throughout the world his fellows of the dusk.[56]

The poem is notable in its presentation of alienation from American society and its pan-African sentiments, looking clearly toward a distinctly black identity.

Johnson also sought to deal with ideals of black distinctiveness by

55. Fenton Johnson, *Songs of the Soil* (1916; rpr. New York, 1975), 1.
56. Fenton Johnson, *Visions of the Dusk* (1915; rpr. Freeport, N.Y., 1971), 48.

writing what he called "imitations" of Negro spirituals, several of which appeared in his 1915 collection. Here he claimed "to give a literary form and interpretation" to the "poetic endeavour" of the slaves. He was particularly concerned to capture "that exquisite Oriental imagery the Africans brought with them"—an imagery that was uniquely black, not borrowed from white religion. For the most part, the spirituals were not written in dialect, but they did make use of the call-response form so often identified with black music, as well as of distinctive forms often identified with black religion:

> Dance the Gospel, honey,
>   Jubal's free,
> Set you feet a-swinging
> Jubal's free;
> Night has changed to morning,
> In her breast the warning
> Of the God of sorrow,
> "They must go to-morrow,"
>   Jubal's free.[57]

In his 1916 collection, Johnson published more spiritual imitations in an effort to evoke that "oriental and primitive" distinctiveness of the folk Negro. By so framing his work, Johnson placed it squarely within the ideas Du Bois and others had sought to encourage, however little he departed from older black poetic forms.

For the most part, even the writers who sought to incorporate Du Bois' ideas in their works were, like Johnson, fairly conservative in their approach. They looked to new sources of authenticity but not to radically new forms or themes. But a few did move toward the creation of an actual literature of black distinctiveness. Certainly, one sees such an effort in the noted poem "Ballade des Belles Milatraisses (The Octoroon Ball, New Orleans, 1840–1850)," written by Rosalie Jonas and published in *Crisis* in 1911. Frankly celebrating the sensuality of the octoroon women as it points up the hideous immorality of the octoroon ball as an institution, the poem also attempts to evoke the exotic rhythms and excitements of the ball:

> The music grows madder! the ball's at its height!
> For beauty and kisses, it's Hey! and it's Ho!
> These women are fair—for an hour a night—
> (Play on! fiddler-man, keep your eyes on your bow!)

57. *Ibid*, 29.

And for all dull to-morrows, to-night who'd forego!
The music grows madder! "Play Trouloulou! play!"
Your women are frail, and your masters are gay!
Cocodrie in the dark marks them flee and pursue!
And the lilt of the old Creole song goes this way:
"Trouloulou! Trouloulou! c'est pas zaffaire a tou!"[58]

Using short exclamations and Creole French terms and phrases, Jonas created a poem with a sensuality that had long been avoided by more genteel black writers, using language in a way that immersed her readers in that sensuality.

Another poem that sought to incorporate Du Bois' ideas was the more obscure "Child of the Night," written by a Washington, D.C., poet named Walter Everette Hawkins and first published in the pan-Africanist London *African Times and Orient Review* in 1912. It was republished in *Crisis* in 1924. Hawkins was an interesting figure. His first volume of poetry, *Chords and Discords*, was published in 1909 and contained several notably iconoclastic poems on such topics as religion and politics. It was forthright in its biases: In one poem, Hawkins described Booker T. Washington as a "traitor." By 1920, Hawkins had moved to a clearly leftist point of view. He wrote for a time for the Harlem socialist magazine *Messenger* and continued to publish poetry through the 1920s and 1930s, showing an increasingly leftist orientation.[59]

At the very beginning of "Child of the Night," Hawkins proclaimed his own black identity:

Child of Night am I—
Night's sable son;
When the elf-children came,
Lo! I was one.

In a recurring stanza, he then asserted the spiritual power of blackness, its strength and its endurance:

58. Rosalie Jonas, "Ballade des Belles Milatraisses," *Crisis*, I (March, 1911), 22.
59. The publication of Walter Everette Hawkins' "Child of the Night" in the *African Times and Orient Review* in 1912 was noted by Hawkins himself in his 1915 entry in Frank Lincoln Mather (ed.), *Who's Who of the Colored Race* (Chicago, 1915), 132. It apparently appeared in a supplement to volume I, although I have not been able to locate that supplement. The excerpts quoted here are from *Crisis*, XXVII (1924), 258. But it is clearly a poem written before World War I. The poem dealing with Booker T. Washington is in Walter Everette Hawkins, *Chords and Discords* (Washington, D.C., 1909), 50. The best evidence on Hawkins' development comes from his own books, particularly *Chords and Discords* (2d ed., 1920; rpr. New York, 1975) and *Petals from the Poppies* (New York, 1936).

> At the great forge of Time
> Making men's souls sublime,
> I stood arrayed in Night
> Ere light was born.

And, with a radical assertion of the distinctiveness of black spirituality, he prayed:

> Cloud me in battle-smoke, night-shrouds attend me,
> The beginning was blackness and so will the end be;
> Black God and black angels, surround and defend me!

Here, along with Du Bois' "The Song of the Smoke," was the most enthusiastic and thoroughgoing poem of black identity of the period, one that fused the celebration of distinctiveness with a proclamation of self and history. The poem was unusual for its time, and even in the body of Hawkins' work. But it was important for showing how Du Bois' ideas could be given shape in black literature in the years before World War I.

VI

The Two Worlds of James Weldon Johnson

The works of such writers as Rosalie Jonas and Walter Everette Hawkins, along with the ideas and efforts of such literary figures as Fenton Johnson and Benjamin Brawley, represent significant approaches expressing the view of black culture and experience that W. E. B. Du Bois' ideas could inspire. However, no one did more to develop a literature in which that view received full play than James Weldon Johnson. Johnson's career was the most remarkable of any black writer's in the early twentieth century. After Paul Laurence Dunbar's death, in 1906, and Charles Chesnutt's virtual retirement from writing at about the same time, Johnson quickly became the most visible black writer of his day. Like Dunbar and Chesnutt, Johnson published widely in the major white-controlled magazines. With the advent of *Crisis*, he also found an outlet for his work that reached the black community as well.

But his career was also more diverse than that of any writer before. At various times a teacher, lawyer, diplomat, politician, and lyricist for popular songs, Johnson was an urbane and sophisticated man who wrote some of the most important and influential literary work by any black author prior to World War I. Moreover, his one novel, *The Autobiography of an Ex-Colored Man* (1912), was a major forerunner of the Harlem Renaissance of the 1920s. And, indeed, Johnson's literary career itself reached over into the Harlem Renaissance. But, most importantly, Johnson's work of the prewar period presents in microcosm the full meaning and the implications of the transformations that appeared in black literature during the early twentieth century. Not that Johnson was in any way typical or representative, for he was not. But his very atypicality helps underline the psychological potentialities inherent in the black literature that emerged after Du Bois, on the eve of World War I.

James Weldon Johnson was born in Jacksonville, Florida, in 1871. His father was a headwaiter in a resort hotel, and his mother was a schoolteacher. His upbringing was fully in keeping with the standards of the middle-class black community that was developing during his day; and Johnson grew up, as he recalled, knowing little of privation.[1] Both literate and literary, the family encouraged young Johnson in that direction. He attended Atlanta University, working during the summer as a country schoolteacher, and graduated in 1894. During the summer of 1893 he visited the Chicago World's Fair, where he met Paul Laurence Dunbar and formed a friendship with him that lasted until Dunbar's death. It was at Atlanta University that he began to write poetry, and a few of his early works were published in the university's bulletin.

Following his graduation, Johnson returned to Jacksonville, where he was hired as principal of the Negro school. He involved himself heavily in his work and brought about major changes in the operations of the school. At the same time, he was seriously concerned about racial issues; and within a year of his arrival, he established a newspaper to serve the black community. The paper collapsed, but Johnson continued to branch out; in 1898, having read law for eighteen months, he passed the state bar. He practiced only briefly, however, maintaining his position as a school principal.

In 1902 Johnson began a new career, resigning his school post in order to join his younger brother, John Rosamond, in New York. Rosamond had always been a talented musician, and in 1890 he had left Florida to study at the New England Conservatory of Music in Boston. After a brief and unsatisfying effort to become a music teacher in Jacksonville, Rosamond had returned to the North to write popular songs. He and James had collaborated on a few efforts during Rosamond's stay in Jacksonville; indeed, during the summers of 1900, 1901, and 1902, James had been in New York working with his brother. They were joined by Bob Cole, forming a team that published a number of hit songs for Broadway shows and revues. Johnson also took advantage of his time in New York to study literature at Columbia University, notably with the influential southern-born professor of dramatic literature, Brander Matthews, who later wrote the introduction to Johnson's first volume of poetry.

During this same time, Johnson was active in New York Republican politics, becoming the president of the city's Colored Republican Club

---

1. Eugene Levy, *James Weldon Johnson: Black Leader, Black Voice* (Chicago, 1973), 7.

in 1905. On the basis of this work and the influence of Booker T. Washington, Johnson was appointed in 1906 to a consular post in Venezuela, and later to one in Nicaragua. During this period he also began to court Grace Nail, daughter of one of New York's wealthiest black businessmen; and in 1910, during one of his trips back to the United States, they were married. In 1912, with the election of the Democrat Woodrow Wilson to the presidency, Johnson left the Foreign Service and returned to the United States.

The next few years were fairly difficult for Johnson. He and Grace went first to Jacksonville, where no opportunities appeared, although Johnson continued to do some writing for his brother and to make a little money from it. In 1914 the couple returned to New York, where Johnson worked as a writer for the New York *Age*. He continued to write poetry and had several major pieces published during this period, including three in W. E. B. Du Bois' *Crisis*. Johnson also joined and took an active role in the NAACP, and in 1916 he joined the organization's staff, becoming its acting secretary. He later became secretary of the organization and in this capacity remained in New York through the halcyon days of the Harlem Renaissance. Johnson eventually returned to the South, to Fisk University, where he taught until his death, in 1938.[2]

There was never a period during Johnson's adult life when he was not engaged in literary work. During his student days at Atlanta University, he wrote prolifically; and even as an American consul in Venezuela and Nicaragua, he continued to write and publish his work. Indeed, much of his *Autobiography of an Ex-Colored Man* was written while he was abroad with the Foreign Service. He was, moreover, not unaware of the works of his black contemporaries. His friendship with Dunbar was strong and lasting. Even as far back as his student days, he pasted the works of black poets, including Albery A. Whitman, in his scrapbooks.

As Johnson developed his ideas about literature, he came increasingly in line with the ideas of racial distinctiveness put forward by Du Bois and Brawley. In one of his early New York *Age* columns (1915), Johnson wrote that black America would furnish the great American poets: "There is every reason for this prophecy to come true; we are more richly endowed for such work than the white race. We have more heart, more soul; we are more responsive to emotional vibrations; we

---

2. Details on Johnson's life are taken from *ibid.* and from James Weldon Johnson's autobiography, *Along This Way* (New York, 1933).

have a larger share of the gifts of laughter, music and song; in a word, we are less material and we are, by nature, more artistic than white people."[3] No one had ever articulated such ideas more plainly.

But Johnson also saw a need to keep a close eye on the main tenets of Western literary tradition. "Although poets are born," he wrote, "they have to be made afterwards" in order to write "acceptable poetry." This meant, he said, "having the necessary tools," for poetry was a "trade" that "must be studied and learned."[4] For Johnson, any distinctive black traits had to be expressed and expressible within the confines of American civilization. Thus he sought to fuse the celebration of blackness with an essentially integrationist perspective on both society and literature.

As one traces the evolution of Johnson's career as a writer from his Atlanta days to the more polished work he produced during the first two decades of the twentieth century, one can see the unfolding of these ideas about black writing. And what one sees is a steady evolution toward the kind of Du Boisian ideas contained in his New York *Age* essay, but an evolution always counterbalanced by Johnson's own strong commitment to what was essentially an integrationist ideal.

Johnson's earliest work, undertaken during his student days and during his career as an educator-editor-lawyer in Jacksonville, was fairly typical of that being done by black writers who were his contemporaries. His student poems included a mixture of romantic verse, poetry on racial themes, and even a little dialect work. His notebooks show him to have been a conscientious young poet. His revisions were thorough, and even then he could be a tough self-critic. In keeping with his later characterization of poetry as a "trade," he worked hard to perfect his work technically. One of his notebooks even contains an outline of traditional rhythmic "feet"—iambic, trochaic, anapestic, and dactylic. Johnson later looked back over some of these efforts, marking those he did not like as "punk," "still more punk," and "juvenile punk"; but a few stood the test of time well for him and even found a place in his first volume of poetry, *Fifty Years and Other Poems*, which appeared in 1917. The mixture of his earliest poetry represented for him, as for other black poets, an effort to create verse that fit into the main currents

3. New York *Age*, January 7, 1915.
4. *Ibid.*

of American popular literature, while not rejecting racial identity as an important element in its composition.[5]

As Johnson began to make his mark as a writer, beginning in about 1900, he continued to work within the confines of black literary tradition, his work capturing all the themes and ambivalences found in works by black writers at the turn of the century. One sees this, for example, in the poem that was his first major publication, "Sence You Went Away," which appeared in 1900 in *Century*. The poem was very much in the tradition of Dunbar's dialect work, expressing a simple but heartfelt emotion:

> Seems lak to me de stars don't shine so bright,
> Seems lak to me de sun done loss his light,
> Seems lak to me der's nothin' goin' right,
>   Sence you went away.

As was true of dialect verse by other black poets, this poem moved beyond stereotypes of the plantation tradition and showed the possibility of melancholy and strong feeling in the people of the rural South— although it did not really go beyond most dialect verse by black writers of the period, at least so far as its theme was concerned. It was, however, a successful work; and it received renewed success when, in 1913, Rosamond set it to music. As a song, it was first performed by Pasquale Amato, a Metropolitan Opera baritone, and was later recorded by the great tenor John McCormack, with a violin obbligato by Fritz Kreisler. According to Johnson, in his 1933 autobiography, it continued to find a place on concert programs throughout his life.[6]

One sees the traditional character of Johnson's early work no less clearly in a piece that was more significant for Johnson's fame as a writer. This was a song he wrote with his brother for Jacksonville's 1900 celebration of Abraham Lincoln's birthday, a song to be performed by a chorus of five hundred schoolchildren. Giving up a plan to write a piece actually focusing on Lincoln, Johnson worked feverishly along a very different line, ultimately producing the words for the song "Lift Ev'ry

5. James Weldon Johnson, Notebooks #2 and #5, ms. volumes, in James Weldon Johnson Collection, Collection of American Literature, Beinecke Rare Book and Manuscript Library, Yale University; James Weldon Johnson, *Fifty Years and Other Poems* (1917; rpr. New York, 1975).

6. James Weldon Johnson, *Along This Way*, 153–54; James Weldon Johnson, *Fifty Years*, 63; John Rosamond Johnson, "Since You Went Away (Seems Lak to Me)," words by James Weldon Johnson, music by J. Rosamond Johnson (New York, 1913).

Voice and Sing." Writing it, he recalled: "I could not keep back the tears, and made no effort to do so. I was experiencing the transports of the poet's ecstasy." Not entirely happy with the versification, he realized nevertheless the power of his words and believed that, in the final stanza, "the American Negro was, historically and spiritually, immanent." The song was performed, and it was a major success. Moreover, Jacksonville students continued to sing it; and as some moved to other schools and others became teachers themselves, the song began to spread through the black schools of the South. The Johnson brothers' publisher received enough demand for it to get out a regular printed edition and then to produce several arrangements of it. It was ultimately adopted by the NAACP and became widely used as the "Negro National Hymn," or "Negro National Anthem." August Meier has seen it as an early instance of an emerging nationalism, which would flower in the 1920s.[7]

In fact, the poem was both within and beyond the tradition of black poetry on racial themes. Like most such poems, it was extremely optimistic, especially in its opening stanza:

> Lift every voice and sing
> Till earth and heaven ring,
> Ring with the harmonies of Liberty;
> Let our rejoicing rise
> High as the listening skies
> Let it resound loud as the rolling sea.
> Sing a song full of the faith that the dark past has taught us,
> Sing a song full of the hope that the present has brought us.
> Facing the rising sun of our new day begun,
> Let us march on till victory is won.

The second stanza traces through the suffering of black Americans— although, as Meier has pointed out, neither this stanza nor the others make direct reference to black people[8]—and does so in a way that, looking back to the tradition of the spirituals, evokes the Exodus story from the Old Testament:

7. James Weldon Johnson, *Along This Way*, 154–55; August Meier, *Negro Thought in America, 1880–1915: Racial Ideologies in the Age of Booker T. Washington* (Ann Arbor, 1963), 271; Levy, *James Weldon Johnson*, 72.

8. Meier, *Negro Thought*, 271.

Stony the road we trod,
Bitter the chastening rod,
Felt in the days when hope unborn died;
Yet with a steady beat,
Have not our weary feet
Come to the place for which our fathers sighed?
We have come over a way that with tears has been watered.
We have come, treading our path through the blood of the slaughtered.
Out from the gloomy past,
Till now we stand at last
Where the white gleam of our bright star is cast.

In the third, and final, stanza, Johnson maintained the conceptual focus of the second, and of the Exodus story, by describing black Americans as a people having a covenant with God and asking His assistance in the fulfillment of their destiny:

God of our weary years,
God of our silent tears,
Thou who has brought us thus far on the way;
Thou who hast by Thy might
Led us into the light,
Keep us forever in the path, we pray.
Lest our feet stray from the places, our God, where we meet Thee;
Lest our hearts drunk with the vine of the world we forget thee,
Shadowed beneath Thy hand,
May we forever stand,
True to our God,
True to our native land.

The poem captured all the idealism of both literary and popular traditions in the black community, presenting the optimism and the faith that had marked black aspirations since even antebellum times.

But for all its traditional character, the poem also moved in directions that showed an embryonic awareness of a distinctively black identity. One may cite, for instance, the line in which Johnson warns against becoming drunk with "the vine of the world," an echoing of other writers' juxtaposition of black spirituality with Western materialism. But this awareness was most notable in Johnson's use of the unspoken analogy linking the destiny of black Americans and that of the ancient Israelites. That analogy had a long and distinguished place in black political rhetoric and folk religion since the antebellum period; it was enshrined, most notably, in the spirituals. It had also played a role in black literature, Dunbar's "Antebellum Sermon" being an obvious instance.

Johnson's specific use of the analogy, however, was unusual for its time. It seems to have represented an early effort to capture the tone and the form of the spirituals in literary terms and to go beyond simply evoking the spirituals as an aspect of the folk past. During the 1920s, in *God's Trombones* and in *Book of American Negro Spirituals*, Johnson moved more explicitly and self-consciously in this direction; but he was constantly experimenting with his writing, and it is not too farfetched to suggest that here, too, was an important step in his evolution as a poet. It was in effectively using the spiritual tradition that Johnson created lines in which, as he said, "the American Negro was, historically and spiritually, immanent." He was not merely evoking a past; anticipating such writers as Wellington Adams and Fenton Johnson, he was trying to create a literature out of folklore. Indeed, even more than they, he used folk tradition to frame his perceptions of the present, anticipating in at least a limited way Du Bois' efforts to write from within the matrix of black culture.

"Lift Ev'ry Voice and Sing" thus represented an early expression of Johnson's giving value to black distinctiveness. To be sure, there was in it no questioning of assimilation as the ultimate goal for black Americans. Its final line makes that clear. But its use of the folk heritage set the work well in line with ideas that would later be articulated by the spokesmen for a distinctive black identity.

As Johnson's career developed, however, his poetry took on a dualistic character that was quite unusual and that emerges with special clarity when one considers the body of his work as a whole. In Johnson's poetry, Du Bois' idea of double-consciousness achieved a dramatic reality as, from poem to poem, Johnson moved back and forth between pieces that expressed traditional assimilationist motifs and those that expressed a radical view of black distinctiveness. Johnson actually became, in a sense, two writers.

One may see the assimilationist Johnson in his popular poem "O Southland!," which appeared in the *Independent* in 1907. Like his "Lift Ev'ry Voice and Sing," "O Southland!" was an optimistic poem, predicting with evangelical fervor a positive future for black Americans. Addressed to the white South, it called on the whites of the region to take responsibility for bringing about change, framing that call within the optimistic assimilationist assurance that

> 'Tis springtime! 'Tis springtime!
> The world is young again!
> And God's above, and God is love,
> And men are only men.[9]

The poem had some impact. Booker T. Washington, who had known Johnson during his early New York years, wrote to Johnson to express his own appreciation for the work. Washington was especially impressed by the technical quality of the poem, writing that "there is real poetry in every line of it." And he was equally impressed with the poet. He told Johnson, "Most of the writing of our people in the form of verse is mere doggerel, but this is real poetry."[10] In addition, the poem was picked up by Du Bois' fledgling magazine, *Horizon*, and reprinted in 1908. Its hopeful language of rebirth was such that people on both sides of the Washington–Du Bois dispute could find meaning in it.

But Johnson's most clearly integrationist poem from this period was his long "Fifty Years," which appeared in the New York *Times* on January 1, 1913, exactly fifty years after the signing of the Emancipation Proclamation. The poem was, as Johnson's biographer, Eugene Levy, has described it, an "inspirational" work, one that, like "Lift Ev'ry Voice and Sing," looked optimistically toward the future for black America. And like that earlier work, as well as like "O Southland!," it was written in a way that managed to suit the followers of Du Bois and Washington alike, in a style that, as Levy has said, "pleased many and antagonized few." Johnson himself considered it, at the time, to be his strongest effort—although he would express some reservations about parts of it in his 1933 autobiography. In relation to the larger tradition of black poetry, however, it was Johnson's most conservative piece.[11]

The central point of "Fifty Years" was that black people, through their contributions to the building of America, had earned their full rights as citizens and that it was their destiny to receive those rights. As in "Lift Ev'ry Voice and Sing," Johnson asserted that this destiny would be achieved in fulfillment of God's plan, just as slavery had been ended when "God, through Lincoln's ready hand, / Struck off our bonds and made us men." In its twenty-six stanzas, the poem surveyed the history of black Americans, from their origins in "heathen kraals and jungle

9. James Weldon Johnson, *Fifty Years*, 8–9.

10. Booker T. Washington to James Weldon Johnson, July 12, 1907, in Johnson Collection.

11. Levy, *James Weldon Johnson*, 142–46; James Weldon Johnson, *Along This Way*, 291.

dens, / To freedmen, freemen, sons of God, / Americans and Citizens." It noted the heroism of Attucks and the continued patriotism of black men called on to defend their country. And it called for continuing courage on the part of blacks, while asserting that, ultimately, God would not let the great efforts for racial justice "come to naught." In its most famous stanza, Johnson stated that black people deserved what they desired:

> This land is ours by right of birth,
> This land is ours by right of toil;
> We helped to turn its virgin earth.
> Our sweat is in its fruitful soil.

Justice as well as destiny demanded equal rights for black Americans.[12]

There was little here that black poets had not written before, but the poem was widely acknowledged for its excellence. The *Times* had commented on this editorially and, in a kind of backhanded compliment, had asserted that the quality of the verses was such that no one "could have deduced it from their peculiarities of either sentiment or diction" that the author was black. Charles W. Chesnutt paid Johnson a similar compliment, writing that the poem "is the finest thing I have ever read on the subject, which is saying a good deal, and the finest thing I have seen from the pen of a colored writer for a long time—which is not saying quite so much." He saw Johnson as a worthy successor to Dunbar and to the composer Samuel Coleridge-Taylor as a black man who could gain "recognition in the world of creative thought." But in its thematic and poetic conservatism, it showed a Johnson who framed his literary goals in essentially assimilationist terms.[13]

The other side of Johnson—the side that stressed black distinctiveness—was no less apparent during these years. Johnson's ideas about black distinctiveness, framed in notions of spirituality and creativity, surfaced strikingly in a 1908 poem published in *Century*. This was his "O Black and Unknown Bards," a poem in which he seriously confronted the main themes that would inform his poetic work and his literary concerns for much of the rest of his career. The poem combined themes of protest with a celebration of black distinctiveness and creativity. Above all, it provided proof of the legitimacy of black literary independence, another major theme in, especially, Du Bois' thought. It did this through an appreciation of the slave creators of the Negro spirituals.

12. James Weldon Johnson, *Fifty Years*, 1, 2.
13. New York *Times*, January 2, 1913, clipping in James Weldon Johnson, "Scrap Album," n.d., in Scrapbooks (of his interests and activities), Charles W. Chesnutt to James Weldon Johnson, January 18, 1913, in Johnson Collection.

Johnson began the poem with a rhetorical question:

> O black and unknown bards of long ago,
> How came your lips to touch the sacred fire?

He asked:

> Heart of what slave poured out such melody
> As "Steal away to Jesus"? On its strains
> His spirit must have nightly floated free,
> Though still about his hands he felt his chains.

Then, in the next stanza, Johnson contrasted the spiritual power of the slave songs with the white assumptions of black inferiority that had been used to justify keeping black people in bondage:

> What merely living clod, what captive thing,
> Could up toward God through all its darkness grope,
> And find within its deadened heart to sing
> These songs of sorrow, love, and faith, and hope?[14]

Having drawn this contrast between the black spirit and the white effort to hold that spirit captive, Johnson began his celebration of the spirituals as such. He wrote:

> Not that great German master in his dream
> Of harmonies that thundered amongst the stars
> At the creation, ever heard a theme
> Nobler than "Go down, Moses."

It was, he said, a "wonder" that such a people could be so creative, and it was truly a distinctive black achievement:

> O black slave singers, gone, forgot, unfamed,
> You—you alone, of all the long, long line
> Of those who've sung untaught, unknown, unnamed,
> Have stretched out upward, seeking the divine.
> You sang not deeds of heroes or of kings;
> No chant of bloody war, no exulting pean
> Of arms-won triumphs; but your humble strings
> You touched in chord with music empyrean.

The last four lines of this passage clearly fit in with the kinds of notions of black spirituality developed by Du Bois. The exaltation of heroes and of bloody warfare was the province of poets who lacked the strong spirituality that characterized the slave singers. Those slaves were

---

14. James Weldon Johnson, *Fifty Years*, 6.

closer to the ideals of faith than were the heroes of a militant life that, by implication, Johnson ascribed to the white world.[15]

There is also in this poem, of course, a touch of the traditional assimilationist irony; but in the closing lines of the poem, Johnson made clear that identity, more than irony, was his chief concern:

> You sang far better than you knew; the songs
> That for your listeners' hungry hearts sufficed
> Still live,—but more than this to you belongs:
> You sang a race from wood and stone to Christ.[16]

The last line was especially important, for it represented a direct reply to those—black and white—who believed that whatever virtues black society possessed came from its exposure to European-derived forms, including those of religion. If Christianity were initially a white man's religion, and if its effects on black life had been positive, the final line of "O Black and Unknown Bards" denied to whites the credit for its promulgation and success among black people. It was the black "singer," with his unique poetry and distinctive spirituality, who made Christianity live among the slaves. This is important, because if it is possible to read the poem in terms of the traditional ironies of older assimilationist black writing—and it is—the stress on the black origins for black religion was not so familiar; and it places the work in a line that goes back more to Du Bois than to, say, Victoria Earle Matthews, at least in its intent.

The poem was a major step, then, in Johnson's effort to set forth a theory of black distinctiveness. It was also a successor to the earlier "Lift Ev'ry Voice and Sing" in its celebration of the spiritual form, in its argument for the distinctive power of that form. And it was an important indication of the future directions Johnson's writing would take, especially in his increasing effort to "find a form which would hold all the character of 'Negro' poetry, and at the same time be capable of expressing deep emotion and lofty sentiment," as he described his aims to Joel Spingarn in 1920.[17] In such a form as that of the spirituals, and in the kind of understanding of the spirituals presented in this poem, Johnson began to move more closely toward his goal.

But a still more militant statement of Johnson's appreciation for black

---

15. *Ibid.,* 7.

16. *Ibid.,* 8.

17. James Weldon Johnson to Joel Spingarn, December 11, 1920, in Johnson Collection.

distinctiveness appears in "The White Witch," published in March, 1915, in *Crisis*. Braithwaite anthologized the poem in his collection of the best magazine verse for that year; and two years later, Alice Dunbar-Nelson requested it for an anthology of her own. Johnson himself wrote that some people found the poem puzzling—although he considered its meaning "quite plain." He also wrote that it had been used in court when a group of black Bostonians sought to have the motion picture *The Birth of a Nation* banned in that city. One of the studio's attorneys introduced the poem as evidence that such a film as *The Birth of a Nation* "was an absolute necessity in the United States."[18]

Given the ideas of whites, the attorney's concern is not hard to decipher, because the poem was a militant call for black Americans to preserve their integrity and distinctiveness and to avoid the seductive charms of "the white witch." Johnson's image of white society was much like the one Du Bois presented in *The Souls of Black Folk*, when he too had called for blacks to avoid becoming corrupted by white materialism. Speaking entirely in metaphor, Johson assigned great danger to the charms of that white world:

> O, brothers mine, take care! Take care!
> The great white witch rides out to-night,
> Trust not your prowess nor your strength;
> Your only safety lies in flight;
> For in her glance there is a snare,
> And in her smile there is a blight.[19]

The white witch seems young and beautiful, but this is a deception. Johnson described her as "twin sister to the greedy earth" and as one in whom "the spirit of the vampire lies." But the real danger lies in the way in which the white witch seeks to use and to ruin black people:

> Oh! she has seen your strong young limbs,
> And heard your laughter loud and gay,
> And in your voices she has caught
> The echo of a far off day,
> When man was closer to the earth;
> And she has marked you for her prey.
> She feels the old Antean strength
> In you, the great dynamic beat

18. Alice Dunbar Nelson to James Weldon Johnson, June 20, 1917, in Johnson Collection; Johnson, *Along This Way*, 306.
19. James Weldon Johnson, "The White Witch," *Crisis*, IX (1915), 239.

Of primal passions, and she sees
In you the last beseiged retreat
Of love relentless, lusty, fierce,
Love pain-ecstatic, cruel-sweet.

In these lines, Johnson caught the essence of Du Bois' ideas of black distinctiveness. Black people were close to nature and the earth, and they were a people of strong feeling—an emotional people—as well. By choosing a frankly sexual metaphor, Johnson presented this idea in the spirit that Du Bois had evoked in his initial description of Zora in *The Quest of the Silver Fleece*. It was a spirit that remained advanced in the context of black literary tradition during the period prior to World War I. But Johnson made it a way of expressing the need for preserving and valuing a distinctive black racial identity, for positively avoiding the blandishments of white American life.

This poem shows especially how Johnson's poetry was, throughout this period, of two minds—and in a way that was more spectacular than the common mixing of, say, dialect poems with more genteel work, in a way that differed from the familiar ambivalence of black literary tradition. The body of Johnson's work expressed not an ambivalence but a contradiction. On the one hand, much of his poetry, including "O Southland!" and "Fifty Years," looked forward to the ultimate assimilation of black people into the American mainstream. On the other, some of his work, including "The White Witch," seemed to claim that black people could find fulfillment only by maintaining a detachment from the larger society, by avoiding assimilation itself. Why should such a contradiction have so strongly characterized Johnson's work?

It is possible to see the roots of this contradiction, to a great extent, in the nature of Johnson's own experiences, experiences that made it difficult for him to embrace either assimilationism or pluralism wholeheartedly. Again, Johnson was not a typical writer. What is important about him is the way in which his career illustrates the psychological possibilities of cultural and ideological dilemmas.

Johnson was well aware of and had experienced American racism, and he was especially aware of how racism had become increasingly strong in turn-of-the-century American life. He saw this in his own experiences as a school principal in Jacksonville. In the early days of his career, he could confidently count on the goodwill and support of Jacksonville's leading whites as he worked to further education in his hometown. By the time he left, however, it was becoming clear that the goodwill and support of the past was being withdrawn and that hopes for good race relations, not to mention integration, were fading quickly.[20] In fact, the language of "The White Witch" may have been a practical warning to his black readers as much as a symbolic one. Johnson had learned the hard way that one could not put too much faith in white people.

At the same time, however, Johnson maintained close personal and professional ties to white America, ties that played an important role in his life. In this, he stood apart from other prominent champions of black distinctiveness. Brawley and Ferris, for example, worked primarily in black institutions. Du Bois, though he had lived among whites as a child and worked closely with them during his years of graduate education and, later, in the NAACP, was noted for his lack of trust in them and his tendency to hold himself aloof from them.[21] Johnson, however, dealt with white people comfortably and often. He had done so in Jacksonville, for a time, and continued to do so in New York as an active politician. As a consular official, he was constantly interacting with white Americans on a social level, as an apparent equal. But perhaps nothing kept Johnson's creative life more closely in touch with white America than the powerful demands made on him as a successful writer of popular songs for the New York stage. And, consequently, nothing did more to encourage his real double-consciousness as an artist.

It is easy to forget, in looking at James Weldon Johnson's literary career, that the bulk of his early creative work was made up not of his poetry but of his song lyrics. And these were lyrics written to appeal to a primarily white audience. The demands of producing such material gave Johnson a special awareness of white literary expectations and a unique appreciation of the importance of those expectations to him as a writer.

The theatrical world that Johnson entered at about the turn of the century had only recently begun to make a place for black artists and performers. Although there had been popular black entertainers before, they had been mainly in minstrelsy, a form of entertainment that drew on the worst stereotypes of the plantation tradition, presenting the black figure as either the most down-and-out of characters or as a clown. This tradition had culminated in New York, in fact, with a large show in

---

20. James Weldon Johnson, *Along This Way*, 184–85.
21. Elliott Rudwick, *W. E. B. Du Bois: Propagandist of the Negro Protest* (1960; rpr. New York, 1969), *e.g.,* 170.

Ambrose Park, Brooklyn, that had involved the re-creation of what the promoters called a "Negro village," complete with a watermelon feast, a cakewalk contest, and an assurance of the show's authenticity. Robert Toll, a historian of the minstrel tradition, has demonstrated how that tradition captured a version of black distinctiveness, but a version based on the white man's fantasies.[22]

At the same time, some black performers tried to break the mold. For example, a number of black minstrel and "jubilee" companies sought to present elements of black folk life without the excesses that characterized Brooklyn's "Negro village." Some even sought to do so in ways that made a case against racial injustice. Performances of plays based on *Uncle Tom's Cabin* were often created by these companies, as was more original material along the same lines. Pauline Hopkins' company, founded before Hopkins began her literary career, was, in fact, precisely this sort of group; and there were many others like it.

It was within this setting that a number of talented black artists began to gather in New York near the close of the nineteenth century. They included Will Marion Cook, educated and Europe-trained as a musician, who began to create shows in the 1890s. Indeed, it was Cook who did the music for Dunbar's successful New York show, *Clorindy—The Origin of the Cake Walk*. There were also Bob Cole, who produced what Johnson called "the first Negro musical comedy," *A Trip to Coontown*, in 1898–1899, and the popular comedy team of Bert Williams and George Walker. Harry T. Burleigh, who had studied with Antonín Dvořák and who worked mainly with art songs, was active in the city's black musical life. And there were Rosamond and James Weldon Johnson.[23]

Johnson saw what he and his fellow black artists were seeking to do during this period as an effort to get away from the excesses of the minstrel tradition. Like many of the dialect poets, they hoped to use the popularity of that tradition as the basis from which to reach a wide audience, but then to present a more accurate portrayal of black life. As Eugene Levy has suggested, theirs was an effort to take the traditional "coon song" to middle-class America and to present it in a way that did not compromise the dignity of those who were its subjects.[24]

The task could not have been easy, for Johnson had to walk a fine line

22. Robert C. Toll, *Blacking Up: The Minstrel Show in Nineteenth-Century America* (New York, 1974), 263.
23. James Weldon Johnson, *Black Manhattan* (1930; rpr. New York, 1975), 100–103, 116.
24. Levy, *James Weldon Johnson*, 88, 92–93.

between his own desires and the expectations of his predominantly white audience. Since Johnson was also in the business to make money, he could hardly ignore those expectations. And, indeed, he often seemed willing to play to them, successfully enough that at least some white southerners were fooled into believing that the Johnson brothers and Bob Cole, their frequent collaborator, were white.[25]

Johnson was the master of dialect songs. These were the pieces on which he built his reputation,[26] and they compose a fairly substantial part of his portfolio. Moreover, he was pleased enough with them himself to print a number as poems in *Fifty Years*. The songs run the usual gamut of dialect writing; they also reveal the extent to which Johnson was able to keep himself in tune with white expectations. "An Explanation," for instance, has to do with chicken stealing; it also plays on the traditional plantation-tradition stereotype of black pomposity:

> Jedge profoun', settin' down,
> Tryin' Brudder Johnsing fer a-lib'lin' Brudder Brown.
> Solemn jury, full o' dignity,
> Wid de pompous manner ob de ol' darkey.
> Jedge arose, den he took a pose,
> An' thus he spake in tones dat rang an' thrilled an' chilled an' froze:
> "Noble bredderen, mo' hones' men,
> Br'er Brown will question Johnsing ob de wherefores an de when."
> Br'er Brown spoke brief:
> "Look heah! 'Splain to me de reason
> Why you said to Squire Lee,
> Der wuz twelve ole chicken thieves
> In dis heah town, includin' me.
> Ef he tole you dat, my brudder,
> He said sump'n dat warn't true;
> W'at I said wuz dis, dat der wuz
> Twelve, *widout* includin' you." [27]

Interestingly, Johnson dedicated the piece to Bruce Evans, one of the leaders of Washington, D.C.'s black community.

At one level, "An Explanation" seems to conform almost completely

25. James Weldon Johnson, *Along This Way*, 196.

26. Levy, *James Weldon Johnson*, 86–87.

27. Will Marion Cook, "An Explanation: Characteristic Negro Verses by James Weldon Johnson, Set to Music by Will Marion Cook" (New York, 1914), in Johnson Collection.

to the white plantation tradition. But as the dedication to Evans—and the later inclusion of the lyric as a poem in *Fifty Years*—helps stress, Johnson was not ashamed of the work. Perhaps putting the song in dialect, especially in setting the scene for the chorus—Brother Brown's testimony—saves it from being simply an outsider's ridicule of black Americans—indeed, removes it even from the traditional detachment that Dunbar and other black writers had relied on in earlier years. Here it is the black narrator himself speaking dialect and seeing the humor in his subjects. Still, Johnson walked a thin line in this lyric; and one cannot easily read the poem without discomfort.

It is a discomfort that, in regard to at least some of the songs, Johnson seems to have shared. One can see this in the career of a 1900 song, done with his brother, that dealt with a subject common in black dialect poetry, the love of opossum. The verses spoke of southern scenery and of the delicacy of 'possum flesh, and there was a chorus warning, "Run brudder possum":

> You better run, run, run I tell you
> Run brudder possum run.
> You better run, run, run I tell you
> D'ole coon's got a gun,
> Young coons all gigglin'
> Cause dey know dere's gwinter be some fun
> You better run brudder possum an' git out de way.[28]

The use of the term *coon* was common in black theatrical work at the turn of the century. Ernest Hogan's song "All Coons Look Alike to Me" was only the most notorious example, as many black performers found themselves working within the confines of the "coon" tradition.

It is not clear, however, that such a tradition was easy to live with. Johnson reported that Hogan himself came to regret the title of his song. Rosamond Johnson and Bob Cole, in performing one of their songs that used Hogan's phrase, substituted "boys" for "coons" because they were unable to say the latter word. Thus, when Johnson published a version of "Run Brudder Possum" as a poem in his 1917 collection, he tellingly rewrote part of the chorus to read, "Old Eph's got a gun, / Picanninnies grinnin' / Waitin' fu' to see de fun." Johnson's aim to elevate the "coon

---

28. John Rosamond Johnson, "Run Brudder Possum Run: A Negro Warning," words by J. W. Johnson, music by Rosamond Johnson (New York, 1900), in Johnson Collection.

song" was never free of the demands of an audience that had well-developed expectations of what such a song should be.[29]

There were, therefore, limits on what he could do as, along with his brother and Bob Cole, he tried to refine black theatrical traditions. About the only consistent approach to revamping the theatrical image of blacks that Johnson and his collaborators found was to "write in our songs the finer feelings of the colored race," while at the same time trying "to retain the racial traits, not only in the syncopated time of the music, but in the lyrics, as well," as Bob Cole put it.[30] They did this, most notably, in one of their most popular songs, "Nobody's Lookin' but de Owl and de Moon," an early piece that achieved great success. In this number, Johnson wrote in dialect; but he wrote what was essentially a popular love song, one that combined affection with an appreciation of southern natural beauty:

> Nobody's lookin' but de owl an' de moon,
> An' de night is balmy, fu' de month in June;
> Come den, Honey, won't you? Come to meet me soon,
> W'ile nobody's lookin' but de owl an' de moon.[31]

It was a song reminiscent of much of Dunbar's work, using dialect to express what were generally acceptable sentiments.

A similar kind of effort characterized the more exotic efforts of Cole and the Johnson brothers, their love songs with an African setting. The references to Africa in these songs owed more to primitivist fantasies than to African ways of life. The most famous number of this sort was the early "Under the Bamboo Tree"—the story of a "maid of royal blood though dusky shade" and her lover, a "Zulu from Matabooloo." Its famous chorus, Levy has pointed out, was a ragtime version of "Nobody Knows the Trouble I See"; and it was written in an unusual version of what was supposed to be an African dialect: "If you lak-a-me, I lak-a-you; and we lak-a-both the same, / I lak-a-say, this very day, I lak-a-change your name."[32]

But the real force of the African songs was to combine the primitivist fantasies with an image of blacks that fit into traditions of American

29. James Weldon Johnson, *Black Manhattan*, 114; ms. note from John Rosamond Johnson to Carl Van Vechten on the sheet music for "Tell Me Dusky Maiden (A Travesty)," words by J. W. Johnson and Bob Cole, music by Rosamond Johnson (New York, 1901), in Johnson Collection; James Weldon Johnson, *Fifty Years*, 79.

30. James Weldon Johnson, Scrapbook, 1905–1910, in Johnson Collection.

31. James Weldon Johnson, *Fifty Years*, 69.

32. Levy, *James Weldon Johnson*, 90.

popular music. One sees this, for example, in a verse to the 1903 song "The Maid of Timbuctoo," a song originally performed by the popular Lillian Russell.

> In Afric's sunny land
> Beyond the desert's sand
> There lived a maid, I've heard it said,
> In a place called Timbuctoo.
> Bold chieftains by the score,
> Would come for miles or more,
> Arrayed in beads and pumpkin seeds,
> This little maid to woo.

Here was no evocation of African roots such as that found in, for example, Du Bois' "A Day in Africa." Here was simply Africa as an exotic setting for a not unusual love song. In its characterization of the young woman as "a little maid," it placed its heroine well within the American mainstream. This impression was reinforced in a later verse, in which it is said that, though the little maid "was uncivilized," she was able to mobilize all the usual feminine wiles to keep those "Zulu guys" under her spell. In the popular "Congo Love Song," one sees a similar treatment of an "African" heroine when, in one verse, the audience is assured that, "though she was but a little Zulu, she did just what other artful maids do." And the verses are accompanied by a chorus that shows how Johnson combined primitivist images with music-hall themes:

> As long as the Congo flows to the sea,
> As long as a leaf grows on the bamboo tree,
> My love and devotion will be deep as the ocean
> Won't you take a notion for to love-a but me?

Johnson did not demean Africa in his songs. Neither, however, were these songs anything like a celebration of an African heritage.[33]

Taken altogether, Johnson's song lyrics reveal a man acutely aware of the beliefs and ideas of his white American audience—and successfully so. They also show (as does his cultivation of white literary mentors and publishers) a man who—like Dunbar and Chesnutt—had strong ambitions for a broad, general audience.

Johnson's experiences as a lyricist point to one possible interpretation of the character of his early poetry, particularly of the real contra-

33. Bob Cole, "The Maid of Timbuctoo," words by J. W. Johnson, music by Bob Cole (New York, 1903); John Rosamond Johnson, "Congo Love Song," words by J. W. Johnson, music by Rosamond Johnson (New York, 1903).

diction between his assimilationist pieces and those focusing on racial identity. To see the significance of Johnson's theatrical experience, it is useful to look at a later work of his, "The Dilemma of the Negro Author," published in *American Mercury* in 1928. Although it appeared over a decade after World War I, and over two decades after much of Johnson's Broadway work and early poetry, it seems especially relevant to that aspect of his career.

According to Johnson, the real dilemma facing the black author was to meet the demands of both black and white audiences. In writing for a white audience, the black author came up against the many powerful conventions and stereotypes whites had of black people. Should the author's presentation of black life stray too far from white ideas, whites would refuse to accept it. But the black author also had to confront a black audience with very different expectations and desires. Should the author stay too close to whites' ideas of blacks, the black audience would be offended and would reject the work. "This division of the audience," Johnson wrote, "takes the solid ground from under the feet of the Negro writer and leaves him suspended."[34] Unwilling to reject either audience, Johnson saw a solution only in a fusion of the two audiences; but, significantly, he portrayed that fusion in social rather than literary terms. The black author's dilemma could not end until racism was effectively challenged, if not destroyed, laying traditional conventions and stereotypes to rest.

Johnson's song lyrics provide an important link between his early work and this later essay. There is evidence in Johnson's theatrical writing that he had a similar perception in his early career. Writing quite purposefully to meet white expectations, Johnson constructed lyrics around the very conventions he decried in his 1928 essay. If he softened those conventions in his songs, he never overturned them to present an alternate portrayal of blacks for the white audience. At the same time, however, when he revised his songs for publication in his book, he took out some of the more offensive features, perhaps in deference to a broader readership, including blacks. He thus seems to have been aware early in his career of the constricting role of the audience in his work. The essay expressed what his theatrical work implied, and it is not difficult to conclude that the problems he discussed in 1928 had become apparent to him much earlier.

34. James Weldon Johnson, "The Dilemma of the Negro Author," *American Mercury*, XV (1928), 480.

If so, Johnson's portrayal of the black author's dilemma helps explain the real contradiction in his early poetry. This contradiction did not involve anything so simple as an attempt on Johnson's part to write for two audiences, doing assimilationist pieces for white readers and Du Boisian ones for black readers. After all, "O Black and Unknown Bards" appeared in *Century*, even if "The White Witch" was first in *Crisis*. Rather, Johnson's characterization of the two audiences in his 1928 essay pointed to a sense on his part of a cultural bifurcation of blacks and whites that resisted synthesis. Despairing of creating a literature that could satisfy both groups, Johnson could see no literary strategy for bringing them together into a coherent whole. Johnson viewed both racial identity and assimilation as valid, valuable goals; and for a variety of reasons, he could find no compelling reason to choose between them. But he also saw them as exclusive goals in the context of a racist society. His poetry reflected his bifurcated world. It reflected deeply held doubts that a Du Boisian synthesis of double-consciousness could ever occur.

The sources of contradiction in Johnson's career were real. Powerfully drawn to the ideas about black life and literature that Du Bois had done so much to crystallize, he was among the first to put those ideas into literary form—celebrating what he saw as a real, positive black distinctiveness, even, as in the case of "O Black and Unknown Bards," a black aesthetic. At the same time, he not only appreciated assimilationist goals but, more than most, had a chance to realize those goals—at least in a limited, professional way. He would occasionally try to bring these ideas and goals into a kind of Du Boisian synthesis. He did so in "Lift Ev'ry Voice and Sing," for example. But in most of his work, such a synthesis is strikingly absent. It is as though Johnson felt compelled to address questions of assimilation and identity as two separate issues with two separate roles to play in his life and thought. Perhaps this was nothing more than a reflection of a division in his own life. Devoted to racial concerns, he also made his living by dealing effectively with white society. It may have been, as well, the product of a deeper sense of the demands posed by efforts to construct a black identity in a segregated society.

The depth of Johnson's sense of the demands to be faced in constructing a racial identity is shown by his 1912 novel, *The Autobiography of an Ex-Colored Man*. Of all Johnson's writing prior to the 1920s, this work has been the one to attract the greatest critical attention—in part, perhaps, because of the unmistakable realism of the novel. Set, for significant parts of the story, in Harlem, it presents a black urban world that is both brutal and exotic; and in this it is, as critic Eugenia Collier has written, an important precursor of the writing of the Harlem Renaissance.[35] It certainly went well beyond Dunbar's earlier effort to portray black life in the urban North, as even Johnson's contemporaries agreed.

It has also attracted critical attention because it was a black novel of unusual complexity for its time. Indeed, it is not even clear whether Johnson intended his protagonist—who is never named—to be a sympathetic character. Certainly he is not the same kind of genteel hero who dominated much of black fiction up to that time. He is a man of weakness who, unlike almost any other black protagonist, turns his back on his race, choosing to take a place in the white world, though not without misgivings. As several critics have noted, Johnson's presentation of the situation encourages a difficult, ambivalent response on the part of the reader.[36]

The Autobiography of an Ex-Colored Man took Johnson several years to write. He began it before he assumed his consular posts, showing some of the early chapters to his Columbia mentor, Brander Matthews; and he finished it before returning to the United States. Prior to its publication, Johnson debated whether to present it openly as a work of fiction, ultimately deciding to let it stand as, apparently, a "human document"—the purported autobiography of a Negro who had decided to make his way in the white world. He would later wonder if the decision had cost him some sales. Some reviewers were fooled. A favorable review in New York's black newspaper, *Amsterdam News*, treated the work as an autobiography and treated the protagonist-narrator with sympathy. William Monroe Trotter's Boston *Guardian* had less sympathy for the protagonist, calling him "a coward," and also failed to recognize the book as a work of fiction. The New York *Times*, which reviewed the book favorably, simply could not decide whether the story was fact or fiction. Johnson himself was especially pleased with the *Times* re-

---

35. Eugenia Collier, "The Endless Journey of an Ex-Colored Man," *Phylon*, XXXII (1971), 372–73.

36. Maurice J. O'Sullivan, Jr., "Of Souls and Pottage: James Weldon Johnson's *The Autobiography of an Ex-Colored Man*," *CLA Journal*, XXIII (1979), 61; Stephen M. Ross, "Audience and Irony in Johnson's *The Autobiography of an Ex-Colored Man*," *CLA Journal*, XVIII (1974), 203; Joseph T. Skerrett, Jr., "Irony and Symbolic Action in James Weldon Johnson's *The Autobiography of an Ex-Colored Man*," *American Quarterly*, XXXII (1980), 540.

view, both because it was favorable and because "it is proven that I am sufficiently a master of the technical art of writing to make it impossible for even so keen a critic as the one on the Times to say that the story is *not* true."[37]

Johnson did a fair job of keeping his authorship a secret; he recalled, in his own autobiography, having once been introduced to a man who claimed authorship of the book. A few people did know fairly early on, however; and the news gradually spread. An old friend, George Towns, wrote to Johnson only a few weeks after the book's appearance to congratulate him on its publication. Braithwaite also knew fairly early. He wrote to Johnson early in 1913, congratulating him "despite the fact that I shouldn't know." In 1914 one mention of Johnson's authorship of the book appeared in the Atlanta University publication *Crimson and Gray* and another in the New York *Age*.[38]

In a long letter to Sherman, French and Company, publisher of *The Autobiography of an Ex-Colored Man*, Johnson discussed his reasons for having written the book and his ideas of what he hoped it would accomplish. Stating his wish to avoid giving the impression that the work was fiction, he wrote that it was not his intention "to make a special plea for the Negro," since many such pleas had been written, but, rather, "to present in a sympathetic yet dispassionate manner a picture of the conditions between the races as they actually exist today." In particular, he wanted to get away from a monolithic picture of black people—to show that the black race consisted of many kinds of people and groups, each of which had distinctive ways of relating to the others and to whites. It was, as well, an effort to illuminate the inner lives of black people, much as Du Bois had sought to do, and—in keeping with Johnson's general literary ambitions—to do so for a white as well as a black audience. "I have been curious to know," Johnson wrote, "if whites would not be interested in knowing the opinion concerning themselves held by ten million people living among them." And finally, and not insignificantly, from Johnson's point of view, the novel was written to show the pressure on at least the Negroes with appropriate physical

37. James Weldon Johnson, *Along This Way*, 193, 238; James Weldon Johnson to Carl Van Doren, December 28, 1922, reviews from James Weldon Johnson, "Scrapbook—The Autobiography of an Ex-Colored Man and Theatrical Misc.," James Weldon Johnson to Grace Nail Johnson, June 26, 1912, in Johnson Collection.

38. James Weldon Johnson, *Along This Way*, 238–239; George A. Towns to James Weldon Johnson, July 1, 1912, William Stanley Braithwaite to James Weldon Johnson, March 29, 1913, James Weldon Johnson, "Scrapbook—The Autobiography of an Ex-Colored Man," in Johnson Collection; New York *Age*, October 15, 1914.

attributes to pass over into the white race. Many, he felt, were succumbing to that pressure. Their doing so was a testimony to the power of
prejudice, as well as to the arbitrariness of racial distinctions.[39]

The Autobiography of an Ex-Colored Man is, then, the story of a
man who successfully passes over into the white race. The plot follows
him through a New England childhood, when he discovers his black
ancestry, through an unsuccessful attempt to attend Atlanta University—unsuccessful because a black companion cheats him out of his
expense money—and into an adulthood on both sides of the color line.
The main character-narrator, who is never named, is a musician whose
music expresses the divisions in his life. A child prodigy with the
classics, he enters the New York club life as a young man and learns the
beauties of ragtime, a black musical form. His abilities with the form
take him to Europe, with the support of a white millionaire who is both
patron and companion. His European experience instills in him the
desire to become an authentic black artist, bridging both worlds by
transforming rough black musical forms into classical music. This decision is to be the turning point of his life, setting up a powerful conclusion to the novel.

In search of black sources, the unnamed narrator goes to the black
belt of the South, where he is greatly impressed by the music and folk
life of southern blacks. Attending a church service, he hears the stirring
black preacher John Brown and drinks in the musical performances of
"Singing" Johnson. In describing the scene, James Weldon Johnson
echoed the views expressed in "O Black and Unknown Bards." Speaking
of "Go Down, Moses," for example, he wrote, "I doubt that there is a
stronger theme in the whole musical literature of the world";[40] and he
noted with wonder that songs of this sort should have been created by
such a downtrodden people as the southern slaves.

Still, despite the protagonist's elation over the church service, his
southern experience is disheartening. Although he sees many signs of
uplift and progress among the black people of the South, he also sees
anew the determination of the white South to oppress the Negro population. Worse, he thinks that too many blacks simply acquiesce to the
demands of southern whites. This belief receives, for him, its final confir-
mation when he witnesses a lynching. Musing on what he has seen, "a

39. James Weldon Johnson to Sherman, French & Co., February 17, 1912, in Johnson
Collection.
40. James Weldon Johnson, *The Autobiography of an Ex-Colored Man* (1912; rpr.
New York, 1927), 181.

great wave of humiliation and shame swept over me. Shame that I belonged to a race that could be so dealt with; and shame for my country, that it, the great example of democracy to the world, should be the only civilized, if not the only state on earth, where a human being would be burned alive."[41] Here is an even worse form of double-consciousness than Du Bois described. Instead of trying to be both Negro and American, Johnson's protagonist feels a strong desire to be neither. He abandons his project and returns to New York.

In New York, the narrator takes on a new life. He shuns the dives he had haunted before and begins to live a life of middle-class respectability. He gets a good job and becomes fairly affluent. And he undertakes to live as a white man. Passing, he meets and falls in love with a young white woman. He tells her of his background; and though she is shocked at first, they marry, keeping his secret between them. Their children, of course, are quite fair and will have no problem continuing to live as white. By the time the book concludes, the wife has died and the protagonist has withdrawn from all society, the better to protect his secret and, especially, that of his children.

The ending is not positive. The narrator is filled with misgivings about his choice, misgivings that increase when, at a meeting, he hears a speech by Booker T. Washington. It reminds him that great men are doing great things for the race, and he wonders if he, too, might not have made a difference. His hopes for his children will not let him acknowledge his past; "and yet, when I sometimes open a little box in which I still keep my fast yellowing manuscripts, the only tangible remnants of a vanished dream, a dead ambition, a sacrificed talent, I cannot repress the thought that, after all, I have chosen the lesser part, that I have sold my birthright for a mess of pottage." As Werner Sollors has said of the passage, in the narrator's very success is also failure. Choosing comfort, the man has lost his soul.[42]

At one level, the message of *The Autobiography of an Ex-Colored Man* is both clear and Du Boisian. Assimilation is not the whole answer for black Americans. There is something in the spirit that demands a racial identity, a synthesis of American culture and black culture, for the individual to be complete. The narrator's failure to create the synthesis is the immediate cause of his spiritual failure, which critic Michael Cooke has described as socially intelligent but privately disastrous. And,

41. *Ibid.,* 187–88.

42. *Ibid.,* 211; Werner Sollors, *Beyond Ethnicity: Consent and Descent in American Culture* (New York, 1986), 171.

indeed, as Cooke and other critics have noted, the conflict in the narrator can easily be seen as not only one of racial identity but also as one between materialism and spirituality. Robert Stepto has referred to the narrator's "mammonism." Stepto has also convincingly traced the narrator's ignorance of his own past and his own culture, and his inability to get below the surface of black life. Unsympathetic to the narrator, Stepto has argued that the real message of the book is its "fresh assertion" of the inability of the narrator really to see what was there to be seen of black culture, whether in New York or in the black belt of the American South.[43]

Such a message emphasizes clearly the Du Boisian purposes of the book. Sollors, focusing on such purposes, has stressed that the narrator's musical ambitions reveal the possibility of creating a synthetic identity, pointing toward the kind of fusion Johnson had called for in his 1928 essay. That the narrator fails to do so makes him, in Sollor's view, Johnson's "antiself"—a kind of object lesson on the consequences of choosing a practical, assimilationist approach to personal and racial aspirations.[44]

In light of Johnson's other work, however, a very different message may be drawn from *The Autobiography of an Ex-Colored Man*—a message that relates most directly not to Johnson's Du Boisian ideas so much as to the contradictions in all of Johnson's early work. To see this, it is useful to return to Stepto's notion of authentication. Stepto has shown how Du Bois was especially significant in turning openly to black sources of authentication for his ideas and even for his own identity. One may see a similar effort to locate black sources of authentication in the cases of Benjamin Brawley, Fenton Johnson, and, in some of his poems, James Weldon Johnson himself. It is not difficult to see such an effort also in the foray by Johnson's narrator into the South in search of musical materials. Indeed, Stepto has chided the narrator in part because of the narrator's failure to see the authenticating power of ragtime in the setting of the New York clubs.[45] This search for authentication is a central theme in *The Autobiography of an Ex-Colored Man*, but Johnson presented it in a way that is not entirely Du Boisian. Ongoing patterns of searching and failure make *The Autobiography of an Ex-*

43. Michael Cooke, *Afro-American Literature in the Twentieth Century: The Achievement of Intimacy* (New Haven, 1984), 46, 52; Robert Stepto, *From Behind the Veil: A Study of Afro-American Narrative* (Urbana, 1979), 119, 125–26.

44. Sollors, *Beyond Ethnicity*, 171–72.

45. See Stepto, *From Behind the Veil*, 63–64, 125–26.

Colored Man less a Du Boisian novel than a comment on Du Boisian ideas.

Johnson presented the two cultures of the black American in such a way that neither is wholly satisfying or compatible with the other. White culture has its ugly racism. Black culture has the kinds of weaknesses spelled out in the narrator's soliloquy on the South. It is also significant that the narrator is cheated out of one attempt to find a place in black life—through attending Atlanta University—by a black man. But more significant for Johnson's work than his characterizations of each culture is the relationship he draws between them. As he makes clear in two of his key episodes, white and black cultures exist not in an uneasy juxtaposition but in a relationship of inescapable antagonism.

In the club scene, the setting for one of the episodes, this cultural antagonism may be seen in the way in which the behavior of club people—marked by imprudent gambling, heavy drinking, and quick violence—directly conflicts with dominant American ideals. Indeed, club life is virtually a negative rendition of what dominant American values prescribe for individual behavior. The narrator himself is aware of the habits and values he must reject in order to enter the clubs. Black and American worlds are, in this setting at least, in flat contradiction. Johnson also had the club setting symbolize a cultural antagonism, through his use of the motif of interracial romance—describing an affair between a white "widow" and her black lover that ends in ugly violence when the man, enraged, enters the club and shoots her to death. As Johnson described the episode, the woman had sought to enter fully into the life of the club. She had entered, however, as a white woman into a black world; and her doing so brought destruction and death.

The second episode is, of course, the narrator's trip to the rural South. Here, again, Johnson described the antagonism between white and black worlds, not so much by a stress on any inherent contradictions as by his portrayal of black and white lives as being lived in two separate worlds. The whites are wholly ignorant of the humanity of the blacks around them; this point is made especially well as the narrator, on the train going South, joins in a conversation with a group of white men who, unaware of his race, rehearse the usual stereotypes. Black people, as Johnson's account of folk life makes clear, find their real spirituality only among themselves, outside the purview of whites. The only actual contact portrayed in the episode between members of the two races comes when a black man is lynched by a white mob.

In each case, then, it is the distance, not the possibility of contact, that organizes Johnson's presentation of events. And, indeed, in their violence, these two episodes stand together in a kind of awful symmetry. In the first, the white woman's murder is the culmination of her life as an alien in a distinctively black world. In the second, a young man's lynching emphasizes his situation as an alien in a world that seeks to be self-consciously, viciously white. The symmetry of the episodes lets us know that they have to do with more than racial oppression, since both black and white characters suffer. The purpose of the episodes is to stress both black and white distinctiveness and to show that, where there is distinctiveness, there are also conflict, brutality, and death.

These are, then, episodes that dramatize the bifurcation of a segregated society. The narrator's efforts to immerse himself in authentically black environments, in the club and in the South, are failures not because of his weakness or blindness but because they increase his sense of the separation of the races and of the difficulty of creating any fusion of black with white. The two realms of experience are too far apart to allow an easy synthesis.

The commentary on Du Bois is obvious. Although Du Bois had himself recognized the conflict between the African and the American—the "warring" of the two selves—he did not characterize that conflict as strikingly as Johnson did. In Du Bois' view, the two selves could ultimately be made complementary, each teaching and learning from the other. Johnson dramatized much stronger barriers between the African and the American, suggesting that in a racist world there is little possibility of ever bringing the two together.

This is not to say that the novel rejects the desirability of the kind of synthetic African-American identity Du Bois had proposed. It is to the point that, at the conclusion of each of the novel's violent episodes, the narrator finds himself in a kind of limbo, situated in the white world but feeling the pull of the black. After the widow's murder, he joins his millionaire friend for the trip to Europe; the lynching determines his decision to pass. But Johnson showed that these are not real alternatives. It is in Europe, for example, that the narrator forms his ambition to create a distinctively black art. His success at passing creates the pangs of conscience expressed at the book's close. When the narrator flees the club and when he flees the South, he has implicitly abandoned not only authentic black worlds but also the Du Boisian quest for synthesis. And in the absence of synthesis, he has become, in a real sense, neither black nor white, prevented by both conscience and feeling from being completely one or the other. The importance of synthesis remains, as even the narrator seems to believe. But, again, synthesis is not, Johnson's story implies, something easily achieved.

Johnson himself did not, of course, flee the task his narrator had renounced. He continued to write poems such as "The White Witch," celebrating a distinctive blackness and even denigrating the surrender to white society embodied in his narrator's life. After World War I, in his verse settings of folk sermons—the remarkable *God's Trombones*—and in his *Books of American Negro Spirituals*, he made even greater efforts to create that fusion of cultures the narrator failed to achieve. In that sense, perhaps the narrator was Johnson's "antiself" and the book was a warning against falling into a literary version of the limbo in which Johnson's narrator found himself.

Still, the trials of Johnson's narrator have a great deal in common with much that we have seen in Johnson's work and career, at least in the years leading up to and immediately following the publication of the novel. Contradiction, not synthesis, marked that early work in a way that dramatized the difficulty of fusing black and white worlds in one creative expression. One can only speculate why this was so. Perhaps the novel—in its portrayal of distinctiveness as, above all, separateness, distance, and conflict—can help us understand. Perhaps, like Chesnutt and Dunbar before him, Johnson believed that any emphasis on distinctiveness was, ultimately, a product of exclusion. Such an interpretation would accord with his narrator's reaction to the lynching, which he sees as a shame to black and white alike.

Perhaps, too, it grew out of Johnson's role as a black artist in a white society. As we have seen, such a sense of the problems of synthesis informed his 1928 essay on the dilemma of the Negro artist, in which he described the possibility of pleasing black and white audiences at the same time. It was something he learned from his experiences as a lyricist, trying to please a white audience while giving dignity to the theatrical treatment of blacks. But whatever its source, this sense of the difficulty of achieving any synthesis of black and white worlds appears at the heart of *The Autobiography of an Ex-Colored Man* and helps emphasize the extent to which the contradictions one may see in Johnson's work rested on contradictions Johnson himself must have seen in American racial life. *The Autobiography of an Ex-Colored Man* is a testimony to both the imperatives and the problems of the Du Boisian task.

The Autobiography of an Ex-Colored Man is also something of a summary statement of the issues and concerns raised by black literature between the close of Reconstruction and the coming of World War I. The contradictions Johnson portrayed in his novel were, in sharp relief, the contradictions that had confronted even the most genteel black writers who sought to find ways to express the sense of racial solidarity and pride they knew to be important, but in a framework that conveyed, without compromise, their desire—their demand—for a place in the mainstream of American society. Despite the Du Boisian rhetorical frame in which Johnson worked in *The Autobiography of an Ex-Colored Man*, he too encountered the dilemmas earlier writers had confronted; and he too saw the validity of both goals while sensing the difficulties involved in achieving them.

Indeed, from this point of view, *The Autobiography of an Ex-Colored Man* becomes a commentary on the post-Reconstruction black literary tradition itself. The narrator's progress through life recapitulates much that we have seen in the history of black literature to Johnson's time. The narrator comes to see a need to create a black identity within an environment that provides mainly mainstream cues—New England, where he was raised—much as post-Reconstruction writers looked for modes to express racial solidarity in a milieu of mainstream, middle-class, genteel literary models. His tentative efforts to connect with black culture—at Atlanta University, in the New York club, in the rural South—encapsulate the approaches to black identity made by black writers toward the close of the nineteenth century. The efforts themselves dramatize the sense so many black writers had that a basis for identity could be found in the evocation of a vital black American folk life. The failure of those efforts mirrors the ambivalence of those black writers—especially dialect writers—who wanted to evoke a black distinctiveness with which they were not entirely comfortable, and without giving up their mainstream aspirations. What Johnson's narrator went through, in other words, was precisely what black literature itself had been going through for almost half a century. And, as we have seen, the issues in that black literary tradition remained as unresolved in Johnson's time as they were for the narrator in Johnson's novel.

The parallel is important, because it points to some aspects of black literary tradition before 1915 that were implicit in other works but that Johnson's novel makes explicit. As noted, Johnson, following Du Bois' lead, wrestled with problems of authentication for black artistic expression. Du Bois had sought to find a source for the authentication of black expression in the black experience itself, particularly in black folk culture. In doing so, he had put black art on a new footing, one that earlier writers had been unable to see or accept fully—just as Johnson's narrator was unable to see or accept it. But Johnson's story, as a commentary on both black literary tradition and Du Bois' ideas, reopened the question of authentication, not just by stressing the difficulties involved in finding a basis for black art and identity out of a synthesis of two conflicting cultures but even more by highlighting the urgency of doing so.

To the extent that Johnson's novel recapitulates black literary history, it implies that the racial conflict that prevented a synthetic art and identity produced the kind of artistic limbo that Johnson himself sought to avoid. Not that Johnson simply rejected what earlier writers had done. As noted, he admired such predecessors as Albery Whitman and Paul Laurence Dunbar. Nevertheless, the novel summarizes a situation in which artists receive cues from many sources, none of which fit well together. Like Johnson's narrator, black artists had to come to terms with a desire to reach a broad, often unsympathetic audience, with their own social aspirations and their own feelings of identity, as well as with the demands of artistic creation. A number of factors affected the black artist's search for an authentic voice; and as Johnson made clear in both his novel and his later essay, "The Dilemma of the Negro Artist," these factors would remain strong and contradictory so long as America remained a racist society. From this point of view, black art would itself remain characterized by the paradoxes and contradictions shown in this survey—until it found the authentic voice that Johnson, like Du Bois, thought was required.

In *The Autobiography of an Ex-Colored Man*, Johnson did not offer an obvious solution to the problems the novel defined. That was not its contribution; indeed, it even adopted a pessimistic stance toward the difficulties and possibilities facing black artists. Nor, of course, was Johnson the first to appreciate the dilemmas confronting black art. We have achieved a sense of them as underlying the work of such literary figures as Dunbar, Chesnutt, Griggs, and Du Bois. But in dramatizing the tensions and paradoxes of earlier black literature and in distilling that heritage so vividly and concisely, Johnson certainly raised his readers to a new level of awareness of them and highlighted their role in the creative process. Thus he set the stage for a more focused exploration of the nature of black American art—of its sociological context and of its social and artistic aims and purposes.

This makes *The Autobiography of an Ex-Colored Man*, in the history of black American literature, a very forward-looking novel. Just as it provides a culmination to the black literary tradition that evolved before World War I, it also indicates significant linkages between the pre-war tradition and what came after—that striking flowering of creative work in the Harlem Renaissance of the 1920s. As noted, Johnson's novel is often tied to the Harlem Renaissance, especially in its urban realism, its stated appreciation for folk culture, and its raising of issues of authentication. And as historian David Levering Lewis has demonstrated, the conflicts Johnson portrayed were not his alone but were those underlying the whole movement.

Indeed, at one level, it is useful to see the novel as an important transitional work between the achievements of the early black literary tradition and those of the Harlem Renaissance, because the writers of the 1920s also wrestled with questions of identity and assimilation, with questions of authentication and its sources, with their own stance as artists toward the worlds of black and white America, and with the function of art in American society. What set the Harlem Renaissance apart from the earlier tradition, however, was the great self-consciousness with which its creators went about their task, constructing theories of black art and culture—and of identity—while creating self-reflexive works of fiction and poetry. In its own recapitulation of black literary tradition, Johnson's novel foreshadowed that self-consciousness and, more importantly, foreshadowed the awareness that most Harlem Renaissance writers had of the real dilemmas confronting black artists in a white-dominated society. Nathan Huggins has shown that the kinds of dilemmas that plagued black writers before World War I were never fully resolved by those who made the Harlem Renaissance. But the background of that work, and the distillation of that background in Johnson's novel, made possible the more clearly formulated explorations of black literary creation that were to come.[46]

46. David Levering Lewis, *When Harlem Was in Vogue* (New York, 1982), 147–48; Nathan Irvine Huggins, *Harlem Renaissance* (New York, 1971).

Index